PORTRAIT OF LANCASHIRE

OTHER BOOKS BY JESSICA LOFTHOUSE

Three Rivers
Off to the Lakes
Off to the Dales
Lancashire Landscape
Lancashire's Fair Face
Lancashire—Westmorland Highway
The Curious Traveller Through Lakeland
West Pennine Highway
North Country Folk Lore
The Curious Traveller: Lancaster to Lakeland
Lancashire Countrygoer
Countrygoer in the Dales
Countrygoers' North
North Wales for the Countrygoer
Lancashire's Old Families
Lancashire Villages
Borders of the North-west

Portrait of LANCASHIRE

JESSICA LOFTHOUSE

ILLUSTRATED AND WITH MAP

ROBERT HALE · LONDON

First published in Great Britain 1967
Reprinted 1969
Second edition 1973
Third edition 1977
Reprinted 1980

Robert Hale Limited
Clerkenwell House,
Clerkenwell Green,
London EC1R 0HT

ISBN 0 7091 6359 2

Printed in Great Britain by
Lowe and Brydone Printers Limited, Thetford, Norfolk

CONTENTS

ILLUSTRATIONS

ACKNOWLEDGEMENTS

The author and publishers wish to thank the following for permission to reproduce photographs: J. W. Price, Langho, Blackburn (Nos. 1, 16, 32); H. Isherwood, Holcombe Brook, Bury (2, 4, 6, 8, 9, 11, 12, 17, 18, 22, 29, 34); P. Anstess, Castleton (19, 24); R. S. Bridge, Bury (26, 27); *North Western Evening Mail*, Barrow-in-Furness (3, 5, 7, 21, 23, 25, 31); *Lancashire Evening Telegraph* (10, 14, 30, 33); Liverpool Information Office (20); *Lancashire Evening Post* (15, 28); P. J. Mark, Lancaster University (13).

PREFACE TO THE THIRD EDITION

In 1966 my *Portrait of Lancashire* covered the County Palatine as created eight centuries ago. In 1974 new boundary changes took away its broad base on the south, "Great Cities and New Jerusalems" now within Merseyside and Greater Manchester; took out four million Lancastrians but not old loyalties. Many will continue to toast their Duke of Lancaster, with the Queen's gracious consent. So Section III, and the Merseyside "Maritime West" of Section IV, I retain intact.

The detached north-west Section VII, "Lancashire Lakeland—Precious Heritage", Cartmel and Furness now in the new Cumbria also. Possession being a state of mind, and all Lancashire loving this enchanted region dearly, it remains in the book with pictures of the well-loved places.

The "Pennine backbone" of Section III remains the eastern border of new Lancashire with four districts extending along the slopes and enclosing its rivers. They are *Rossendale* (with 62,000 people) from Whitworth to Haslingden, and *Hyndburn*, *Burnley* and *Pendle*, their 261,000 people living within sight of ancient royal forests and always with the hills rising proudly around them. Included in their number are a pocket of rather reluctant Yorkshire folk from the Barnoldswick and Earby area.

Four more towns to the west with their adjacent rural areas, *Blackburn*, *Preston*, *Chorley* and the largest, *Blackpool*, account for 304,000 of the new county's population, leaving the rest of "Lancashire without Chimneys", Section V, unchanged. Here the truly rural Lancashire covers two vast open areas of great beauty and variety. The larger with the smaller population is *Ribble Valley*. Clitheroe and Longridge are the only sizeable towns and there are many lovely villages along the river by the Hodder; part of Ribblesdale and Bowland Forest has been brought in from Yorkshire. Almost as extensive and as beautiful, with Lancaster,

Morecambe and Heysham and Carnforth to boost its otherwise meagre numbers, is *Lunesdale*.

Rural Lancashire's new areas include the Yarrow and Douglas valleys with Ormskirk on its edge, *West Lancashire*; *South Ribble* with Leyland along the estuary and the lower valley; north of Preston, *Fylde* from Kirkham to the seaside towns near Blackpool; and taking its name from the estuary at Fleetwood to Garstang and the fine fell country Over Wyresdale, the very beautiful rural district called *Wyre*.

There are fourteen new districts, of which six only are urban and industrial. The new Lancashire is a good place to belong to and live in and visit.

Langho,
Blackburn,
1977

J. L.

INTRODUCING THE PORTRAIT

TO COPE with the impossible task of portraying all Lancashire in one book, I have been compelled—most unwillingly—to limit to paragraphs certain topics deserving pages. Also the First Industrial Revolution has minimum treatment; a fascinating subject, but now ancient history for we are well into the Second Industrial Revolution which is making Lancashire 'not what it was'.

A picture of Lancashire as a Landscape Without Figures would be unthinkable so the first and last sections of the Portrait are about Lancastrians, who we are, the forces which made us what we are, our speech, manners, customs and reactions to outside influences; and also about how we cope with our climate and at the same time get the best out of every month as it comes, enjoying the seasonal changes with native fortitude, good humour and zest—in 'The Lancashire Year'.

Note well, I treat the Portrait subjectively as Lancastrian born and bred and proud of it. But being part Yorkshire, and having travelled often and far beyond the North-west, I can stand back, survey landscape and people objectively and say, "Lancashire, with all thy faults I love thee still".

The five middle sections reveal the five faces of Lancashire. Where else is such diverse character of life and landscape in so small an area—one million acres compared with Yorkshire's four millions! My love for my native county was inborn. Mine was a purely country town childhood, but my work has taken me from Liverpool to Lakeland, first teaching, then lecturing county-wide, writing in numerous newspapers and collecting material for my North-Country books—the last always pleasurable. I have been fortunate to meet the people at all levels: cottage door, farm kitchen and baron's hall, against backgrounds urban and rural. The outlook from my window: Ribble Valley, Pendle and the fells above Stonyhurst seen in detached pieces, and Clitheroe where I began.

Ten minutes walk up the lane and in one vast encircling panorama I can look on each of many faces. Eastwards, the wild, bare Pennines and wind-raked moorlands with half industrial Lancashire hidden in their folds, the gritstone country which put hardihood into the working millions; and westwards the greenest, most serene pastures and meadowland watered by clear brooks and the coiling Ribble, one valley of the many I write about in 'Lancashire without Chimneys'. South and east, many towns and hundreds of thousands of people. South-west, lowlands verging the Irish Sea, purely agricultural, the countryfolk bucolic, concerned with potatoes, lettuces, tomatoes and food for the five millions; and the coast, the Ribble estuary, and—of course—Blackpool Tower. All are 'in my sights'.

Liverpool and Manchester I cannot see nor guess at from my moortop viewpoint, for thirty-five miles of rolling hills and valleys and many towns intervene. Nor, because of fells between, can I see Morecambe Bay or Lancashire Lakeland; on top of Jeffrey Hill—five miles west, they too would be visible, inviting.

If I had wished my enthusiastic Lancashire-loving and all-Lancastrian photographers could have provided crowd pictures—Cup Ties, Grand National, Point to Points, Blackpool's Golden Mile on Whit Monday, Manchester or Liverpool's crawling shoppers on any Saturday—but we all preferred other aspects, less publicized. Only for purely documentary purposes, for town archives before demolition wipes them out, are they likely to photograph dark cobbled streets with uneven pavements fronting long straight rows of uninspiring terraced houses, with backdrops of factory walls, slag heaps and chimneys pouring black smoke in banner headlines against grey skies.

"Now, that is really Lancashire," declared an American visitor looking down from the railway outside Blackburn on the succession of identical streets each with hundreds of identical houses with the south-west wind blowing plumes of smoke in the same direction from every one of their chimneys. Not once had she used her ciné-camera during visits to our finest buildings, loveliest villages, fairest valleys and most beautiful lakes. No, this was what she was waiting for, and this is what her friends in Washington D.C. will see, and this only, to represent Souvenir of Lancashire.

In July 1966 viewers saw a similar series of shots of Blackburn's surviving, but earmarked for demolition, back streets as most suitable to go with a feast of choral music—the town being famous for its sweet singers. The television cameramen seized upon the dismal picture, just ahead of the bulldozers,—and the viewers probably said "that must be typical of Lancashire".

With the two cities, Liverpool and Manchester, falling over themselves to present a new image, each town renewing itself and bent on housing its people in brighter if not always better homes; and after amputation of over half its oldest mills to make way for the Second Industrial Revolution—all electric, all automatic, smoking chimneys rare. Darkest Lancashire comes clean. Once, scores of coal pits; now less than ten.

So, before they are too late, I suggest that authorities who want to perpetuate the 'typical and traditional' should earmark a derelict factory with all its obsolete machinery, a back alley or side street with its corner pub and fish and chip shop, and stock up a supply of clogs and shawls, so that when required folk can trudge along the preserved streets dressed up in traditional style, Lowry-like, or perform as spinners or weavers in the museum-piece factories. Too touristic? Industrial archaeology is a popular study. Many students flock to Lancashire to see buildings local councils plan to demolish—derelict mills, cotton-workers' terraced houses. Modern residents are eager to wipe out the Victorian image; and who can blame them? But Helmshore has shown the way by reconstructing most faithfully at Higher Mill the early woollen industry, authentic machinery in full working order, the great wheel with its racketty clatter, the old oily smell, dim lights—all as in the bad old prosperous days.

No need to create museums when old industrial communities remain intact, as at Helmshore, Barrow Bridge and Eagley, models of the nineteenth century. There is a chance for Wycoller to revive the early handlooming cottage industry days. Lancashire must preserve its heritage where it belongs before the old communities become 'sites of' and component parts become museum pieces later to be sought after, collected up and put in a new 'folksy' setting.

Most demolitions have been in urban areas. In the rural, handloomers' cottages become desirable residences, mills are converted into mansions, ruins are ripe for conversion.

The character of the people remains constant.

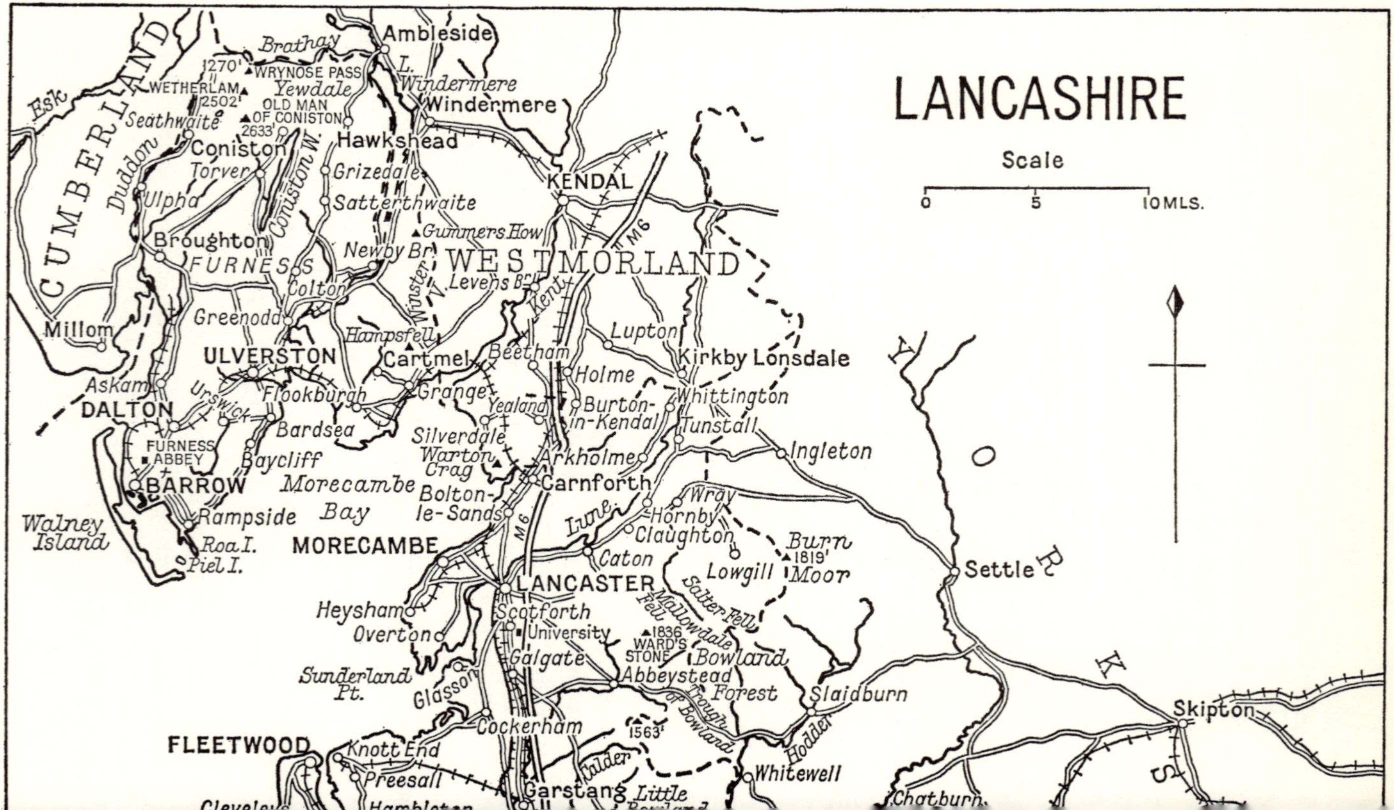
LANCASHIRE
Scale
0
5
10 MLS.
CUMBERLAND
WESTMORLAND
Y O R K S
Esk
Duddon
Brathay
Ambleside
L. Windermere
Windermere
Wrynose Pass
1270'
Wetherlam
2502'
Yewdale
Old Man of Coniston
2633'
Seathwaite
Coniston
Hawkshead
Torver
Grizedale
Coniston W.
Ulpha
Satterthwaite
Kendal
M6
Gummers How
Broughton
Newby Br.
Furness
Colton
Levens Br.
Winster V.
Kent
Greenodd
Hampsfell
Millom
Ulverston
Cartmel
Beetham
Lupton
Kirkby Lonsdale
Askam
Urswick
Flookburgh
Grange
Holme
Whittington
Dalton
Bardsea
Yealand
Burton-in-Kendal
Tunstall
Silverdale
Furness Abbey
Baycliff
Warton Crag
Arkholme
Ingleton
Barrow
Morecambe Bay
Carnforth
Bolton-le-Sands
Wray
Walney Island
Rampside
Lune
Hornby
Roa I.
Piel I.
Morecambe
Claughton
Burn Moor
1819'
Caton
Lowgill
Settle
Lancaster
Heysham
Scotforth
Salter Fell
Mallowdale Fell
Overton
University
1836
Ward's Stone
Bowland
Galgate
Sunderland Pt.
Glasson
Abbeystead
Forest
Slaidburn
Trough of Bowland
Cockerham
1563'
Hodder
Skipton
Fleetwood
Knott End
Calder
Preesall
Whitewell
Garstang
Little
Chatburn

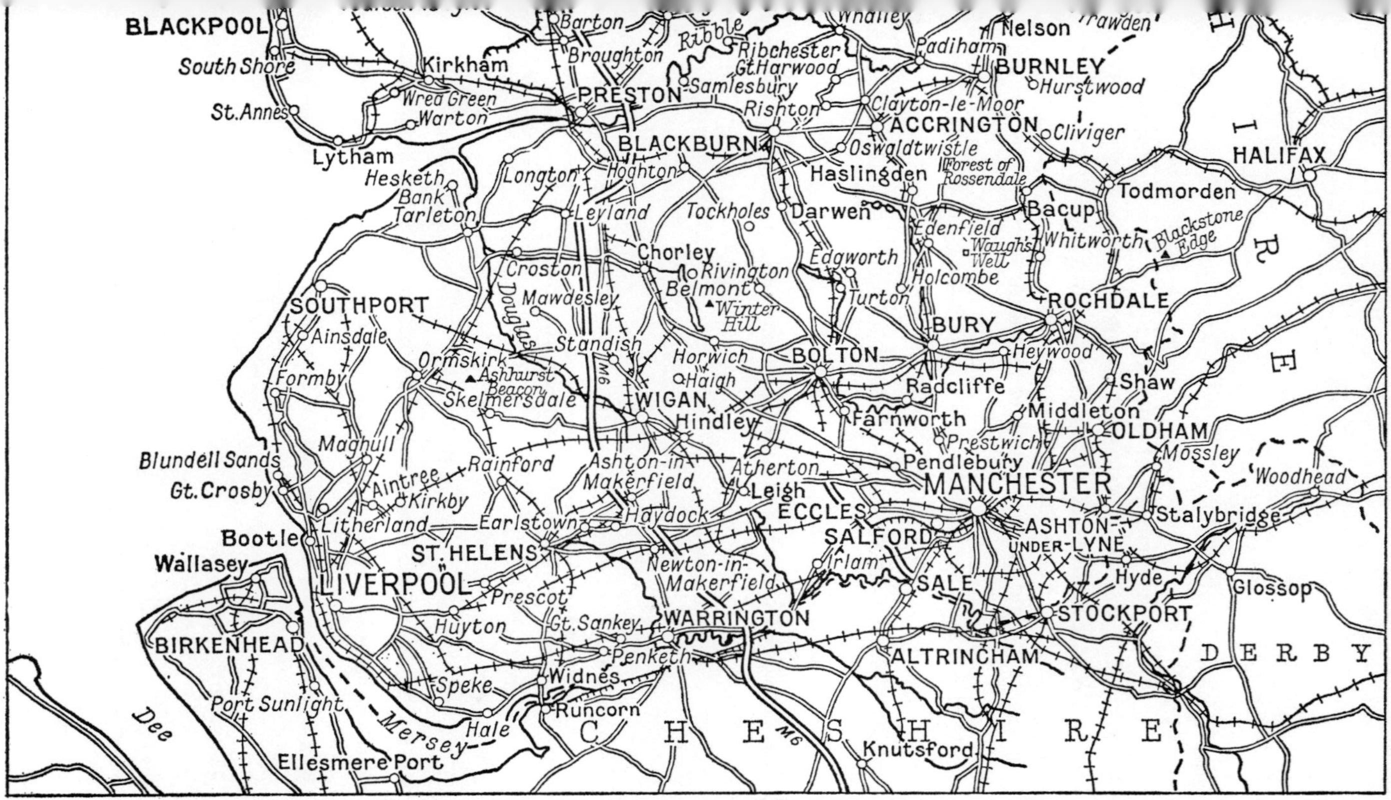
BLACKPOOL
Barton
Ribble
Whalley
Nelson
Trawden
South Shore
Kirkham
Broughton
Ribchester
Gt.Harwood
Padiham
BURNLEY
Hurstwood
St.Annes
Wrea Green
Warton
PRESTON
Samlesbury
Rishton
Clayton-le-Moor
ACCRINGTON
Cliviger
Lytham
BLACKBURN
Oswaldtwistle
Forest of Rossendale
HALIFAX
Hesketh Bank
Longton
Hoghton
Haslingden
Todmorden
Tarleton
Leyland
Tockholes
Darwen
Bacup
Edenfield
Waugh's Well
Whitworth
Blackstone Edge
Chorley
Croston
Rivington
Edgworth
Holcombe
Belmont
Winter Hill
Turton
ROCHDALE
Douglas
Mawdesley
SOUTHPORT
BURY
Ainsdale
Standish
Horwich
BOLTON
Heywood
Ormskirk
Ashhurst Beacon
Haigh
Shaw
Formby
M6
Skelmersdale
WIGAN
Radcliffe
Hindley
Farnworth
Middleton
OLDHAM
Maghull
Prestwich
Mossley
Blundell Sands
Rainford
Ashton-in-Makerfield
Atherton
Pendlebury
Woodhead
Aintree
Kirkby
Leigh
MANCHESTER
Gt.Crosby
Haydock
ECCLES
Stalybridge
Litherland
Earlstown
ASHTON-UNDER-LYNE
Bootle
ST.HELENS
SALFORD
Wallasey
Newton-in-Makerfield
Irlam
Hyde
LIVERPOOL
Glossop
Prescot
SALE
Gt.Sankey
WARRINGTON
STOCKPORT
Huyton
BIRKENHEAD
Penketh
ALTRINCHAM
DERBY
Widnes
Speke
Port Sunlight
Runcorn
Dee
Mersey
Hale
CHESHIRE
Knutsford
Ellesmere Port
HIRE

In memory of my friend—
RACHEL KAY-SHUTTLEWORTH
Whose roots were deep in Lancashire's past
Who enriched its present
And gave so much to its future

I

LANCASHIRE FOLK—
THE FIGURES IN THE LANDSCAPE

What Makes a Lancastrian?

To anyone really interested in Lancashire history it is surprising that rarely do books include any mention of it before Kay's fly shuttle, Hargrave's Jenny or Crompton's Mule, as though we had not till the mid-1700s emerged from the Dark Ages.

School histories always disappointed me. I came to mistrust them. I knew my town had a history though it rarely had a mention.

Being a Lancastrian was something to be proud of, though I have a Yorkshire name. Where I was brought up was a little of both, Clitheroe being a border town. On market days Lancashire and Yorkshire farmers were in evidence. They talked and looked the same. Only when excursion trains emptied their Manchester and Liverpool loads and I heard them speak did I realize there were differences. These strangers were as foreigners to us.

How can a Lancastrian be distinguished from Yorkshire, Cheshire and Westmorland neighbours? Does the true Lancashire man only live in the south-east; do the residents of Coronation Street represent him rather than small-town folk of Ormskirk or Kirkham, villagers of Chipping, Hornby, Urswick or Broughton-in-Furness? And are cloth-capped Evertonians or Manchester United fans yelling themselves hoarse at a Cup Tie more typical than cloth-capped hill farmers from Cliviger, Wyresdale or High Furness pondering silently the merits of penned ewes and tups? Can we tell the native from the 'off comed'un'?

Names are clues. When surnames became compulsory many chose villages from which their forefathers hailed. Look in any Lancashire telephone directory to prove this. Especially common, small-town names as Whalley, Barton, Brindle, Hornby, Formby and Dalton as well as most inconspicuous hamlets and villages—by modern standards—Bailey, Thornley, Bradley and Holden, Dewhurst, Dutton, Ashworth, Haworth, Entwistle and Birtwistle, Walmesley and Greenhalgh. Larger towns like Bolton, Blackburn, Oldham, Worsley, Farnworth and Walkden are represented too. But where the Manchesters, Salfords and Liverpools?

The likelihood is families who took these names originated in villages settled by seventh-century Angles who arrived west of the Pennines, chose sites above our rivers for their Tuns and Hams and Leys, attempted clearance of scrub and woodland for farming and were our 'founding fathers'. They spoke Northumbrian English. Later came a second wave, Mercians from the Midlands, to gain the upper hand.

Penda, their bloodthirsty king, had sworn to sweep the worshippers of the White Christ from the North. He overcame and murdered the saintly King Oswald—as Lancastrians we like to think the martyrdom was at Winwick—and gave his Mercians the chance of filtering into Northumbrian land. They swept from the Midland plain, through Cheshire and fanning out took their pick of south-east Lancashire—not good land but worth the having for landless men.

Their speech was West Midland English, in which consonants hard in the Northumbrian tongue—'c' and 'k' as in Lancaster, Hincaster, Casterton and Castercliffe, Kirkland and Kirkham became the soft 'ch' as in Chester, Manchester, Childwall and Chadderton, Ormschurche and Cherchdale (Kirkdale). There has been much jiggery-pokery with place names, but as written down from the mouths of eleventh-century folk—in Doomsday Book—they reveal their mixed origins.

The Ribble was territorial and language boundary between Northumbrian and Mercian and later the border line between Angle and Norseman. The Danish invasion was confined to the east of the Pennine barrier—except for a few outliers around Manchester and in the upper Calder—so the eighth and ninth centuries saw little change between Mersey and Duddon. A thin population—less than ten thousand souls—was scattered across the region. The Celts were still herding their animals in the Lakeland fells, the English farming in their woodland clearings, fishing and wildfowling around the estuaries and on the fringe of the great meres between Ribble and Mersey, Ribble and Wyre, accounting to their thanes at their Hundred meetings—at West Derby, Leyland, Salford, Blackburn and north of Ribble, in Amounderness.

They were good Christians, peacefully inclined—but when need arose the fighting spirit of their invading forbears was strong in them. They could be tolerant and fair-minded and adapt themselves to change, attributes which were to serve them in good stead when off their untroubled shores the black-sailed Viking ships were sighted.

About the time the Danes invaded England, Norwegian sea-rovers also had the urge to travel, their seafaring carrying them to remote shores; many however chose to settle in Northern Ireland, in the isles off Scotland and in the Isle of Man. Their warring kings eventually turned their sights on England, finally in the tenth century their successes leading to the founding of a Northumbrian kingdom, centred on York and linked with Dublin. Norse settlement increased, thick along the west flowing rivers, Eden, Lune, Kent. Eventually their ships probed up the estuaries of Wyre, Ribble and Mersey. They were encouraged to form a 'buffer' state around Chester. Some took a look at the Wirral, others prospected along the coast. Nothing of the blood-mad sea-dogs about these newcomers; they were Irish Christians, their speech had Irish inflections. They were family men, their only wish to settle down to farming and fishing; if they decided to plant their dwellings near the Anglian villages, why then, they would be good neighbours.

Follow them round the map of Lancashire. Toxteth and Croxteth named their staithes or landing places, Fishwick and Salwick creeks where their boats drew in. 'Byrs' were farms here as in Norway; near Mersey find their water-side homesteads at Crosby, Formby, Roby, Kirkby and Derby (West). Was Thingwall their local Tynwald, their new place of assembly? Bekan's mound we know as Becconsall; the headland with the crosses, Crossens.

In the Fylde, the Anglian flatlands renamed after a Norseman, Agmundr, as Amounderness, there must have been successful co-existence, one feature being 'paired' villages, Norse side by side with Anglian. There is Ribby with Wrea, Medlar with Wesham, Catforth with Cottam, Westby with Plumpton, Elswick near Eccleston, Nateby near Churchtown and near Barnacre, Bonds.

The reformed sea rovers even carried on the old Norwegian seasonal movement from lowland to hillcountry in summer; Grimsargh and Goosnargh, the airdhs or dairy farms of Grim and Gosan were their shielings. They were contented to remain small community folk. The Anglian villages grew into larger centres of religious life, marketing, trade—at Kirkham, Poulton, Lytham, Singleton and St. Michael's.

The mark of our Norse ancestors is strong by the Wyre, in the Lune valley, especially up the small tributary dales like Hindburn and Roeburn, with Wray and upland 'saetrs' at Salter and Winder, Backsbotton, Outhwaite, Ivah, Lowgill and Harterbeck, keeping themselves to themselves well away from the Anglian valley villages, each with its old church, at Halton, Caton, Gressingham and Whittingham, Tatham and Bentham—though Arkholm was a Norse dairy farm by the Lune levels.

Even thicker on the map are Norse names 'north of the Sands' and around Morecambe Bay. The Angles never strayed far from the reasonably good land near the coast and above the mosses. Warton, Bolton-le-Sands, Dallam, and Ulverston, Dalton and Broughton-in-Furness sat low with their backs to hinterland of knotts and swamps, ignoring wild fells and rocky mountains where the Celts still lived on, caring for their poor flocks and small fields of corn. There was plenty of space left for Norse landseekers whose names have the authentic hard tang in Biggar, Urswick, Scales and Thrang, Mansriggs and Blawith, Thorphinsty and Tilberthwaite, Gummers How, Arnside Keld, Nettleslack and Wrynose.

For surnames most of them adopted their father's and became Casson, Tysons and Gunsons. From the North Lancashire telephone directory the Wilsons, Harrisons, Simpsons and Richardsons, Atkinsons, Dixons, Hodgsons and Dawsons appear in long columns so the old patrynomics still hold.

Bensons, Dickinsons and Robinsons appear with Butlers and Burrows among Morcambe Bay fisherfolk—not unexpected for they have always claimed to be of good Norse stock—especially in Flookburgh.

We inherit more than we recognize from our Norse fore elders. They were tough, hardy and not prone to run away from difficulties. They subdued the wanderlust of their ancestors and stayed where a reasonable living offered. They indulged in lively imagery, colourful speech; their humour was of the robust sort: horseplay and practical joking, leg pulling and apt nicknaming. They were great tale tellers, fond of subjects strange and grim, and—when comic—told with dead pan faces and flat expressionless voices. They could sum up a character or a situation in a pithy phrase. They were born psychologists. They enjoyed fighting and wrestling, music and singing, drinking and all forms of conviviality but could retire into long brooding silences, heavy with deep thought.

They were prey to inherited superstitions and beliefs. They believed in demons, active in the underworld of potholes and caves, in devils from their 'home country', in supernatural beings, ghost hounds, in signs and portents. It does not need scholarship to identify ourselves with this Norse in us; and behind that the good firm foundation, solid Northumbrian English and Mercian English virtues. Maybe a drop of Celtic too, from those Cumbrians who held fast to their native hills throughout Roman conquest and English invasion.

Unless we belong to one of the ancient families possessed of a family tree with its roots in pre-Norman times we cannot be certain 'how far we go back'. There were only about 10,000 of us in A.D. 1066. Now there are around five millions. Apart from population 'explosion' there has been considerable drift to the north-west, a great flood of incomers in the last hundred and fifty years, to account for this.

So, let us forget the typical Lancastrian who probably does not exist, not more than the mythical John Bull. In Lancashire as in Britain, 'it teks all sorts to make a world', and a good mixture can be a very good thing. Especially so in our language—a very rich mixture.

The Way We Speak, the Things We Say

What is Lancashire dialect? A form of spoken English which has in it Northumbrian English (as spoken in Yorkshire) with a good admixture of West Midland or Mercian English (as spoken from Cheshire to Staffordshire), a plentiful sprinkling of Old Norse words and phrases to give an added zest, and a little Old French surviving from the days of Norman conquest. Hardly a 'pure' form of speech, but capable of a score of rich variations which dialect speakers draw from unconsciously, only the dialect experts knowing how and why.

I am all in favour of keeping dialect fresh and bright with constant use. Only a few old folk keep up a flow of dialect talk and one must travel farther to find them, and often meet with disappointment. Most of us are content to use dialect words and phrases, in inverted commas as it were, to improve a story, enrich comment and conversation which would sound bare and bald without them. Talk is spiced with dialect. For backchat, banter when we are with friends, humourous asides—instinctively the old words are used. And for dealing with the stupid, careless and slaphappy a well-chosen 'bit of Lancashire' gets over at once, and no hard feelings.

"Tha gaumless fooil"; the clumsy creature who has earned this does not retire in high dudgeon but grins and tries again.

"Theer's nowt so queer as fooak," said in sheer exasperation is accepted as a fair comment, and no ill will understood.

"You're as queer as Dick's hatband to be sure," has the same mild salutary effect; both make the obstreperous observe patterns of normal behaviour, and no offence taken.

We say that a dialect phrase has more telling power than a torrent of abuse.

What of this for an example of brevity; a conclusive business transaction in six words!

The office door opens, the traveller looks in.

"Morning," he says, and "Morning," replies the manager.

"Owt?" he asks, and "Nowt", is the answer.

"Morning," from the one, "Morning", from the other and, with the door shut, all is ended.

Entertainers always find Lancashire voice goes down well with audiences. Stanley Holloway adopted the voice and asked a Lancashire writer to produce the very funny monologues for him—Albert and the lion, Sam and the musket, and the Ark above the Floods on Blackpool Tower. He discovered the acquired Calder valley accent allowed him to get away, literally, with 'murder'. In none other would the B.B.C. have allowed the ghost with her head tucked under-neath her arm to walk the 'Bluddy' Tower. Broad Lancashire, yes, can be endearing and much is allowed of it. It has become an actor's valuable asset on modern stage and screen.

England thinks it can recognize the Lancashire voice. Did

George Formby, that amiable Mad Hatter, speak for Lancashire? Does the March Hare, Ken Dodd? Or the whimsical gnome, Arthur Askey? I think not. Gracie Fields' voice rings more true, and Al Read's telling of larger-than-life but founded on fact altercations, against authentic Lancashire backgrounds. The characters in Coronation Street have their origins in the industrial towns of the south-east—but they represent only a part of a section of the county. Lancashire has spoken, and speaks on, with many voices.

To hear 'pure broad Lancashire' poured forth without inhibition, board one of the workpeople's buses anywhere between Colne and Burnley, Blackburn, Bolton or Wigan, when after a day's work in pit or factory good humour flows free, in many variations of the voice and dialect. Dialect has never been standardized in Lancashire.

School buses too are revealing. "Grammar School, and speaking like that!!" Freed from restraining influences of higher education they revert to Basic Lancashire. A stranger might ask for an interpreter, and be told that the best people, the greatest scholars, have often confessed to 'putting on their dialect with their house slippers'.

There may be Irish, Pakistani and Jamaican conductors in evidence but the natives hold their own, the platform their stage, their humour their own brand. Ridiculous familiarity? Not a bit of it!

It is a bitter cold day. The Blackpool conductor rubs his hands before collecting fares. "Na then," briskly, "warm up your pennies!"

"Single to Oswaldtwistle," says a passenger. The next, "Same again". "Nay, we're not going theer".

"You want a return to Darren? You'll *want* a return if you're going *there*."

"It's a fine day. What about turning round and all going off to Blackpoo'?"

A passengers offers a handful of small change. "Good King Wenceslas! Carol singing starting early this year!"

A girl steps on laden with autumn leaves. "Thinking of building a nest, are you, luv?" Always 'luv', We expect it everywhere in Lancashire; it is warm, friendly—and means nothing at all.

Occasionally a conductress will try new words. 'Ducks', she says to one fare, 'darling' or 'sweetheart' to a child, 'honey', 'macushla', 'mavourneen', 'leibchen'—and when one reached me I gave her quickly, 'cariad'. What she carried on with on the upper deck I do not know but there were gales of laughter.

We recall amusing incidents and smile-provoking phrases. I remember two women on a Windermere lake steamer. A perfect afternoon of glitter and dazzle, dancing water, warm sunshine, and mountains heavenly blue. "E-eh, we couldn't ha' chosen a bether day," sighed one, then pulled out a True Romance paper back and, with her head in it, did not look up again till the *Teal* bumped at Waterhead Pier.

That is an expression to be brought out, dusted frequently and repeated with requisite emphasis whenever our plans are blessed with sun and shine—"Nay, we couldn't a' chosen a bether day".

We remember a dear old soul who beamed on the assembled guests in a large hotel lounge who were sitting eyes averted from forty coach tourists newly arrived after a long journey. She was first out of the 'Powder Room'. "After that I feel med ower," she informed them with immense satisfaction.

"Dayleet's a fool to it," was the comment of Stonyhurst villagers on seeing the first gaslight installed at the college—in the 1830s. We repeat this with relish whenever electric light illumines dark corners. And on finishing a do-it-yourself job, "I've made it all out of mi own head, and there's plenty of wood left to make another", as a Chatburn wheelbarrow maker informed his admiring neighbours.

"I've taught you all I know, and still ye know now't."

"He never stops talking. And when he finishes he's said nowt."

All worth remembering—typically terse Lancashire comment.

Often incomprehensible to strangers as this, heard in a railway compartment at Warrington, three natives joining travellers from London. One patted all his pockets and found no matches and his cigarette at the ready.

"Any on yo any on yo?" he asked looking around. Blank faces.

"He means he's baht," explained one companion. And the other, "He's getten noan".

It must have been during childhood I heard and tucked away dialect words heard from old folk. They needed no translation, subtle and obvious differences understood. "Thrutching in t'corner" and "Cowering in t' nook" were not the same, A 'feckless' creature, improvident, was not as the 'sackless' lass who lacked spirit. A person who came in 'clemmed'—hungry, needed different treatment from one who declared he was 'starved', cold through and through. A too busy mother who was 'throng or thrang', or too bothered with many jobs, 'moidered or moithered', was very different from one who was 'powfagged', brain weary. 'Chunnering', grumbling under ones breath, 'camping' for gossiping, 'fratching' for quarrelling, and 'marlicking' for boisterous play, all meant something.

So did so many Old Norse words in common speech—'brast oppen', burst open, 'stop skriking'—stop screaming or crying, 'greeting' for weeping, 'riving' for tearing. A watering can was always a 'degging can', heavy cakes were 'sad' and dark days, 'dree'.

Every community has a handyman who can 'fettle owt', and when 'he gets agait' completes his repair job without delay. "Na then, frame," he says to his slow helper who make little headway.

'Leika' is a Norse word for leaping and playing. "Have childer got their laikings?"—used as a noun, and "Are you laiking?" was a question often asked during days of mill closures. "Aye I'm laiking. We're shut down another fortneet."

Wriggling children who could never keep still were 'wick as snigs'—eels being the most squirming of creatures. Ready for his bath, a dirty boy was 'black as up luvvers', though his mother did not know that the 'louvre' was a smoke vent and therefore very black.

The state of one's health was expressed in many ways from "Fairish", "Not so badly", to "Nobbut middling", or "I'm noan so clever", to "Reet poorly".

Old fashioned names for garments. Aprons were 'brats'. Devil's bratstrings broke when he overloaded with stones. A family tale told of our brass pan discovered by a farmer's wife "whose brat strings brast, she tried to carry so many spade ace guineas". Braces were 'galluses', a word associated with hangings—a conscience-stricken murderer in Gallows Lane near Ribchester, a man betwitched behind Huntroyd 'hanged wi' his own galluses'.

The highest commendation in Lancashire is 'reet champion' or 'it's jannock' or 'gradely'. "Theer's nowt wrang wi gradely folk—and if gradely's not in your dictionary, it's not a gradely dictionary."

It is in modern dictionaries, meaning excellent and thorough, handsome and comely, real, true and proper; its derivation honourable from Middle English 'greithlic', Old Norse 'greithlyr'. What is gradely, good and wholesome is also 'jannock'.

Jannock according to Webster is a provincial name for bannock, a bread made from oatmeal. A Lancashire/Yorkshire dialect word, origin unknown, for what is straightforward, honest, genuine, says a 1964 dictionary, Jannock was a staple diet in the past and oatcakes to Lancashire what porridge was to the Scot.

Every cottage had its rack laden with large oatcakes suspended over the kitchen fireplace. "Are they dried washleathers, chest protectors?" wondered strangers.

A young man was cautioned about chosing a thrifty wife. "Watch how she butters the oatcake," he was told. "Wed not the unthrifty lass who spreads butter on the rough side, but take the one who can make it go twice as far on the smooth side."

Often people say, "I don't mind dialect but I do dislike slovenly speech". But what is slovenly and careless, apart from enunciation? Condemned words are often of long and honourable lineage—as 'owt and nowt', 'nobbut and summat', 'sithee and sista', 'tha knows', 'hasta bin' and 'arta going'. So are 'I mun' and 'you munna', and the rarely heard 'did hoo' of Darwen and 'dud hoo' of Blackburn, genuine dialect used by our Old English and Old Norse forbears.

"Did hoo ax thee?" Old English for "Did she ask you?" 'Sithee and sista', for "Do you see; dost thou see?"

One might think treatment of the definite article careless speech when it is in truth of Scandinavian origin; Hole i' t' Wall, Cat in t' Window, Hall i' th' Wood, Bottom o' th' Moor, Top of' t' Hoof, and recent addition—'Back o' t' Spouts', a rendezvous for the young of Bolton by the new fountains in the Town Hall Square.

A Lancashire man is a born philosopher and what he does not think out for himself has already been summed up in well-worn adage. Living has always been a serious matter; none of the necessities of life, shelter and warmth, food and clothing, or the money to get them, came easily. Therefore money and money-making were serious subjects. Brass and the 'addling of brass' gave rise to many a pregnant saying.

"Them as don't work, don't eat."

"Wilful waste brings woeful want."

Wilful waste is a deadly sin in many a family where grand-parent's tales of the Cotton Famine are remembered. What did the old grandfather say when a child left food on a plate? "When I was your age we had twenty meals in a week of nothing but thin meal, and watery porridge. Every meal, porridge, except a piece of bread with dripping for Sunday tea."

Many a Lancashire family prospered and became wealthy as a result of dogged hard work. The father laboured—but his son spent freely and the grandson squandered what was left.

"Where one'll rake, another'll strew."

"Three generations, clogs to clogs."

A flour miller of Feniscowles near Blackburn was so close-fisted a friend once reminded him that "money were made round to go round". The miller retorted dryly, "Aye, and it were made flat to pile up".

"Ha'pennies make pennies and pennies make pounds and pounds look after themselves."

"The first hundred pounds takes the longest to save."

Thrift encouraged as a primary virtue is less apparent nowadays. In spite of dire warning, young folk gaily embark on married life with millstones round their necks, mortgages and H.P. repayments.

No one now damps ardour with gloomy sayings as "Laugh before breakfast, cry before night", or "Evenings gay lead to mornings grey". And never are there reminders that life is more likely to be a vale of tears than a bed of roses, moralizings gleaned from Victorian churchyard tombstones. A long time since our poets wrote:

> "Owd Time-he's a troublesome codger,
> Keeps nudging us on to decay."

And in the words of the Wigan poet, John Critchley,

> "Man must not lie on sunny leas
> Counting the daisies on the sward.
> Duties well done must purchase ease."

Unconscious humorists excelled on the subject of death, or the end approaching. When death could not be avoided it was said laconically "He mends war",—improvement reversed! "A short cough and a long stocking"—the end was in sight!

A Job's Comforter looked around the sickroom with a worried expression. "Them stairs—and that bad bend half way down. How the hangment do you think they'll get coffin down yon?" The sick man did not know. He was past caring.

Love, courtship and marriage were treated with dry humour. Each stage was watched from behind lace curtains and reported with gusto. Lizzie's 'getten a chap'. She's 'walking out'. They're 'coorting strong'. Maggie, a homely lass 'better to follow than to face' has at last 'got a lad'. When two equally unattractive people find a mutual attraction the neighbours comment, "Well, they wont spoil a pair". or "They haven't got much, but they must have fondling ways". A rich man was a 'Long Oliver'. Of an unfortunate girl left on the shelf to dream of a wealthy husband it was "Clogs weren't good enough—and shoes wouldn't come!"

A stuttering lover was a figure of fun. His proposal, "M' begum, Emma, isn't it time we were wed?' became a byword round Hurst Green.

So did the laggard pair after long years of 'coorting'. Said she hopefully, "Don't you think it's time we settled down?" He thought long then said, "But who do you think would have us now?"

"What I admire most about you northerners is your ability to endure your weather," said a newcomer.

Weather is of vital interest to us; everyone is something of a prophet. I have inherited from my mother, grandparents' lore.

"Rain before seven, fine before eleven", and "Such a Friday, such a Sunday". And Pendle has always proved more accurate than B.B.C. forecasts.

> "If Pendle hill do wear a hood
> Be sure the day will ne'er do good."

A grey cloud cap askew and ragged over its brow is a bad sign, but a white cloud worn straight as a straw boater—very good.

We make jokes too. Blackpool Tower, visible from every hilltop, is a foreteller of rain for if we see it plainly it is surely going to rain and if we cannot see it, it *is* raining!

Bitter cold, winter winds are less common west than east of the

Pennines, but grandmother used to say when biting east winds raked the valley, "They're the only winds Robin Hood never went out in!" and they were "Lazy winds that went through instead of round you"; "Too cold to turn out a cat", and cold enough "to freeze a brass monkey".

Keeping warm has always been a major problem. "Get something warm in you". "Let your clothes warm you, not you your clothes". "Good fires save doctor's bills", old folk use to say. In Lancashire today is no raking out fires in May and ferns and flowers in the grate until October. Fires, hot water bottles and electric blankets are always on hand.

Good fires, good food; first priorities. Food interests everyone, eating to live rather than living to eat. Though most are as familiar with new, continental and foreign dishes generally as the next, and sea foods, chicken baskets, chicken barbecues are 'fashionable' there is no sign of the rank and file's rejection of fish and chips, hot-pot, taty pie, black puddings, tripe—and other north country dishes with Lancashire and local variants.

Yorkshire pudding in Lancashire? We eat it not only with roast beef but as a batter pudding with sweet white sauce. Tripe? Charlie Chaplin expressed a wish to eat it again as in Blackburn of his youth—"as it comes from the shop, every hole full of vinegar" —and that, our longest established tripe dresser tells me, can be done only in Lancashire, for having the purest soft water processing results in tripe quite delicious, without cooking being necessary as in other counties; in hard water areas, uncooked, it would be quite unpalatable.

Whatever cook books says, the true Lancashire hot-pot must be made of neck end of mutton, not stew beef, with layers of sliced —or quartered—potatoes alternating with layers of meat and onions, the top layer of overlapping scalloped potatoes cooked to a crisp brown.

Hot Pot suppers? Centre piece of all 'dos' in town or country. At Ulverston, where Sunday School parties were a last fling before Lent, the hot-pots were of two kinds, with or without black puddings.

Black puddings? Made after November pig killing, as a Mawdesley farmer's wife described to me: as the blood from the hanging pig, newly killed, flowed into a waiting bucket it was stirred vigorously to prevent coagulation. Then it was boiled, groats added, garlic for seasoning, and small pieces of leaf fat, without which the pudding loses much of its attraction. The home made were much the same as the large scale commercially produced puddings. Where the high percentage meat content the Government insisted upon in 1966? The ignorance of Whitehall set blackpudding eating Lancastrians rocking with hilarity.

Mr. Ashworth, whose Old Original Bury Black Pudding Shop I tracked down in a dark backwater, was amused too. Casewells started black pudding making over a century ago; they are sold on markets, in shops and sent to places as far afield as Cornwall and the Outer Hebrides, where the haggis-minded appreciate them. Danish customers eat theirs with strawberry jam!

In Westhoughton families enjoy 'rice pudding with a crust on'; odd maybe, but made rather like a custard pie in a pastry case and served piping hot and liberally springled with currants and sultanas—just the dish to give the stomach a comfortable lining on a winter day.

So back we come to the weather, and the cold and damp mists —the reason scholars like to think for our many superstitious beliefs and the prevalence of witches. One wrote of the Pendle witches in the 1630s:

> "Needs must strange fancies poor old wives possess
> Who in those desert misty moors do live
> Hungry and cold—"

We are still slightly superstitious, but do not always confess to it. We would rather not break a mirror, or find a picture cord snapped, or a bird trespassing in the kitchen; or hear birds crying in the night or a dog howling—age old premonitions of death or disaster. And we wish on seeing the first black lamb, the slim new moon and an all-white horse in a field. Harmless ritual, turning over our money at the first cuckoo calling, and counting magpies from 'one for sorrow' to 'seven for a secret'.

Old Nick, Old Demdike—and suchlike

Early in 1612 Lancashire came into the news. It was known that the King, who had written a book in demonology, had sent north an astute witch-finder, Thomas Potts, and that Master Roger

Nowell of Read Hall, a new J.P., had sworn to wipe witchcraft from Pendle.

He did, for a time. Members of the two most powerful and rival families of witches, the Demdikes (the Devices and their grandmother who styled herself the devil's chief agent in these parts) and the Chattoxes, together with other Pendle Forest members of their coven were caught at a Good Friday meeting and haled off to Lancaster. In the Shuttleworth Accounts, money is put down for payment to the constable who took a Padiham suspect, 'Pearson his wife' to the Castle.

Potts' *Trial of the Lancashire Witches* gives all the details, the deposition of the accused—who professed amazing powers—the evidence taken down by Nowell at Read Hall, and at The Fence and within Pendle and later at the trial. Out of their own mouths, and the accusations of the nine-year-old Jennet Device, they were condemned—fantastic to our way of thinking, but not to our ancestors around Pendle who firmly believed a witch could maim and kill by pointing a finger. Fear could kill—as in the case of the Huntroyd man who believed he was 'witcht'.

In 1633 nineteen unfortunates accused by a boy, Edmund Robinson, trained in witch-hunting by his father, were found guilty at Lancaster Assizes and seven sent for further interrogation to London. The King's Examiners acquitted all, but four had died of terror. Witch-finding ceased to pay. Edmund, false witness exposed, languished in London's Gatehouse Prison.

Poor and half-witted old hags no longer feared arrest and hanging, but their neighbours did take precautions against witchcraft, to prevent a witch milking cows in the fields—rowan tree wood and red thread plaited in their tails; crossed brooms on the threshhold would turn away a witch—and better still, a cross cut in the stone. No hag could enter a stable if a horseshoe, heel upward was nailed to the door.

My father's great grandparents lived in a moorland farm high above Ribblesdale. The girls' bedroom was over the stable. They were wakened at dead of night by commotion below, a great crashing noise, and the sound of thudding hoofs and wild cries borne away on the wind. Next morning the 'hag ridden' horse, black with sweat, was in his stall; the door still fast bolted!

Queer goings on are remembered in unexpected places. Within sight of the Ribble Valley Bridge on M6, is a churchyard with a witch's grave, the stone cracked and signs of old rivets upon it; the hag obviously tried hard to break out. On the Ribble Banks there were diabolical dances; men like devils with Samlesbury witches for partners.

The Fylde is innocent-seeming landscape surely, yet Old Meg Shelton lies under a heavy ice age erratic in Woodplumpton churchyard, near the scene of her various depredations and disappearing tricks; but she wandered to Grimsargh and Whittingham where folk long cursed her name. On Cow Hill she did what was unforgiveable—milked the fabulous cow (which had given milk to a half starving countryside) until it dropped dead. Old Rib Farm near Longridge preserves a (supposed) bone of the cow.

Of Pendle it is annually expected it should give some recognition to its old reputation. Hallowe'en for witches rides—on motor bikes and horseback. I remember a night ride of witches, a cavalcade a hundred strong strung out against the Sabden Valley skyline and the stars, all in peaked headgear, flowing capes and red rearlights in each mount's tail—a precaution I am sure old Demdike and Chattox never took. At every cottage and farm gate families watched them ride by, and at each they obligingly gave their most bloodthirsty and eldritch screeches. A pony club 'do'.

Lowland Lancashire dealt in spirits, mostly evil, of bog and pool. Fiery headed dobbies, tempting lights over dark meres went with the draining of the mosslands as did ague and rheums. But Jenny Greenteeth, being useful to keep alive as a warning to venturesome children, still haunts deep pools clad in pond weed and slime.

Our Celtic ancestors left us as well as fairy lore, 'tree magic', the rowan with especial virtue against evil things and witchcraft, and taboos on cutting blackthorns and felling hollies, or ill luck will surely follow.

I played on the superstitions of Irish labourers sent by estate developers to fell a holly at my gate!

At Thornley Hall near Chipping a roof high holly of great age must never be cut down—or else! And in a most lonely clough near Parlick Pike and Wolfen Fell, high above the Vale of Chipping, at the gate of Wolf House farm there stood a venerable yew; it was there when watchers gave warning of wolves marauding in hard winters, and when the Derby tenants rode forth to Tudor musters—and it was known that "when the yew

Lancashire Contrasts: 1, *Great House door, Gawthorpe Hall*

falls so will the fortunes of Woof'us". Some years ago a howling gale tore across the Bowland fells leaving in its wake trees uprooted, and the yew tree torn asunder. The catastrophe was at once reported to the Earl of Derby's agent; a young yew next day was planted within the roots of the old!

Boggarts familiar to our grandparents and our remote ancestors still troubled us as children. We did not really believe in them, but when older companions urged us to run quickly with eyes averted past a barn because there were boggarts in it, or when hurrying home at the edge of dusk through a clough reputedly the haunt of boggarts, we did not feel very happy about it and would rather not have known.

Boggarts thronged my part of the Ribble country. Old Clitheronians had a saying, "It keeps turning up like Old Hall boggart", referring to the appearances of a fearsome creature who patrolled the streets of the borough at the midnight hour. He was a horrid apparition who made night hideous with howls and clanking chains. But a much pleasanter boggart, who took lodgings with a spinster at Well Hall—near the Manchester bus terminus, left only kindly memories behind him. He made himself useful, spun the thread, did the housework and it must have made a cheerful picture to see the two of them, the boggart on his three-legged stool and the old woman sitting with her chair drawn up to the fire, 'camping' before she went upstairs to bed.

Lancashire folk knew what was expected of them when a boggart came as uninvited guest to pass the winter months beneath their roof. If they were to be on good terms no reward was to be given for work done, no prying on his actions tolerated, no iron or wood to be used on his behalf. These rules remembered, and they would find the cows herded to the shippon, sheep rounded up, unpleasant tasks performed most cheerfully. But—what happened when children peeped through a knot hole at boggart's quarters under the stairs? And when a tiny pair of new clogs was put down for him? A terrible scene, tantrums, screams and stamping as he jumped about crying "New clogs, new wood, boggart'll never do any more good".

At one Pennine farm the boggart made himself such a nuisance to escape him the family were forced to 'flit'. The old home was broken up, all the gear loaded on the cart, the door locked for the last time, the key safely in the father's pocket. All ready for off, a

Lancashire Contrasts: 2, Cottage door at Firwood Fold; 3, Cottages at Cartmel

jerk at the reins, and away! Then from a rattling milk churn a shrill voice, "I'se flitting wi' you too". So, as the farmer's wife decided, it was a case of "What, flittin' wi' us too? Then turn the horse's head and home again!"

Boggart Bridge at Towneley Hall? The last resting place of a troublesome imp who after a spell of waylaying travellers, terrifying horses, buffeting and tripping up the unwary, was 'laid' here by the priest with a promise never to bother folk again "as long as a green leaf grew in the clough". Hollinhey Clough is never without its green leaves; the evergreens were planted specially!

Just off the Longridge-Hurst Green road near Knowl Green there is Written Stone farm. Centuries ago another boggart made himself objectionable to all who travelled the lanes hereabouts so he too was well and truly laid, under an eight foot long gritstone slab from the Tootill Height quarries. As the writing upon it lets every one know "Rafe Radcliffe laid this stone to lye for ever". That was in 1655. The first attempt to remove the stone, to a new dairy not many yards away, led to such a series of mishaps that the new tenants of the farm were only too ready to replace it. Hollies were planted against it to make assurance doubly sure.

As in the days of the Norse settlers the spirit of evil stalked through Lancashire—till the devil disappeared at Hell Hole bridge near the Clitheroe borough boundary. So legends say, and who are we to doubt them?

Lancashire was devil-conscious. A thousand years ago two devils walked the north, Nikkr and Scratti who had followed the sea-rovers on their wanderings. Christian priests conveniently combined the two, the new devil being known as Old Nick, or Old Scrat. They knew him well in Rossendale. At Hell Clough, near Stacksteads, he sojourned in a dark ravine where with great rocks he dammed a deep pool for his daily bath; when water ran low he called up a storm. One day he found he had excelled himself, such torrents descending his dam was carried away and the breach torn in The Thrutch, littering the valley below with debris. He never succeeded in repairing it. Usually he was an excellent mason and builder, witness the Devils' Bridge over the Lune at Kirkby Lonsdale, the most beautiful in the north, surviving centuries of floods.

He wandered alone around the countryside, anxious for company. Many times he made a foursome at a card game, all going well for him until at a three lane ends near Chipping, a keen eyed country lad glimpsed the cloven hoof beneath the table, and the end of his tail draped around a stool leg. He joined in a game of football with some lads at Crawshawbooth, and they shouted approval at the mighty kick which sent the ball flying; but when it continued skywards and disappeared from sight—and one lad saw the cloven hoof and tail just before the stranger vanished in a blaze of fire—they all were aghast. That was what happened to Sabbath breakers!

His kick was noteworthy but his aiming at a given target not so good. How lamentably he failed to tumble down Clitheroe Castle from his stand on the hilltop above the Wellsprings inn. Though one breach in the thick wall of the keep has been called the 'Devil's Window' his aims misfired; stones dented with his finger marks are scattered around Pendleton and the pile he dropped in disgust on the hill side is still there, the Devil's Bratful. And two footprints, one cloven, on a rock slab above Craggs ruined walls on the Sabden side of Pendle mark where he jumped.

"The devil is ten thousand years old and growing daily in cunning." So it was written centuries ago, but without foundation. Not outstandingly learned people got the better of him—the Cockerham schoolmaster, a priest at Hothersall Hall near Ribchester, the Clitheroe parson—with the same trickery; his memory was very poor. Each asked him to weave ropes and knit knots in sand.

Good tales: worth remembering, if only for the children.

What We Say of Ourselves

We have a pretty shrewd idea of our own virtues and failings, and we know what others think of us—that we are friendly, straightforward, blunt and 'nosy'. I know what I would put first among good points and bad, but to make sure my opinions were general I have asked hundreds of people, from Furness to Merseyside, what they consider makes a Lancastrian.

Friendly, yes. Quick to make overtures to the stranger, to make him feel at home, to make him 'one of the family' not within months but within a few days of arrival. "Smiles cost nothing", a child is taught; ready smiles at bus stop, in shops and market and as a London traveller once remarked on arriving by train at Warrington, "I can tell I'm in Lancashire, everybody's smiling."

The fact is we like people and, hoping they will like us, we at once put all our cards on the table. This proves disconcerting and alarming to southerners who are accustomed to introductions and time to make up their minds before conversing with a stranger. Reactions are amusing to watch. A Lancashire man enters a railway carriage or public place oozing camaraderie, hail-fellow-well-met, eager to make friends with the whole world. He ignores class distinctions and is incapable of seeing that though *he* feels matey no one else does. How he tries to warm up the frigid atmosphere!

He is extremely helpful to strangers in difficulties; not only will he tell you the way but go half way across the town to deliver you safely at the place you want. On the other hand, he will stand half an hour, quite lost, at the entrance of Euston Station and drive half a dozen times round an unfamiliar town rather than show that he is from 'up north' and he 'does not know'. TV is a godsend; he can shut himself up with the 'tele' and through informative programmes become expert on diverse topics—without revealing his former ignorance.

He is expansive with utter strangers, and—especially if a country man, readily stops for gossip with every passer-by. Not to greet any one on the road is highly suspect. From earliest childhood I was taught that only undesirables did not return our 'Good mornings', so much so that countryfolk in Wiltshire, Hampshire and Dorset who passed without a word, I considered very odd.

What would be a southerner's reaction to a greeting as given to us one foggy November day on the moors above Belmont? "A grand day for a murder!" commented an old man heading east. It was too—just such a day when James Henderson the Scotsman was 'done in' on Winter Hill; it chanced to be November 9th, the anniversary of the foul deed.

Friendliness, homeliness, hospitality, are virtues which go together and have done so for generations.

"E-eh, I'm that glad to see you. Come in, and take your clothes off. Jean, make room for Miss Lofthouse's clothes ont' spere."

So did the mayoress of a Rossendale town welcome me in—and warmth and kindliness radiated from her.

Teddy Ashton knew of such greetings.

"Sit thee down, draw up to t'fire
An mak thissel at hoam.
Here's a jolly good health,
Here's luck and here's wealth.
Whenever th'art passing this way
We'll allus be glad
To see thee owd lad,
Thar't welcome as t'flowers i' May."

The words change slightly but the welcome is as well meant; no longer "I'm gradely fain to see thi, sit thee down", but a friendly direction towards the table with "Sit down and get thi feet under". This is a commonplace today. Some believe good neighbourliness, characteristic of the close-packed terraced houses where clan spirit and helpfulness were as strong as in the villages from which the folk came, is of the past, wiped out in 1939. They talk of neighbourly combined-aid when trouble came upon a household; how one did the baking, one the washing, another cared for the children, another did the shopping—all taken for granted. It was always done in the old days—but not now, not in new towns, new estates, new flats, they say.

Friendliness and hospitality is ready enough, especially in the Rossendale area. Coming down from the Waugh's Well unveiling from Fo' Edge, New Hall Hey and Plunge to Edenfield, I was invited home to his snug stone-built cottage by a typical Lancashire man. I had missed my 'bus, there was a long wait, so it was, "Come in. My wife will have a cup of tea ready." In his home they made "as many cups of tea a day as Lyons", said he. "And if front door wasn't open; back door was just closing after a departing guest." Easy hospitality too, welcomed as though it was the most natural thing in the world to have a complete stranger sharing a meal. "Reach to", said his wife. "Reach to, you're very welcome".

Rochdale has a very large Pakistani population. In 1966 they took the largest hall, a thousand of them, to give a thank-you dinner to the townsfolk who had made them so welcome and been so helpful during their ten years in Lancashire.

Straightforwardness, being forthright, downright, honest, we recognize in ourselves, and in calling a spade a spade; and, getting down to brass tacks with no beating about the bush, a definite tendency to bluntness.

"I never realized how blunt and outspoken I could be until out in Singapore it stood out a mile", said a home returned Lancashire exile. "I had to learn there to wrap up my feelings, to think before I expressed opinions. I learnt a little finesse."

What voice is invariably chosen for those dominant, bull-dozing characters in radio and TV plays who are go-getters, beating down all opposition in getting to the top of the tree? Lancashire accents for successful business tycoons, self-made millionaires who have bludgeoned their way to a fortune. They are out for all they can get, they rub people the wrong way—but in the end are shown to have hearts of gold.

Times Have Changed

Have all the old virtues disappeared. Have Lancastrians changed?

Are we as thrifty as we used to be? Is the war the dividing line, between those adult before '39 who knew hard times, and those growing up after '45 whose chief struggle has been to keep up with the Jones's rather than work for necessities?

"Lancashire is not what it was," say the older. "And aren't you glad it isn't?" say the younger.

A farmer from Broughton Beck told me of the threepenny piece his mother brought from her carefully hoarded 'brass' to give his father when off for a spree in Ulverston. "Tak that," she said when he patted his pockets and found them empty. So off he went for the evening. At midnight he was home again. "Here lass," he said, as he handed back the threepenny bit. "I didn't break into it." "Nay lad keep it. You nivver knaw. You might need it some day."

Are we as buoyant, resilient, refusing to let hard times get us down and, surviving, ready to face the future with good humour where lesser breeds of men would become sullen, cowed or rebellious?

Certainly the 'old breed' was like that.

I was asked to judge a large number of essays written by members of the Over Sixties Clubs in the Fylde. The subject, "Times have changed". Many were born in the 80s and 90s. They knew adversity, but what was known as Lancashire grit pulled them through.

As half-timers at twelve or thirteen their 2s. or 3s. weekly wage was welcome addition to the family budget. At thirteen as full timers, working round the clock from 6 a.m. to 6 p.m.—and factory gates locked on the dot to catch out late comers—6s. was a week's pay for a two-loom weaver. A fully trained weaver with four looms queued up after work on Friday night for her 25s.

"Men were stunted in growth, women bent and worn before they were old, flat chested and undersized. Cheap shoddy clothes set them apart."

"Thank God," wrote an eighty-year-old, "we shall never see the like again." Neither will barefoot children ever crowd the gates of Merseyside shipyards begging from the workers, "Any bread, mister, please more bread". Nor will infant mortality ever again be so high that, as a seventy-eight-year-old woman wrote, "I remember playing in his father's workshop with the undertakers boy and we were given tiny brass nails to hammer in 'boxes'. Tiny coffins were stacked in piles, and little shrouds waiting, ready made, all with rows of forget-me-knots sewn down the middle of them. Infants died like flies."

There are many of the old hardworking breed still around, whose motto is "Hard work never killed anybody", and from whom the highest commendation is, "She hasn't an idle bone in her body".

I walked along with a woman the other day, one of five sisters, all taught weaving, for as their father, a farmer, knew, "it was a good thing to have a trade in one's fingers". Forty years ago, in the same mill where she still works, her wages "£9 clear", it was 25s. a week for three looms, if the 'sorts' were good. She had her own sweeping, lifting and oiling to do; but now 'sweepers' do the heavy and dirty work—and her day finishes at 4.45. Time after that lies heavy on her hands. With the five-day week 'weavers don't know they're born', with the shorter week the work-hungry Lancashire man and woman is now able to take on a secondary employment to 'put time on'. The weaver works evenings and Saturdays in a café.

At Rampside church near Barrow is an epitaph to a man who died "for working too hard!"

The New Industrial Revolution which has amputated the old, outworn mills and methods, brought in new techniques, new fibres—and new automatic machinery—is now reducing the forty-five-hour-week to thirty-seven-and-a-half hours. Shades of the past, the twelve-hours day and the weary start of '6 o'clock i' t' morning'.

In one essay a Preston woman born in the 1890s wrote of her mother's hard day's work. To make a living her mother, who kept a grocer's shop, was compelled to remain open till midnight perchance a customer might want something, if only a halfpenny candle.

A grocer's daughter of today was incredulous. Her parents are home every evening, they have a caravan on Windermere shores, a boat on the lake, two cars—and she hopes to go on a ski-ing holiday again with her school at Christmas and pony trekking at Whitsun.

How could she hope to understand that her parents would have been happy as youngsters to go for a week to Blackpool in July, and her grandparents remember throughout the year a day trip to the Isle of Man?

Times have indeed changed, and not one of the 'over 60s' seemed to regret it. They enjoyed their bright new flats and bungalows, the light, heat and hot water. They looked back with slight nostalgia to childhood days of black-leaded grates, polished brasses, gleaming fenders and fire irons, blazing coal fires, and the tin bath on the hearth filled laboriously by ladling can from the boiler to the left of the grate, and the delicious smell of the family dinner cooking in the oven to the right of it.

Each regretted the hard work their mothers of the early 1900s had endured. In Lancashire working class homes in the cotton towns mothers were weavers. Factory hours were long and wearisome, one form of labour replaced by others when they reached home, all the baking, washing, ironing and mending, scrubbing cleaning, polishing, waiting to be done. And it was done, and well, the house kept spotless, and when she had finished inside, out she went to scrub and donkey stone the door step and the window sills, to swill and sweep the 'flags', the pavement fronting the house. She was not satisfied until the flagstones were "that clean you could eat off them".

No woman in the days when her pride was in home and family and all her pleasure wrapped around them, grumbled that "a woman's work is never done". In her little world her word was law. Long after they were married and off her hands her children treated her with utmost respect. "I always watch out what I say to our mother, though I am turned fifty. She stands no nonsense from any of us"—this from a prosperous mill manager. Matriarchy is common.

One or two regretted that some of their youthful pleasures were denied young folk of today—the jolly music of the street barrel organ, Italians with their monkeys, the Russian with his dancing bear at Preston Whit Fair, German bands playing in the streets, the borough band on Christmas Day waking them with "Hail, smiling morn, smiling morn"; the balloon man, the rag-a-bone man who gave you in return for jam jars, donkey stones, rubbing stones or a balloon; the muffin and crampet man with his basket over his shoulder: and rides high above the world on the top of a jolting horse-drawn tram, feeling like a Queen; Sunday School field days, and slow, slow dreaming voyages along the canal to Whittle in a horse-drawn barge.

And what pleasure there was in spending a Saturday penny—weighing the lasting merits of four ounces of boiled sweets, one pound of damsons, four strips of Spanish ribbon, or four toffee sticks! When one became a worker the young apprentice—who worked fifty-three-and-a-half hours for 5s., his father paying his 10s. for lodgings, knew the value of his 1s. weekly spending money. A night out in Preston in 1910; his budget—fish, chips and peas, 4d., pop—2d., a packet of Woodbines—2d., and a seat in the 'gods' at the Hippodrome—4d.

Family gatherings were round the piano on Sunday evenings, or sing songs round the American organ. "At 9.30 prompt Dad locked the door with due ritual pronouncing, 'All good folk should be in bed for 10 p.m.' "

"We knew how to enjoy ourselves. We made our own fun. When life was most grim we cracked most jokes; we had to, or we would have gone under." Some grew an extra protective skin.

At work, fun and good humour was the leaven which made toil endurable. The old hands sent raw recruits to fetch glass hammers, left-handed screwdrivers, bundles of post holes, and tins of elbow grease; generations of youngsters were taken in. They were inveterate leg-pullers and there are even now more clever mimics off the stage and screen than on it. They 'took off' the boss, the overlooker, and made fun of the high handed superior person as well as the simple, gormless and gullible. Even the Arm of the

Law was not free from ridicule. In Bacup a story was told of a local 'bobby' who was so poor a scholar that before he could write out his report of the finding of a dead horse in Henrietta Street, he had to drag it into Gas Street!

Tale Telling and Lancashire Humour

Tacklers Tales are a Lancashire speciality. They date to the last century when overlookers in cotton mills were the butt of a thousand stories, all derogatory. The weavers were so dependant on their tackler, and he on them—his wages being based on their earnings, that more often than not there was bitter antagonism between them. Making him a half wit, a simpleton, they got their own back.

A newcomer to Lancashire was advised by a neighbour how to make a good, cheap but nourishing meal for her family. Ask the butcher for a 'tackler', she was told. He hooked down a sheep's head for her. "But I asked for a tackler," she remonstrated.

He went on preparing the head for her. "It'll be a tackler all right," he assured her, "when I've taken all 't' brains out."

A tackler's head "not overstocked with learning" as in William Baron's verses.

> "But a tackler requires none you know
> And if he's as numb as a great lump of wood
> He'll nobbut be same as em 'o.
> What he's lacking in knowledge he has in conceit.
> He's a mighty big man in his way,
> An if suppin' flat pints makes a qualified mon
> He's fit for a tackler today."

That was a century ago. In the 1960s a 'tackler' is a skilled technician, his a specialized job in the modern mechanics of textiles.

The best tales are remembered, collected and told-by tacklers. Two arrived at the seaside on an annual cheap trip by train. Both ceremoniously removed their footwear for the annual dip. Said one to the other, "By gum, Bill, thy feet are mucky!" Retorted Bill, "Well don't you remember, I missed trip last year!" A definitely 'dated' tale!

Bill was the type who explained his accustomed late arrival to his boss, "I know I'm late, but how the hangment can I hurry when I live on t'doorstep?" And when told to make sure all the incandescent gas mantles were in working order, when gas light was an innovation, did as bid. Returning, he said, "They're all bad 'uns. I tried every one on 'em, and they're all soft".

What happened when a tackler showed his wife the nine-foot clothes prop she had ordered him to buy? "But I want a nick in t' top," she declared. Nine feet high and he but five feet six inches. A problem. He went to his neighbour, also a tackler, to borrow a ladder. "You don't want a ladder to put nick in t' top," cried he. "All you need to do is to prop it agen t'wall, go upstairs, open bedroom window and then you'll be reet height for t' job!"

In the spinning areas, that is in Greater Manchester and from Oldham and Rochdale to Bury, Bolton and Wigan, the butt of the jokes is the spinner, the overlooker or minder of the mules (for the uninitiated, the spinning machines and named so when Samuel Crompton combined the virtues of James Hargraves' jenny and Arkwright's invention). The spinner is no simpleton as the tackler is made to appear, but a mean skinflint and every tale exaggerates his carefulness and miserliness. His job was to see to a pair of mules, and he required helpers, a side piecer and a little piecer, one an experienced man who had to wait for the spinner to retire or die before he could reach promotion, and the other possibly a half-timer. Their pay came out of the spinner's wages, as little as possible, hence his reputation for meanness. In fact spinners were the élite, the aristocrats of the spinning industry.

How mean could he get? Well, in the days when chewing twist was a substitute for smoking—forbidden in the mills—one spinner chewed all day, then took out his squid and placed it very carefully on a hot rail; this he took home, sliced and smoked in his evening pipe.

Once an accident robbed a spinner of two fingers. A search was made, high and low, but no fingers could be found. Until someone dropped a half crown on the floor. At once, up popped two fingers to close round the coin.

This is my favourite. A certain spinner, too mean to buy watch or alarm clock to waken him each morning, was asked how he managed to be on time at the mill. Did he pay a knocker-up to knock him up? His method was simple, he said, cost him nothing and never failed. When he woke, with no idea of the time, he took up the bugle he kept at his bedside, shot up the bedroom window and blew a loud reveille over the sleeping street. Within a few moments irate neighbours were opening bedroom windows. "Who the hangment," they shouted, "is blowing a bugle at 4.30 in the morning?" Much better than TIM!

Not at all like the tacklers' tales! Care of money and thrift have always been outstanding in the spinning towns, especially in Bolton. According to the Trustee Savings Bank 1966 report the town saves a million pounds a month, its savings per head of the population is double the national average.

As he worked for me, a painter and decorator recalled for my benefit the daft doings of a certain Darwenner I will call 'Old Fish'. The tales filled an afternoon, and the next day he had remembered more—and all true!

Old Fish was late home for dinner. His waiting wife spied him an hour late progressing very slowly up Hacking Street. She went to meet him calling, "Your dinner's been ready this hour and more". "Don't dinner me," cries he, "And don't send me to buy shoes at Co-op no more!" She looked at his aggressively new footgear. "Tha great gaumless fool," she exclaimed. "Tha's not cut laces!"

One Saturday morning he arrived at work dressed as for Sunday. "Aye, I'm going to niece's wedding this afternoon," said he "and, I'll be short o' time. So I thought I'd don my best clothes and when I get home I'll have nobbut mi singlet to change."

The often repeated old tales are hardly likely to be forgotten, though completely out of date. New ones will be thought up too, as long as Lancashire men keep that old sense of humour.

We say a Lancashire man is quick on the mark, he sees a joke at once, whereas the Yorkshireman will clap his sides and the funny side dawning, laugh the next morning.

No doubt about the Lancastrian sense of humour. Maybe it is not always recognized as such. Take the visit of a Lancashire technician to an engineering works in the south, proud of its products. After a tour of the various sheds and hearing a succession of experts extolling their fine degree of accuracy 'to two thous' he remarked dryly—"That's nowt. Where I come from we get ours *reet*."

Who but a Lancashire workman could summarize the doubtful capabilities of a new worker in so few words as this. "You want my opinion? Well, he starts at nowt—and tapers off."

Remember, Lancashire folk enjoy playing up to an audience. It is quite likely the 'scouse talk' put on by two hail-fellow-well-met Liverpudlians is for the benefit of baffled eavesdroppers. So was the remark of a prosperous Rossendale slipper manufacturer at a conference in the Savoy Hotel, London who announced he was not climbing any stairs, he would "Go up in t' hoist". Leg pulling is the breath of life to many of us. If 'broad talk' is expected, then broad we can be!

So, naturally, if others have the idea we live in the backwoods, are roused by 'knockers-up', stump about in clogs and are incapable of coherent speech 'we have only ourselves to blame'.

Having written all this I wonder how accurate a picture I have drawn, not only my own but from a concensus of opinions?

A Liverpool friend remarks, "The virtues claimed are no more than you would expect from any Hottentot villager".

When London friends newly come to the North declare our chief fault is intolerance of southerners I feel they have a case, but reserve judgement. There is something about a pronounced southern drawl which makes some Lancastrian hackles rise; they wrongly believe it implies patronage. Nothing silences a northerner more. No one is more touchy. He is tolerant of everything—except snobbery and affected superiority.

"How mercenary Lancashire people are," a retired officer settled on the Fylde coast told me. That comes of living in Blackpool, thought I, where from Easter to October is concentrated money-making.

Adverse criticism I can understand. Is it not well nigh impossible to draw a picture of the 'standard' Lancastrian when he is so complex a character, a 'compound' who emerged late in English history?

Townsfolk and city folk everywhere have so much in common. So have countryfolk. I have found dalesmen in the Tyrol, in the hills of Donegal and the heart of Wales very like the High Furnessians. I know that in the villages of East Bergholt, Brent Eleigh and Kersey, Taynton, Lower Slaughter and Painswick, Dinas Mawddwy, Dolgelley and Llanelltyd—to mention but a few where recently a common love of flowers and gardens and all things old and comely has been for me open sesame to homes and hearths—friendliness has been as warm and ready as anywhere in the north.

And who was to know whether they were 'natives' or off-comed 'uns. We are all so mixed a population these days that virtues and faults are little clue to place or county of origin.

Most of what I have written is doubtless true of Lancashire before 1939, can still be true of the older parts of towns and cities not yet demolished, and of villages little affected by overspills and development. About the rest I refuse to commit myself. There are un-neighbourly neighbours 'who don't know you are alive', travellers on bus and train who hide behind newspapers or sit with lips tight shut, unsmiling queues, and lonely people—as anywhere else.

Being proud of my Lancashire/Yorkshire ancestry I would like to say one is less likely to meet such 'north of Trent', and even fewer north of Mersey.

II

LANCASTRIAN LAND

What is Lancashire?

Lancashire is one million acres of north country compressed into a very odd shape, its head gripped by Westmorland and Cumberland to stop it floating away, its feet firmly planted against Cheshire, its bony back braced against big bully Yorkshire. In '74 comes beheading, elbow-pressure easing when Bowland and mid-Ribblesdale come in from the West Riding.

A late-comer into the shires, it was taken in 1168 in two large pieces from Chestershire and Eurwikshire, and later a very precious part of the Barony of Kendal added, land beyond Morecambe Bay. Of all counties it is most varied in its underlying rocks, landscape contrasts, its tone and colour, and the way Man has made or marred it.

Its foundation stones range from the New Red Sandstones—accounting for the colour of Merseyside from Liverpool to Warrington and underlying Lancashire's west from Liverpool to Ormskirk, Preston and Lancaster to Low Furness—to the Silurian slates, and the hard volcanic rocks which make the grandest mountain scenery in the county, embracing Coniston Old Man and all the giants around him.

In between the oldest and the newest come the Carboniferous, coal-bearing measures, shales and limestones, lending every gradation from blacks and browns to pale grey and white to the landscape. The full horror of what Man has done in the name of Progress is here displayed. Within a short distance of natural beauty, untouched, inspiration of poets.

Just a century ago experts were complaisant about what industry had done to the face of Lancashire. About four hundred collieries were yielding thirteen million tons of coal a year from over two hundred square miles of coal measures. With four million tons estimated 'still left to dig at', it would last another 250 years. At the same time, the gritstone moors of the Pennine edge and the hills from Billinge and Parbold to Rivington and Anglezarke were providing the building stones for scores of towns still a-growing, their factories, monotonous streets, massive Victorian Town Halls; paving stones for their sidewalks; cobblestones for roads; and for roofing, the thin Haslingden flags.

Where the country looked 'dreary superficially, the riches that are obtained from under the surface made ample amends'. So men thought in the 1860s. Muck meant money, and where smoke belched from chimneys meant wheels whirring, looms working; so who cared that the clean grey, yellow-brown and biscuit-coloured buildings turned black as if hewn from coal? The skill of her workers, the wealth from her own under ground, flung Lancashire high on a wave of prosperity. But everything within miles was ravished, ravaged, blasted, blackened.

For a century and a half, writers have painted Lancashire in none but the darkest shades, not putting the blinkers on to hide the ugliness—as Lancashire folk have done for generations, coming to terms with it, making light of their surroundings, but refusing to see the bright side, refusing to let in a glimmer of sunlight or a gust of clean air. Firbank's 'hundred miles of prison in which all the inmates are lifers' of the '40s is being repeated in the '60s by writers who find the 'only depressing thing about the towns is the scenery', and that in travelling through the county they look in vain for a break in mile after mile of dismal, drab and uniformly ugly landscape. Such as he came by car, keeping to highways. Anyone with his eyes open in the 1970s must recognise vast changes, reclamation, 'environmental improvements', and not too soon.

With these unpromising industrial and near industrial scenes I deal in their own sections; they are not tourist areas, but are far less drab than they are painted. The rest, nearly three quarters of our million acres, is rural or nearly rural. This 'truly rural' covers much of my native Ribble valley and eight rivers which, running from Pennines, or Bowland and Wyresdale Forests, to the Irish Sea, make sweet music and water a green and pleasant land. With gritstone breaking through, it is wild, whaleback moorland, clad in ling and heather, home of grouse and blackcock. When limestone takes over, from Clitheroe to the Hodder, from the Lune to

Lancashire Contrasts: 4, Sky over Peel Tower; 5, Sky over Furness fells

Keer and Kent it is pure water-colour landscape, in delicate washes, for the rock is dove grey and in sunshine looks to be made out of moonbeams; pastoral from the beginning of time it is unspoilt; very precious countryside.

And so former Lake Lancashire, shared with England and the world. Five star beauty here, the oldest rocks, highest peaks, and within it the southern part of the great Cumbrian dome thrust upwards when the world was still writhing in the agony of creation. The Ice Age gave us our loveliest dales, Duddon, Crake and Leven dammed them for lakes left dark cwms hanging among sheer crags high above them, cupping lonely tarns like those in the shadows of Coniston Old Man and Dow Crag.

The Ice Age travelled along Lune, Ribble and across south Lancashire leaving a liberal coating of boulder clay—the unresponsive stuff we have to contend with in our gardens—and scattering alien boulders.

The water and lakes drained from some of the valleys, like the Duddon, eventually but not of their own accord from the almost flat saucers between Mersey and Ribble, Ribble and Wyre and Lune. Mere and moss, marsh and swamp, accounted for half the area thousand years ago and encouraged but few dwellers who occupied the low ridges of the Fylde and the mere fringes of south-west Lancashire.

In fact, when the surveyors in 1087 were compiling the Doomsday Book they accounted for no more than 13,000 people who lived thinly dispersed over one sixteenth only of our million acres. It was not very impressive, much marsh and swamp, more woodland and dense scrub, and only two or three reasonable ways of getting into or out of the region. With the descendants of the early Celts or Cymry still herding in the mountain fastnesses of Cumbria, a few Angles established in their hamlets and villages on the well drained slopes above the rivers and near the heads of estuaries, and considerable Norse settlements where the Angles had not attempted to bring into cultivation fell side and dale head or coastal creeks, life was pretty well at a standstill. They stayed where they were—those who had survived the bad times of Earl Tostig's revolt in 1065 and William's harrying of the north in 1067.

Even the Conqueror's henchmen who were given the largest estates as reward for aid during the invasion, cannot have been

Lancashire Contrasts: 6, Bridgewater Canal at Worsley; 7, the Tarns, High Furness

enamoured of their holdings north of the Mersey. William shared out the lands formerly held by Edward the Confessor and Tostig and a handful of Anglo-Norse thanes, to kinsmen and close-followers. None was worried about outside interference and few saw need to erect strong castles to guard coastal approaches—the coast looked after itself; nor to make any show of strength on the inland passes—the unfriendly Pennines were their own defence. Small motte and bailey castlets sufficed to watch fords and the few highways, and to protect the garrisons from unwelcoming natives. The only permanent castles guarded important crossings at Ashton, Penwortham, Clitheroe and Lancaster; others did not appear until medieval times and the period when halls were fortified against the Scots.

So much was unproductive, waste and 'deserta'—with no income—that hunting-mad Norman kings seized it and designated vast areas for 'forest'. Half the county between Mersey and Lonsdale was so taken. Pendle, Rossendale, Trawden, Little Bowland, Wyresdale and Lonsdale were reserved for the chase.

In the royal forests folk had to watch their step. Where natives had little freedom of movement no wonder outsiders made no attempt to come in. The Irish Sea, the Pennine barrier, the even more formidable northern approaches, either by the Cumbrian mountains or the dangerous oversands crossings, cut us off for centuries; a most wild and inhospitable part of the north, outsiders considered it as some (not knowing them) think of the Outer Hebrides or the far west of Ireland.

Has any other county come as far in nine centuries? Has outside opinion changed as rapidly? There are still some who think of Lancashire as among the least attractive counties, under a perpetual pall of smoke or obliterated by fog or rain, and not a blade of grass to be seen. In fact, artists complain all is *too* green!

Our weather repels people. As a maritime county with none of us much more than thirty miles' crowflight from the sea, we have full benefit of sea breezes and rain-bearing south-west winds. The highest mountains draw down the darkest clouds; High Furness can expect an annual 80 inches close to the Coniston range, but Low Furness around Barrow gets away with 30/35 inches. The Pennines are also cloud gatherers, the cotton towns of Calder valley and Rossendale enjoy that damp humidity 45 inches of rain gives them—so necessary in the early days of the textile industry but less attractive now to folk who have tested the sunshine of Torquay, the Channel Islands, the Costa Brava and San Sebastian. At lower level, the area around Manchester shares 40 inches or thereabouts, but down the Mersey a mere 30 inches falls and the Southport and Blackpool coast have rather less.

We talk a lot about the weather. Our part of the north is not so bleak as it is painted and rarely do we live up to the weather forecasts; usually we listen unbelieving to weather reports. Promised 'bright intervals' have meant ten hours continuous sunshine, and the worst depressions coming in from Ireland have been broken by good dry periods. No—you do not need to be supermen to endure our climate; and you can chose what you want.

Some days an assortment of weathers are going on at the same time. I have dropped from rain-swept Wrynose Pass to sun-drenched Coniston, from mist-curtained Rivington Pike towards Southport living up to its continental type posters, from high winds on Pendle to dead calm and sunbathers on Blackpool sands. Take your pick!

No, our weather is not so bad as painted, but what of the country, the county? Are we proud when we bring new friends across our borders in that narrow Manchester-Ashton gap, the inescapable tentacles of Cottonopolis clawing? If they turned tail and bolted we could hardly blame them. And this the Classic Ground, work-begrimed and a sorry mess—*almost* as bad as the less advertised parts of London, Birmingham and Glasgow—which so many northern writers and playwrights have been so clever in painting as the true image—and succeeded only too well.

Yet changes are coming, swiftly. South-east Lancashire in the melting pot and a Brave New World taking shape. In ten years time it will be unrecognizable, having been taken in by Greater Manchester.

Meanwhile travel M6 and M63, splendid motorways, for swift, smooth progress from south-east Lancashire into a green and pleasant countryside where rolling hills take over, smiling villages look up at clear unsmudged skies and motorway bridges carry us over clean shining rivers, part of my 'Lancashire Without Chimneys'. So there *is* a Lancashire where we can walk tall and be proud to say, "Look, all Lancashire, and all beautiful!"

When I first heard of plans to erect a tall observation tower on M6 near Forton I had my doubts. Not now! It is just the best 'display stand' we could possibly have. There should be a visigraph and arrows (as pointers) to all points of the compass, naming the swart fells tumbling over themselves just eastwards and the shadowed dales gripped between their knees, identifying the farms and villages on the flat lands westwards, the shoreline landmarks, the jagged peaks of High Furness looking over the Cartmel fells, and the inlets and creeks probing deep within those fells, and the headlands and islands. What a panorama!

> "Straight mine eye hath caught new pleasures
> Whilst the landscape round it measures."

We do not need to be poets to appreciate this. I have stood side by side with Americans, Swedes, Germans, on the glass-screened balcony. They enjoyed the prospect—all free!—but for me there was a special pride, as though I had made it all myself.

I belong to Lancashire—to country like this, to the towns to which I was transplanted, most unwilling, at the age of ten, to the great city of Liverpool where I worked. Town and city made me love the country all the more.

I grew in the town—a hundred and twenty mill chimneys Blackburn had then, all smoking, its looms adding up to its reputation of being the largest cotton producer in the world; I could bear it with Clitheroe only ten miles away and not at the end of the world as I first thought when uprooted.

I enjoyed Liverpool too, from the start, the bustle of city life, the activity on the river front, the people of all colours and nations. "Of course," said my friends, "Liverpool is not Lancashire, it's international." My friends included Welsh, Bahamian—and South African.

When as a student in London I accepted an offer for a post in Liverpool my college friends, amazed, cried, "Why go back north—why to Lancashire?" I had realized 'up north' seemed remote to them, and that northerners were somewhat different from the rest. So thought relatives of my friend from the Cape when she, given a choice of posts, chose one in Liverpool; they saw her off from Euston with tears of regret that she had opted for banishment! It was not long before she invited them to join her; she liked the north. And they were agreeably surprised on arrival.

Like so many she became the most enthusiastic 'adopted northerner', was soon accepted, and inevitably found herself one of those many non-Lancastrians who is helping to run charities, clubs, institutes, guilds and the like. Surprising but true, in every activity such as these a fair proportion of southerners are working with us, keen as mustard, doing work which never came their way before they transplanted themselves to our not-so-alien soil.

My first book, *Rediscovery of the North*, claimed that from Blackburn it was possible to keep on walking for a hundred miles heading for the border with four thousand square miles of the Pennines—fells and dales—to explore, all away from 'public haunt or dwelling'. In the Lancashire Pennines the sheep population outnumbers that of humans. Within sight of them—excluding Liverpool, which sets its sights on the Welsh mountains—live half of the five million Lancastrians. Where else are such startling contrasts?

How should I tackle the Portrait? Start with town or country, mountains or coastline, or with the Backbone of England which put hardihood into the Lancastrian—the Pennines? Or with cities and towns of the Classic Ground—darkest Lancashire with its new Jerusalems, the Counties of Merseyside and Greater Manchester.

Exiled Lancastrians make for Trafalgar Square when homesick. The new stone pavements are Pennine flagstones from Whitworth quarries in Rossendale.

Lancashire's New Image? We grow rather tired of seeing the Old Image perpetuated. Take the Media. When it was suggested there was too much about slums and old mills in programmes, it was insisted that always a 'fair picture' had been shown, it was "necessary to show the unattractive side" whilst recognising there was delightful countryside in Lancashire, rich cultural activities, recreational possibilities. . . . .

In my book *Lancashire Villages* I have shown how many thousands of townsfolk have opted in the last decade for living in the country. Among them are a number, who, realising the unspoilt charm of certain rural backwaters, would rather no one came to know about it. The 'new protectionists'! At the same time others are eager to get Lancashire a place on the tourism bandwagon! We cannot have it both ways.

III

GREAT CITIES AND NEW JERUSALEMS

Liverpool and Manchester: Past, Present and Future

After talking with the planners of the New Liverpool and Manchester some of their enthusiasm brushed off on me, and I could almost bear to walk their streets with pneumatic drills to the left and bulldozers crashing through on the right, without too much despondency. Everyone called all this urban renewal thrilling, and to be a witness of the birth of New Jerusalems a great privilege.

I was shown Manchester's plan, with bright and beautiful tall buildings, massed proudly above the small black models of the 'Old historic' and begrimed, and riding high above all, the road opened in 1967, Mancunian Way. Smacking of Rome? And why not? Was not Julius Agricola the first to realize this 'great potential', as road centre of the north-west, as long ago as A.D. 79? Modern Manchester with becoming modesty blows its trumpet: 'Capital of the North-West, Focal Point of the Largest Industrial and Commercial Area in the Country!'

Capital of Greater Manchester? Is there not a population of two millions on its doorstep, and three millions, with baskets at the ready and full purses clutched, within a radius of fifteen miles, and 8,500 shops (annual turnover £140 millions) waiting for them? We are promised shopping which will be at the same time a dream and an adventure in urban landscapes, with splashing fountains and traffic-free streets.

Liverpool wants approval for its plan, Graeme Shankland's vision of a city good to live in, pleasant to visit, keeping the best from the old and creating the new to enhance it. For visitors—two millions from its hinterland—a dual carriageway is planned on a motorway to fly in a three-and-a-half mile circuit over the city until, 'on the southern edge of the tipped saucer which is the city's topography', it will sweep to ground level below the two cathedrals. Such is pride in its magnificent cathedrals that "all other buildings must be kept low so that they will retain their serene dominance of the skyline".

There is pure poetry in Liverpool's plan. From shopping expeditions made pleasant "on the biggest system of pedestrian walkways, outside Venice, devoid of traffic", there will be quiet backwaters for sauntering, the "grandeur of Albert Dock combined with the humanity of Leather Lane". "Tall buildings north and south of the centre will combine with the Pier Head group like spikes round a crown", whilst southern approaches will be beautified by a "green swathe of parkland which, combined with tall buildings alongside, will make this entrance as dramatic as river front and Pier Head do now over the water".

With "hope and imagination", says one, with "courage and stamina" says the other, we must decentralize, decongestalize!

The cities created by the Liverpool gentlemen and the Manchester men a century ago should now be complementary. Neither should try to steal the glory of the other. But I am slightly worried about Manchester's three million potential customers. There is always the chance they will stray to Liverpool when whim decides! Or stay in Better Bolton and Rochdale Reborn!

I have just been reading Liverpool's first charter in the local history section at the Picton Library. King John granted it eight years before he was forced to put his seal to Magna Carta, when he was involved in plans for conquest of Wales and Ireland, and saw the creek as a good anchorage for his ships. He offered burgages, the first in a new town, at one shilling a year rent, and made a few vague promises which his son ratified later, recognizing a merchant guild and the 1207 charter—at a price. His castle on an elevated site—now levelled and with Queen Victoria surveying the city traffic—was in command of harbour and estuary, the creek, the forest land reaching out to West Derby and Toxteth, the hills of Wirral, and the sea beyond the sheltered basin. A fair spot then, its motto, "God has created these pleasures for us", could be that of the new city planners!

The burgesses disliked the castle, constant reminder that they depended on good behaviour for keeping the royal favour; the

Constables kept too close a watch upon them. There was a ferry, "the King's boat in Mersee" and great numbers wishing to cross because of Liverpool's markets. "Great Contrarity of weather and frequent stormes" often hindered them and on the Cheshire bank was no lodging. So in 1318 the prior of Birkenhead was authorized to erect lodgings, keep provisions at hand, "support men to cross the said arm of the sea". The ferry became more busy and the market and fairs more prosperous.

Nine years later, soon after Bannockburn and ferocious Scots raids, the Constable was compelled to shelter fugitives—and the name of Leverpol appeared for the first time on any map. By 1361 it was the naval base for Edward III—ousting Chester—with ships of war, and men and supplies always at the ready when trouble flared up in Ireland. Liverpool's fortune was linked with Irish expeditions. When the Wars of the Roses caused waning interest in Ireland the town and port suffered, but the Stanleys who had fortified their riverside house, Tower of Liverpool, in 1406 had ships tied up there and Sir Thomas, Lord Lieutenant of Ireland,

"Without all doubt at Liverpool
He tooke shipping upon the sea."

Tudor kings recognized the port, and Liverpool revived.

The town, developed so enthusiastically by King John's burgesses, had grown from creek and pool towards Town Fields, Heath and Breck. It had St. Nicholas chapel and St. Mary del Quay, both near the water, a Martinmas Fair and Saturday markets—the liberty stone in Castle Street marking its limits—with merry minstrelsy in Juggler Street near the High Cross. The Lord of Liverpool claimed rents, tolls and revenues.

The Molyneux, (the *X* is sounded by the Earl of Sefton, who ought to know) descended from the Norman Molines who came to Sefton in the eleventh century, leased Liverpool from the king. Generations were Constables of the Castle and in Tudor times erected a comely brickbuilt hall at Croxteth in West Derby, to be near the town; this house is surrounded now by Queen Anne, and William and Mary, plus Victorian wings, a great mansion with a new Liverpool encroaching around its Park.

The Stanleys frowned at Molyneux from their water-side Tower, like gamecocks red in the comb and spurred for combat, as in 1425 when the two families and armed supporters prepared to do battle on the Heath, neither accepting role of second fiddle. At Knowsley, which the Earl of Derby built in the 1490s to welcome his stepson Henry VII, they were near neighbours of Croxteth. And both are still there.

Both families have Lancashire at heart. Their histories would each fill large volumes. Enough to say that the Stanleys—who for generations were Kings of Man, refused another crown a century ago. As Disraeli said when the Earl of Derby put aside the throne of Greece, "A dazzling adventure, but Stanley will prefer Knowsley to the Parthenon and Lancashire to the Attic Plains".

How did Manchester stand when the Tudors came on the English scene. Little was left of the Roman fort, a five-acre site with barracks for a thousand men. Salford, chosen to name an Anglian Hundred, had been superseded in Norman times when new Barons of Manchester, the Grelleys, chose a spot at the confluence of Irk and Irwell to set up their Barony Courts, eight generations of them. Their estates were vast; their forests extended north to Rivington and Horwich.

Chetham Hospital includes part of their Hall above the rivers and this was the De La Warrs' who succeeded them, and given in 1422 to the college of priests 'to keep hospitality together', as they did until the Collegiate came to an end.

Any who doubt Manchester's long history should look for the Angel Stone in the cathedral, a precious fragment from a pre-Norman church. In that blackened building—about to be relieved of its centuries' coating of grime—glorious Perpendicular, and flooded with light through tall windows, see how the early Wardens laboured, raising magnificent choir and nave. Bishop Stanley in 1450s set skilled carvers to work on ornate choir screens and canopies, introducing the eagle, his family's badge, instead of angels in the roof beams, and the eagle and child on the bench end of his pew.

A deep and wide impassable ditch below the church was bridged by the College in 1422, the 'Hanging Bridge' in Deansgate, a road along the dean. Manchester's streets then were Blackfriars and St. Mary's Gate, Long Millgate and Fennel Street, Market Street and Four Acres Field, where markets were held and the fair when the corn was cut.

Except for the 'Wellington' in the Old Shambles, miraculously surviving the 1940 blitz (the plan to preserve it involves buildings round a courtyard with the inn islanded in the middle), no half-timbered Tudor buildings remain.

Seventeenth-century Manchester was a jolly town, "music and dancing and things very plenty", and the folk "passing fair and beautiful". Kind too to strangers, with landladies at the inns "like mothers" to penniless travellers, according to John Taylor in 1618.

> "Oh, all, you true worth men of Manchester
> True bred bloods of county Lancaster
> When I forget what you have to me done
> Then let me headlong into confusion run!"

"A town or city without its old buildings is like an old man without a memory." Let Manchester and Liverpool cherish what they have for posterity's sake.

By the seventeenth century both towns knew where their futures lay. Of Manchester it was written as early as 1538, "it is the fairest, best builded, quickliest and most populous town of all Lancashire"—with 8,000 people; and in the 1690s "a thriving place", with two street lengths on market days taken up by linen, cloth, cotton, tickings and yarn. Cottonopolis in the making.

Liverpool knew also. The world was its oyster and the shipping of the seven seas was about to enter its waters.

From the start there was no real competitor. When we were at war in the seventeenth and eighteenth centuries and all sea routes hazardous, Liverpool had a north-west approach to give her ships security. Chester she saw out of commission in the fifteenth century, Bristol was outpaced in the eighteenth century. Lancaster had no chance, and neither had Glasson, whilst Fleetwood had to leave the port pre-eminent in her own field and "stick to fishing". It all began when the Pool was converted into the first wet dock in 1715. Trade gained momentum during the next century with the three-legged voyage of her own ships; first south to West Africa to exchange goods for slaves; the middle passage to the West Indies or the port of New Orleans, profits in the slave markets, purchase of rum, tobacco, molasses, cotton; and a return home with hold full of rich cargoes—and a handsome return on all Liverpool money invested by Liverpool's gentlemen.

These imports were the raw material for Liverpool's new dockside industries, and for its hinterland as soon as Lancashire inventors had found new techniques for dealing with cotton instead of the traditional wool and linen for textiles. When slaving was declared illegal, Liverpool provided two of Wilberforce's chief supporters to force through the Bill—Rathbone and Roscoe—and instead of decaying, as foretold by prophets of gloom, port and town leapt forward into greater prosperity.

New roads, canals and, in 1830, the new railway were needed to carry the increased trade, and as transport improved from port of landing to towns of manufacture so population rocketed. Liverpool's 77,653 in 1801, was 223,002 in 1841 and industrial towns increased accordingly.

The Hungry Forties and the Cotton Famine—tragic episodes Lancashire lived through with native fortitude—only halted progress. They led to many leaving England—in immigrant ships sailing down the Mersey.

Shipbuilding gained impetus, and ships fitted for new ventures filled the docks. Local families like the Holts founded shipping companies, their sights set on Far Eastern trade; two brothers thought it out in the garden of their father's Liverpool home in 1865. They were part of the middle phase of local enterprise.

In 1830 there were 435 founder members, most of them styled 'merchants', in the Chamber of Commerce and Industry, wealthy and prosperous with handsome houses on the outer southern fringe of the growing town. Some built elegant Regency houses near Lakeland—like the Fords at Yealand Manor, and the house the Wordsworth's rented, Allan Bank, Grasmere, built by the Crumps, and the great mansion at Storrs on Windermere shores erected by the Liverpool shipping family, the Boltons. To be a Liverpool merchant meant something solid, respectable, prosperous, and enormously rich.

These Liverpool gentlemen wholeheartedly disliked the idea of admitting as new members those who called themselves manufacturers. "Liverpool was turning its back on the sea," said they. But change came; they had their port, their ships, but enormous additional prosperity came with the manufacture of raw materials close to the port of landing.

Now, merchandise and manufacture share the Liverpool scene, inter-dependent: sugar refining—from a Dale Street kitchen boiler in 1665 to the world famous Tate and Lyle refineries of today; flour milling—a long way from the Lord's mill to the extensive multi-storeyed mills dominant on Liverpool's skyline today; rubber—which came in as a milky fluid sailors had seen as a hard outer skin covering the feet of Amazon natives, now used for countless rubber-consuming goods including the Dunlop's factories, the newest providing work for the population of Skelmersdale New Town; tobacco blending, tanning, malting and brewing produce a rich aroma along the Dockland roads; Merseyside special! As for the industrial estates ringing the city you can tell when the day's manufacture is raspberry or lemon jelly, or when marmalade making is in full swing.

The slump of the 1930s hit both cities. But, as everyone says, pushing the memories aside, "that is ancient history". So is the Second World War when both had a battering, and Liverpool endured the worst continuous bombing—the never-to-be-forgotten May blitz of 1941—in which the city centre and dockland were left shattered. And, phoenix-like, both have risen out of their own wrecks.

Urban renewal in Liverpool covers Speke, industries wooed there by civic backing; Aintree; the six square miles of Kirkby, the most extensive housing estate in Britain; and Huyton with Mr. Harold Wilson as its member in Parliament. Coming to the end of rebuilding within its boundaries—what spectacular flats in the green valley below Childwall—the city has embarked with great vision and little ill feeling on New Towns. Skelmersdale I saw when the first three hundred families had moved in as settlers in a new world. I imagined the place ten years hence when the seeded avenue verges are like green lawns and the trees planted along them are fully grown, and every family can "sit under its own fruit tree" now staked in each garden, and creepers—already trained to grow up the high grey walls of flats—are scarlet drapes in Autumns to come. Liverpool is good with trees; its older residential areas like Mossley Hill and Woolton are beautifully avenued and bird song in Childwall gardens is as fully choral at dawn as in any Surrey wood. So Liverpool gives trees to its new towns, flanks squares and piazzas with conifers and wherever flowering shrubs can find a home there they are already growing.

Manchester having shown how pleasant life is on its perimeter, Wilmslow and Wythenshawe, plans to develop at Sale and Whitefield, is making of Hulme, "the greatest development in the country, maybe in western Europe", and its new satellites of the 1970s/80s will "permit city folk formerly condemned to pass part of their lives in dismal surroundings, to live full and happy lives" and city children will know the smell of green grass and growing things.

Manchester's most sensational new buildings are its 'biggest and highest' skyscraper blocks. Liverpool's, the two cathedrals which will rank as outstanding achievements of this century. Four sovereigns have visited the great cathedral on the Mount since Edward VII laid the foundation stone in 1904; plans have been modified and work goes on, masons in the workshops, cranes lifting blocks of stone, men on scaffolding putting them in place; the largest church in Europe though size is not its outstanding attribute, but a solemn grandeur enshrining great tranquility, rich and glowing colour of the fabric heightened by brilliant stained glass. It remains as much a haven today as in the war years when thousands entered as on pilgrimage, from distant and dangerous places, from the war-ravaged city near its walls, to thank Providence that Liverpool still stood where it did. The Metropolitan Cathedral on Brownlow Hill, completed in 1967, shows a clean break with tradition in discarding Sir Edwin Lutyen's plans for Frederick Gibberd's designs, 'the shape of things to come'.

I find modern Liverpool exhilarating; bracing winds come round corners—and surprises too. The place is on its toes—waiting. There is noise and bustle; but silence too, and sunshine trapped in the city's heart at the Exchange Flags; peace-making sounds of pigeons 'cru-cruing' and their clapping wing beats; on the terraces behind St. George's Hall, people dreaming among flowers and children—white, black or brown—playing round Gladstone's feet, or gazing up at Wilberforce Square fountains, fascinated.

Beauty catches hold of you—from the new balconies of the Pier Head, white wings against blue sky, sleek dignity of big ships, the far-away gaze of folk leaning against railings—especially beauty Man has created, for Liverpool has had its golden times. The Town Hall, John Wood's work of 1754 with Wyatt's additions, is emerging from its first wash in two centuries, rosy, glowing; what fine work those French prisoners of war put into the capitals of the Corinthian columns, and how well the war-shattered masonry of 1941 was replaced! The Georgian Bluecoat School of 1717 looks fine too, and the Georgian to Regency houses in the terraced Rodney Street, a delight with its ornate fanlights, distinguished looking doors and rows of brass plates to match.

Following the Railway Age—the first train left Liverpool for Manchester in 1830 with its full complement of V.I.P.'s—the city produced its most impressive buildings, sign of the highwater mark of wealth and prosperity. On its Acropolis of St. George's Plateau, the Greco-Roman Hall—which is an odd marriage of concert hall and courts of Assize—is considered the best example of English classic, and near by the long range of library, art gallery and museums, all pillared and porticoed with many steps one mounts as to the Parthenon. Being on hills Liverpool's stature gains much, as Edinburgh's.

So much to see. There is a green bronze door in low relief at Martins Bank in Water Street, and at Lewis's store Epstein's 'Liverpool Resurgam', a naked man springing into the future—and milling shopping crowds below him, unaware. There may be kestrels teasing the Liver Birds on the Pier Head skyline. . . .

For Nature—with the assistance of the city's gardeners—where does she sit more beautifully than in the parks along that 'green swath of the southern approaches'? Princes Park and Sefton, the glorious gardens at Calderstones, and miles of rock terraces, green sward to walk on along the new waterfront, at Otterspool where once was barren shore. Here was a city tip, and the dumping ground for rock brought out of the Mersey tunnel excavations; now it is a promenade for the citizens to watch the river's ebb and flow, the passing ships, the changing colours as day ends in sunset spilling over the Wirral hills.

Museums dull? Not on your life, not if like the new one in Liverpool. Fascinated, I am drawn to it every time I pass and enjoy watching eager youngsters, wandering round rapt with notebook and pencil, pestering benign attendants with their whys and whats, in bright faced clusters round 'teacher' and later dragging in parents to 'see' for themselves, I know I am but one among thousands who finds it thrilling. And good in clearing up the hazy bits in How The World Began. What happens under the sea when fishing boats go out, etc., etc., etc. How ships developed from coracles, triremes and quinqueremes to modern vessels. How Liverpool became what it is. And what each civilization, since man emerged from his cave, has given to mankind. No mental indigestion afterwards and all confused from overmuch culture. Enough and well chosen riches from the tombs and temples of the early civilized world.

First things? A dinosaur's footprint from a quarry near the Mersey. And, most appealing, in the entrance hall, a single piece of statuary—as impressive in its entirely different way as the Winged Victory on the stairway of the Louvre—an immense figure in stone of St. Christopher with the Christ Child on his shoulder and his bare feet planted in the waters among the fishes; this they believe once stood near the Mersey crossing at Fiddler's Ferry.

Liverpool is stimulating, as every city should be—or it is half dead. Nothing is standstill about it; everywhere great activity though it is clouded by dust and powdered rubble. But one can escape into the Walker Art Gallery to the serenity of the old Masters and Holy Families, the unruffled elegance of a Gainsborough portrait, and the brute force of Holbein's Henry VIII, for contrast; then back to the present with a modern art exhibition down below—papier maché lady painted like a totem pole reclining in tin bath tub, or a baby doll's head planted in a block of wood. It all 'makes for variety'. I always liked kaleidescopes!

What of the Mersey Sound which has encircled the world? The 'Phil', one of the nation's great orchestras, or the Four Young Men who could have been sold to America to pay off the National Debt—which will be remembered longest? Meanwhile, be glad of the Beatles, all taxpayers, for their dollar earning-power and what they have done towards the balance of payment. To have shared the same Liverpool sky with them—ah, that is great!

Manchester is in its own way as stimulating as Liverpool, with past and present jostling for elbow room, crowds jamming shopping streets, pavements and side streets full of memories and odd incidents. You never know what you will see next—a human skull shrunk by primitive tribesmen to the size of a tennis ball, in a Building Society office window; people packed round corner stalls and ranged three deep before florists and seedsmens—because Manchester folk have such a love for flowers; a score or so city gentlemen, who ought to be using their rolled umbrellas as shooting sticks, all looking at a shop window, so silent, so motionless—the time is noon and from TV sets pictures of the Test match in triplicate! A knot of long-haired youths and maidens with blanket rolls, laugh and talk in Piccadilly Gardens, and when I look for a seat in Albert Square I find one woman occupying the full length, fast asleep, an arm hiding her face. Everywhere subjects and objects with question marks above them, waiting for some radio sleuth, microphone and tape at the ready, to roll them over with "our listeners would be pleased to know why".

A green armoured security van draws close to the pavement outside a narrow door and helmetted men begin to pass out boxes to waiting hands. I stop to watch, "Want one?" asks a strong man, and makes as to throw one to me. Obviously I do not look a bank robber.

On the fifth floor of the Town Hall Extension where I talk with a planning officer of the future, a blown-up aerial photo of the New Jerusalem already realized covers one wall. Ivory towers, glass walls, tall flats caught within sungleams—these are Manchester's 'soaring signposts' to a brighter future. Is the Age of Miracles just beginning? Remembering the Cité Universitaire near Paris' Porte d'Orleans, I like the new Higher Education Precincts and University Village on the plan, but wonder if 'green-fingers' along Irk, Irwell and the Rochdale Canal showing the way into sweet rural backwaters are but a pipe dream. And are those ivory towers going to house standardized Lancastrians who cannot indulge their individual idiosyncracies in plots, gardens, backyard whimsies, pigeon lofts, hen 'coits' and doorstep gossip?

Nothing foiled the planners of Victorian Manchester, nothing mean, niggling, gimmicky then. The Town Hall; Sir Alfred Waterhouse's essay in romantic Gothic—obviously agreeable to Prince Albert who looks on—proclaimed that the city had arrived, and so did the Square. In 1877 the Town Hall cost every penny of one million pounds; grand of scale outside and in, with long dusky vistas; Ford Maddox Brown murals—in which it is good to read Manchester history and Lancashire achievements; stained glass and statuary on stairways—and far more below ground. I remember running the gauntlet of blank eyes between white marble ranks of superannuated city fathers draped in dust sheets. Lost in the labyrinth on my way to a meeting, after hours!

Flowers, pigeons and often bells pealing (City Police ringers) make Albert Square alive as a Grand Place in France; with brilliant sunshine too, on days when weather forecasts are for rain! Almost continental noontide somnolence fills the side streets behind Brazenose buildings. Tucked away in Mulberry Street, St. Mary's —named by Cardinal Vaughan, 'the hidden gem'—has flowers before statues, hundreds of candles flickering before marble altars

Upland pastures: Holcombe
Midwinter frost over Irwell Valley

Waugh
1890

and sunlight pouring down on choirs of angels and serried ranks of saints. Not a sound except the shrill voices of little Cypriots outside a corner café.

Halfway down Deansgate it is goodbye to the sunlight through the gloomy portals of John Ryland's Library. Until the Dead Sea Scrolls brought thousands in March 1966 to Manchester, I doubt if one per cent knew this precious casket for the world's most amazing treasures even existed. It has taken only sixty-seven years of air pollution to achieve that funereal coat, and to overlay the gothic halls and the stone stairways—which would grace a palace—and to seep into the holy of holies, the long fan-vaulted Reading Room. Here, between tall perpendicular pillars, are a series of alcoves 'arranged to ensure freedom from distraction'—solicitude for students' comfort being a constant care. They sit with lights illuminating their books—booking a 'carrel' for three months if their researches require it—and they have riches, more than any emperor could command, for their own. Deep hush; cloistral calm.

John Rylands, a Lancashire self-made man, left great wealth, and his widow gave this magnificent pile behind a deceptively narrow frontage, to be a memorial, and shrine of biblical art. Soon the concept widened with the buying of the Althorp Library and the Earl of Crawford's manuscripts so that now, apart from priceless 'holy books'—thousands dating from before 1501—there are rare classics, charts, and traveller's tales to go with them; and not only books but writings on skins, leaves, silk, rice paper, stone, bark, clay and bamboo. As for the priceless jewelled bindings, only two libraries in the world contain more.

From its superfluity of treasures the Rylands was able to present a nucleus from which the annihilated Louvain University Library could start building up again after the First World War.

It is said with truth that there is no better way of studying the history of printing than through the bible. I was shown in the Bible Room so much, from the earliest Gutenberg's in 1436, a Spanish polyglot bible of 1514—the Pope clamped down on such productions—Tindale's English version of 1523, and an American missionary Red Indian Bible of 1663, all in phonetics as no written language existed. And, of course, I found that misprint which ruined the printer and thrust upon puzzled readers the 'wicked bible', exhorting all 'to commit adultery'. From the earliest to the

Waugh's Well Centenary, 1966; Pennine moor edge cottage near Edenfield

most beautiful printed and bound 'collectors' bibles of modern printers and binders, a feast for the book lover is here at Rylands.

In the Reading Room I saw a priceless scrap of papyrus dating from the early part of the second century with words from six verses of St. John 18, in Greek; the first block of a St. Christopher which in 1423 heralded woodcut printing; a pocket sized Virgil of Ardus Manutius who introduced italics in 1501 and the writing—Petrarch's—from which it is said the first type was copied.

A lifetime's enjoyment—and so few even know!

For literature coming up to modern times, there is St. John Street with the Braille Library at its Deansgate end, and Georgian front doors with row upon row of brass plates naming physicians, surgeons, consultants, and eye specialists. In one house in 1846, whilst waiting for her father to have an operation for cataracts, a woman placed an exercise book before her and began to write, "There was no possibility of taking a walk that day . . ." it was page 1 of *Jane Eyre*.

The Civic Trust's mark is upon St. John Street with excellent effect, charm, and eighteenth-century elegance on either hand; in King Street too, though this is part of the financial side of the city. In 1772, a doctor's most pleasant house was taken by a prosperous tea merchant and his four sons to start banking as a side line; finance became all important and within a short time Jones and Sons' bank was the 'District'. Very handsome this, and with the fine house next door, face-lifted and pristine clean, shows what must be hidden behind scores of grimy façades in the city centre. In the same street in 1846 the Bank of England's architect, C. R. Cockerell, planned a noble building, an 'essay in Grecian' to replace the temporary premises of the new agency—the first outside London—occupied in 1826; how grand and heavy with dignity, 'safe as the Bank of England', indeed!

Other 'essays in the classic' are Barry's Royal Institution, now the Art Gallery in Mosley Street, and the nearby Athenaeum. The Portico Library, a little jewel in the same street, the design of Thomas Harrison, was completed in 1806—a 'members only' library, an early subscriber being Mrs. Gaskell's husband, minister of Cross Street Unitarian, and its first honorary secretary a man whose work was concerned with words, Peter Mark Roget of the *Thesaurus*.

Mosley Street leads into St. Peter Square—with memories of

the Peterloo 'Massacre' of 1819 when the Manchester Yeomanry, to disperse a peaceful assembly of men, women and children—hungry, unemployed, and workless ex-soldiers among them—needlessly slashed at them with their sabres, leaving terror and bloodshed behind. If Englishmen indulged in siestas this square or Picadilly Gardens would be the place for it. Instead, the benches in the square are packed with quiet lunchers and very little is said. The pigeons have rather a thin time of it but flutter around hopefully.

Modern Manchester is facing; the Library not only Central but circular, something of an achievement as a spherical building, with curving Library Walk on one hand and a curving road on the other coming to St. Peter Street. Here Richard Cobden, no other, gave a piece of land—for ever made sacred to lovers of freedom because of Peterloo—to the free traders known as the Anti-Corn Law League in which he and Bright were leading lights. A third building on the site was the famous Free Trade Hall—shades of Dickens and Disraeli, of great Victorian thinkers and reformers, of massed children's choirs singing that best selling recording of 'Nymphs and Shepherds'—and of the Hallé from 1858, its earliest days. The Hallé is still here, under Lancashire's own Sir John Barbirolli, and men feast on music as in the old building. German bombers destroyed much of Manchester in 1940, the Hall was gutted and the outside scarred. But, with old wounds healed and stone grafted to replace the damage, its Palladian façade rises proud and glorious withal—especially when floodlit and reflections are thrown across the rain-wet street.

Music has always gone well with Manchester. Prince Charles' lament 'Farewell Manchester' is as poignant as any highland ballad. John Byrom's Christmas present to his daughter, 'Christians Awake' has sounded round the world. And in its way the Chetham Hospital boys carol service is as much an event as the King's College Chapel Nine Lessons and Carols.

In the early years of the Commonwealth, Humphrey Chetham, who had purchased the very much war-damaged Hall, formerly owned by the earls of Derby and before them occupied by the priests of the Collegiate next door, to become a Bluecoat School for poor boys. He also provided for a library to be 'public for ever to students and others well affected', his own collection arriving in 1663. Rare and valuable the books were too precious to be left around however 'well affected' the borrowers. For some years they chained the books to the reading desks; later they chained in the readers—or rather locked them in the library alcoves! Still a 'free' library, you may present yourself as a reader, joining a select company including almost every Manchester writer who needed old books for research into Lancashire's past—which naturally places Harrison Ainsworth as a most voracious reader here.

After spending some time in the Library I walked out and round the outside walls of the courtyard to the dark gateway of the Hospital—alias Chetham Hospital and Nicholl Hospital School, the ancient foundation brought up to date, now an independent grammar school in a five-centuries old building. Not all was as old as that, I was to learn from three boys who pounced upon me at the gate asking would I like to be shown round. They often do on Saturdays, when in the mood and games pall.

What antiquities did they show me before I was led to the new block, the swimming baths, the labs and woodwork rooms? First the refectory, adorned with carved woodwork when the Derbys were here. I like Tarquin the giant devouring, whole, little boys. And the impressive Audit Room where the Devil—a crony of the schoolmaster, Dr. Dee, Queen Elizabeth's fortune teller—left a proof of his visit and a pact witnessed by a print, like a scorch mark or burn in the polished table. One old chair the boys informed me, in trio, was where Raleigh, smoking a quiet pipe, was drenched by a pail of water thrown by a terrified servant.

They took me into the cool cloisters, showed me the whipping post where recalcitrant brethren were punished, the Scurvy Court where those with skin diseases were isolated, and of course, Fox Court. One day as the Derbys were hunting by Irk and Irwell, excellent for sport in their time, a fox was chased into the Hospital, fled into the inner court, leapt down the deep draw well—and is still there, eyes blazing! They have fun at the expense of a raw new boy. He is brought unsuspecting to the well and told to look through holes in the well lid. Three holes; as he gazes down a hand covers one—and the fox winks back! His eyes winked at me, most realistically.

What else adds up to a portrait of Manchester today? The cleaning of the Cathedral's 'carved out of coal' stonework; the splendid post-war reconstruction of the regimental chapel destroyed in 1940; the modern wall hangings covering the exquisite Lady

Chapel; and Sir Charles Wheeler's shawled Madonna and adorable kneeling angels outside the east end. For contrast—exhilarating exhibitions of the good things of the 1960s in both the Design Centres, one concentrating on textiles, the other on building. And art galleries, museums, shops.

I almost wish I were a stranger, or a foreign visitor let loose to enjoy for the first time the good things in Manchester as described in a selection of folders, leaflets, brochures—one 'for the visiting business man', another for 'delegates without necessary time to see all the sights'—together with mouthwatering itineraries, in four languages, too!

Manchester, "Britain's second city, commercial heart of a great industrial area, frequently maligned by those who never knew it, regarded with affection by those who did"—welcomes you! New Manchester with the cosmopolitan air, "foreign restaurants staying open until two o'clock in the morning so that no one need go hungry to bed after a good night out, and delicatessen introducing foreign delicacies to once-conservative Lancashire tables". Name your sport, Manchester has it: football, cricket to stock car racing at Belle Vue, ten pin bowling at Kirkmanhulme Lane—fun and games at Boggart Hole Clough, Blackley. . . .

One almost envies visitors who arrive by air. Remember two Manchester men, Alcock and Brown, and their first non-stop crossing of the Atlantic by air in 1919? Did you know that 60,000 allied paratroopers were trained at Ringway? A two hundred square-foot stained glass screen is their memorial.

Sweetness and light, and in a city which pioneered smoke-free zones, the most fog-free airfield in England. Is that surprising? Perhaps the giant chandeliers of the Ringway concourse, each containing 1,300 pieces of Venetian glass "clear grey and amethyst glowing at night as from a hidden source of light", are symbolic.

If the brightness of Manchester is too piercing there are always possibilities of retreat to the not-so-distant Peakland caves—or to the aforementioned Boggart Hole Clough!

New Towns from Old

North of Manchester, on the Irwell and its feeders, the Croal from Bolton and the Roch from Rochdale, are a score of towns which would be very big fish in smaller pools, each with its own special flavour and none over-enthusiastic about the Local Government Commission's changes making Manchester capital of the new metropolitan county, Greater Manchester, with its reiterated two millions in ten miles, three millions within fifteen miles' radius.

City and towns have already submerged many other lesser and rural neighbours in their time, Oldham swallowed Roundthorn, Smithy Fold and Priesthill in 1770–1810; Ashton-under-Lyne its numerous satellites, and Royton and Chadderton are involved with the outer edges of Oldham and Heywood; Castleton and Milnrow with Rochdale; Heywood and Radcliffe with Bury.

You might call this Darkest Lancashire, the background for Coronation Street, a brave-hearted corner of the county where the green oases between towns are very precious though their waters are polluted and tree trunks are blackened. Schoolchildren always choose black crayons to draw their trees, knowing nothing of the subtle colouring of common birch and silver birch, oak trunk and beech boughs—not yet, though smoke is becoming less dense and snow can lie a day or two without becoming too be-smirched. Black trees in green parks surround great empty mansions, immaculate lace curtains hang at windows of black terraces—launderettes once offered 12 lb. wash for 2s. on Cheetham Hill; at Blackley is more green belt country and the Irk lost in a deep ravine haunted by a boggart, as all know, but so pleasant for lingering that town clerks go there for lunch break. Manchester longs to build houses here. Public opinion in 1967, 1972 and again in '73 said 'No!' Blackley's 'vigilantes' are vocal.

"Culture starved, strangled in the Bingo Belt," it is written of towns like those linking Manchester with Rochdale. But that is superficial, and 'clever' summing up. Middleton—ancient, around the church which was in part memorial to the Flodden victory from which the Asshetons brought Scots trophies—goes as gay as maybe with flowers in open spaces, from daffodils and masses of hyacinths to dahlias. Castleton splashes bright paint to relieve dingy walls; pointing of walls is done in white, yellow and blue to match up with brightly painted doors

And Rochdale, that virile town, should be notable not only for its export of great singers and comedians but because of its Pioneers of 1844 who at 31 'T'Owd Lane started the co-operative movement. This flourished so amazingly among the working population of Lancashire that John Bright knowing them, in political speeches declared vehemently that such men, reliable and trustworthy, should be given the vote. Rochdale's Bright and Liverpool born Gladstone won the vote for the working man.

And now Rochdale is rebuilding—towards the stars; up go the flats! Look over the Irwell Valley. Far and near the many storied buildings stand boldly against moors or misty valleys.

> "Behold, behold, with wondrous eyes
> The towering hills that reach the skies,
> The fertile plains and vales below
> Where the lovely streams of Irwell flow."

from the pen of the Lily Hill gardener, a century ago!

One must appreciate what the flats are doing—housing the thousands, putting an end to appalling slums, and saving the country for what it was intended. Every town is repeating the pattern—with local variations—on all the Irwell feeders and the canals linking Manchester with its lesser neighbours. When the new tenants have moved in and lights at dusk appear at scores of windows they are even more impressive than the spinning mills which with the nightly switch-on took on the appearance of fairy palaces. Lawns are laid about them; mature trees planted on their approaches; and, to make travel more pleasant on the once dreary highways from town to city, verges are seeded, green grass is tended carefully and gardeners are constantly at work on flower beds and many garden spaces, as from Farnworth to Pendlebury and Irlam o' th' Heights.

I make no attempt to describe the towns as they are, changing week by week so that natives are baffled and lost in once familiar places. In demolition Lancashire is above all thorough. Sweep away the lot! Let's have a new start! Naturally there is grumbling, hints at dark doings of Big Business and millions going into developers' pockets.

In old towns everything before the 1850s is being wiped out, tumbling down the Waterloos and the Trafalgars but leaving for a later phase Crimeas, Balaclavas and Inkermans. First victims, old markets, empty chapels, old houses impeding 'Progress'.

Bolton is proud of its Civic Centre and newly-washed buildings floodlit by night. Blackburn's new market precincts cover the river at Salford, where two thousand years ago native Britons traded and bartered, and Roman troops halted en route from Manchester to Ribchester; the cruciform cathedral is three quarters complete and the nave, a transformation of the 1826 parish church, flooded with sunlight, is under the powerful influence of John Hayward's 'working Christ', a thirteen-foot figure, "a simple massive column with large capable hands—a Man in the working world who wears His apron like a scapular, a symbol of work made holy".

Burnley is so rejuvenated, exiles returning know it not; the town was first to build an ultra-modern hotel fit for the reception of those V.I.P.s and industrial and financial potentates Lancashire is wooing with hopes of new business coming north. Preston, the county's administrative 'capital', with its own new image in mind has levelled square miles with great vigour, so that a stranger might think a tornado had followed upon an earthquake to lay so much bare. Everywhere is wholesale, rarely piecemeal, demolition leading up to construction on a grand scale.

Sir Hugh Casson, who travelled through the county in the '50s, saw "a vast ocean of ugliness, hopelessly, helplessly depressing" with miles of dereliction, "backyards, dustbins of industry—in a smoke-stained, unloved wasteland". Changes are coming, rapidly. Air pollution the greatest evil, is diminishing and a black-smoke-belching mill chimney becoming a rarity. The blackest spots have their smokeless zones. The skies are clearer, paintwork less grimy and snow stays white.

Much remains to be done, especially to the eyesores, thousands of acres rendered sterile in 'lunar lanscapes' of mining slag, abandoned works and scrap heaps—from Widnes and Warrington to Wigan and Westhoughton—'filthy, featureless, cratered like a battlefield'. Now at last reclamation is under way.

Yet one June afternoon in 1966 we took a walk over this 'battlefield', through waving hairgrass and bentgrass, over mats of sweet white clover, and climbed Indian file up gullies to breezy hilltops, to gaze over wide landscapes under cloudy skies full of larksong and peewits calling. Beyond, miles of meadows running under the wind, and fields new mown around stone-roofed farmhouses. A man with a gun moved round a field verge. Many motionless figures, rod in hand, meditated round a blue pool. Westwards, gentle green countryside—and this the South-west Lancashire coalfield.

Some years ago travellers on A6 at Four Gates near Wingates

wondered why a man on a mare rode up and around road edge slag banks. At the 'bus stop, folk waiting were immensely curious too. So were all the residents of Everest Road, Atherton in 1964 when—after the Lancashire County Council had completed large scale afforestation over acres of the Pretoria pit slagheaps, working parties arrived in the valleys and rolling hill country beyond their garden fences. There was great surprise, too, among the householders along the highway at Westhoughton just after Easter '66 when thirty-seven people of assorted ages and sexes began to swarm over a large round 'kopje' near the railway.

These are three of the many sites where Michael Graham, C.M.G., O.B.E.(mil.), M.A., a returned Lancastrian, famous fish biologist and anthropologist, author of *Fish Gate* and *Human Needs*, experimented in reclamation of slag and shale, backed by the Lancashire Community Council. His work is known worldwide, as I discovered talking with Canadian Fisheries scientists at Nanaimo. He died at New Year, 1972.

Graham became enamoured of these 'mountains of accumulation', not for their use as hard core of motorways and new highroads, nor for levelling into dull flats for agriculture, but as the most exciting places for children's play. Watching bands of lads careering up and down mining tips, disappearing into deep gullies, slithering down steep slopes and racing away to still more undulating landscapes piled up by a century and more of colliery waste, he realized what lucky youngsters they were. Here, at the edge of towns, was a vast natural adventure playground—no tame concrete 'rec'. Where else such freedom? Certainly not away from the north. Liberty is denied, and often in agricultural counties like Norfolk and Suffolk access to fields forbidden.

The spoil heaps need treatment, the movement of slag halting by planting of grasses which thrive on shale and ash. Helpers are called in, preferably the children who will inherit the particular plots of earth, to hammer in willow and hazel pegs to form terraces for the grassing. Like miniature vineyard slopes they look. A few weeks later, green grass is a haze over the grey-blue mounds; the slips have struck. In a few years the hills are clad in greensward, willow groves and hazel copses growing gaily, and not only clovers and hawkbits, but foxgloves and lupins, comfrey and alien self-sown plants scattered over the dips and slopes. No eyesore now, but green 'up and down land'.

One of the most tragic disasters in Lancashire mining history was the explosion in the Pretoria Pit when over two hundred men were entombed. Abandoned for years, the county attempted to plant the vast wasteland above it, and succeeded. The sealed shafts are surrounded by twelve-feet-high spiked railings; old pit roads are half way back to nature; finches and chaffinches carol from the oaks and birches, and there is a fluttering of wings in every glade and copse—as pleasant as Hampstead Heath without the crowds! At the edge of the slag heaps, where a large new housing estate was built almost into the shale, grass planting failed; the tenants looked upon 'miles of tip'.

Michael Graham was called in. He discovered new seeds and ways of cultivation.

I was with him at the housing estate when smiling folk came up with "It's coming on fine!"—meaning the seeded acres. Ladders were placed against backgarden fences so that we could climb over to the new green banks where children play wild westerns and dogs are exercised, and beyond to where folk take evening strolls through glades of birch, oak and hazel—and youths are discouraged from dirt track racing down the planted gullies!

One might say, having watched Michael Graham on 'his slag heaps', there is more joy in seeing a tip growing green than in many fields of ripening corn. Scores of ecologists, students, environmental bodies are the richer for what he pioneered.

As Lewis Mumford, the American, realized, 'a terrific act of energy made Lancashire the hole it has become', and with the same energy directed to restoring it there is no reason why it should not again be a garden. No reason why the pointed pikes of the mining tips, like miniature Alps dramatic in silhouette against the setting sun, should not be as pleasing by day.

We have some beautiful parks in Lancashire, many of them created, like Blackburn's, by workers during depression, cotton famine or unemployment. Why should the affluent society not make an equal contribution? We have Sefton Park and Prince's Park in Liverpool, the beautiful gardens of Calderstones, and Manchester its parks at Wythenshawe, Heaton Hall, and Fletcher Moss gardens; Preston's Avenham Park by the Ribble, and Moor Park for play; Bolton's Queen's Park and the most enchanting rock gardens at Moss Bank; and Wigan's magnificent woods leading to the enclosed gardens of the Earls of Crawford and Balcarres at Haigh Hall—what variety! Fine and historic mansions stand proudly within public parks at Astley Hall, Chorley and Towneley Hall, Burnley; at Worden Hall, Leyland; at Hopwood and Alkrington Halls near Middleton. One might list a dozen more, as well as 'new parks' on the edge of every industrial town, the pride of each community. We are indeed very good at parks, in the past we have been un-excelled in attempting to make gardens bloom in the dreariest places. Now the gloomy corners are disappearing we will still go on creating gardens.

If Lancashire people are lovers of beauty, let them have it, in pleasant urban landscaping—and in making deserts of waste blossom like the rose. Give every encouragement to those who want to make a little bit of England of their gardens. Nine out of ten make a go of a garden, but the odd one, the over reluctant gardener, with no interest at all in such things should not be compelled to take land with a house. Manchester has introduced green 'painted' surfaces for those who cannot or will not grow grass!

Lancashire has spent enormous sums in the last five years, on Operation Springclean—when the grime of nearly one hundred and fifty years was removed from old buildings; Operation Eyesore—eleven millions on this; Environmental Improvement—far greater sums poured out with good effect; and responded to 'plant a tree in '73' with gusto. This is where the same energy which went into making a mess of the county in Victorian times is being used to make some slight amends.

Who would have thought that Manchester Cathedral and Liverpool old Town Hall, Preston jail and Blackburn's Richmond Terrace could be restored to such surprising beauty? Or that from Whitworth to Bacup and The Valley linear landscaping could have improved the dark narrows and old railway track so effectively? Or that the canal enthusiasts could have wrought such wonders by herculean efforts on waterways 'deathly and death-dealing'?

IV

PENNINE BACKBONE AND GRITSTONE

From Blackstone Edge to the Gorge of Cliviger

The Pennines, gaunt moors which made us what we are, sheltered our forefathers from wild north-easters, let them dig their gritstone for hamlets, villages and a score of towns. The towns look up to the hills, a love-hate relationship between them.

Few roads ever forced a way across them, those wild heights of many moods—"high lights and deep shadows, gentleness and savagery, steeps of moors black as thunderclouds, great cloughs, ravines and gullies slashed into the breast of the hills by the axes of time and storm".

Only two main routes linked Manchester and Halifax, Lancashire and Yorkshire until the new Woodhead motorway was cut through the Pennines. But when winter comes, fog, ice and blizzards will still have their way and with all modern devices to make motoring comfortable, when the driver puts his nose out of the window he will realize what stern stuff early travellers were made of, to venture over this Great Divide as they did. Remember Camden invoking the protection of the Almighty as he paused on the brink of Lancashire the Unknown. And Celia Fiennes valiantly facing up to "moorish ground, precipices, mist and rains almost perpetual". Daniel Defoe was baffled by snow and 'cold, acute and piercing'—in August!

Blackstone Edge can certainly prove menacing, but for an appraisal of Lancashire it is magnificent. The Old Coaching Road which branches from the main A58 at Littleborough gives the best picture of the past. Both meet and soon 'cross hands' near the Roman Camp; thereafter turnpike road and packway sweep in figure-of-eight towards The Edge. A third road ignoring both climbs direct, with grim determination, to the skyline. This is the so-called Roman Causey though it is not certain if the Romans made it, used it or put down that impressive stretch of metalling—a paved way 16 feet 6 inches wide between cambered gutters and upended stone kerbs—or when and why was the shallow groove down the centre created. The groove, subject of endless controversy, was possibly a skid pan for carts and sledges, or maybe filled with turf to prevent heavy loads slipping in icy conditions, to give packponies and human porters a grip on slippery stones.

Up to the skyline, a hard struggle with the wind against you, and there on that escarpment, with nature the only architect and Kinder Scout gritstone the only masonry, it is like surmounting the ramparts of some crag-perched castle. Without human agency the defences were raised and only time and the elements threw down the huge rocks, as though a giant after taking the stronghold had cast down its outer walls in spite.

Roman or not, one can but be impressed at the ancient road building over such inhospitable terrain.

Greater Manchester looks gentle spread out below; little sign that the south-east is all industrial for towns are hidden in friendly folds of grey, green and dun moors. Two million folk live within sight of these hills, thronging the valleys and the plains melting into the blurred distances. Winds buffet us so we clamber down the rampart to Robin Hood's Bed, "Where no winds ever blow", there to look on "Old" Lancashire in greater comfort.

The Pennine Way northward from The Edge, careers over the tops, 1,200 feet up, through wind, wet and wildness, the world well lost. A lower, level route gives a better and more intimate picture of county border country. Here the Rochdale canal plays hide and seek with the Todmorden railway, and enters a gorge crammed with factories, houses clinging to the rock walls like cliff dwellings. For a mile the railway disappears from view; the Summit tunnel, described by an astonished traveller of 1844 as "in the midst of the stupendous works of Nature, and the highest triumphs of human enterprise".

Summit, Warland, Shade—all expression of human endeavour when mill towns began to grow like dense plantations in the narrow valleys. Warm hearted folk took root there, in close-packed neighbourly proximity; inhospitable moors overhung them, dark gritstone walls leapt to the cloudy sky, broken walls dribbled down into the 'bottoms'. Watch a man going home from the office, suitcase in hand. He leaps from the bus, grips his case, then like a mountain goat, finding grips with his free hand and firm footholds, takes a short cut up a rock overhanging the highway, mounts a wall on top and disappears—on the last lap!

Ramsden Woods, Walsden thrown about its church and soon, in the very heart of the High Pennines and built from it, Todmorden, a border stronghold with formidable factory walls for cliffs, streams tunnelling under houses and the towering railway viaduct stalking over the town centre dwarfing its homely open market.

The sky and the racing clouds are only seen when heads are tilted far back; the clouds are in a hurry, having made up their minds where to drop their rain—a choice of county, east or west of the Rigging of England, the watershedding of the two Calders.

The Lancashire-Yorkshire border should be easily defined, a simple matter 'as heaven the water deals', but in fact skyline watershed and boundary do not quite coincide. On the highroad however, three miles west of Todmorden, a road sign "YOU ARE NOW LEAVING THE IRON DUKE'S COUNTRY" used to impress on the stranger that Yorkshire was being left behind.

A lonely green hollow is a funnel for the keening wind; a few farms are rolled about like pebbles in the bowl. Maybe Roby's farmer lived in one. Said he, "Aw live at riggin o' t' world aw reckon, fur the watter fro one side o' t' roof fas to th' east sea and t'other t' west sea".

Large scale maps define the border prosaically: "The Ouse Catchment Area (Yorks) behind us, and meeting the same boundary, Mersey (above Irlam Weir) and Irwell (above Hunts Bank) Catchment Area." The wildest part of this frontier is in Stipersden, a dark ravine cutting deep into Black Hameldon and Blackshaw—'black' indicates a boundary—with pastures steep tilted and gay with flowers in summer, and farms scattered haphazardly above Redwater Clough and Dawk Hole. The Long Causeway, a prehistoric-medieval-monastic-Duke's Highway, runs above, highlevel and out of sight.

The farther we come into Lancashire the more dramatic it is, even diabolic, in wildest moods. So travellers heading into Cliviger saw it in the past, a place of crags where rock eagles had nested "time out of mind and longer than the memory of man runneth", according to Dr. Whitaker. Loynd Wife, a local witch 'took off' from Eagle's Rock—and somewhere in this wild place the Devil used to bide his time, waiting for more mischief.

The Whitakers lived for generations at Holme-in-Cliviger where Cistercian monks had a grange and humanized the medieval landscape. Holme lies snug, very tranquil after what we have seen. The Tudor hall is comely in itself, smiling into the sun, but plantings done by the 'learned doctor' who took in 130 acres, improved the scene and covered with forest trees, rocky brows and gullies. Backing the Hall are some of his 422,000 trees planted between 1784 and 1799—wartime afforestation.

Thieveley Pike looks into Holme from across the valley. I like its old name, 'T' Skirts'. It is a viewpoint to watch the meanderings of the infant Irwell and the upper reaches of the royal forest of Rossendale; a beacon site, naturally, a prehistoric defence point, and Old Dike, a very old boundary, running across its shoulder.

North and south of Cliviger is good for looking at a Lancashire not so overwhelmingly changed that you 'cannot see the wood for the trees'. In 1770 the region was 'near waste' supporting but one person to nine acres, with only a few farms northwards towards the Forest of Trawden, and southwards over Rossendale almost as desolate. Both had been 'deserta', used as hunting grounds for Norman and Plantagenet kings and both were once within the wideflung parish of Whalley which stretched "from The Cross above Wycoller called Watersheddles Cross" to Sharneyford and Irwell.

Folk had long memories, and though you are not likely to find old men in chimney corners nowadays to talk of boggarts and fairies, ghosts and hauntings, they will agree this was a good place for them, 'long sin'. I would enjoy hearing the tale of Dick of Cinder Hill's meeting with the Devil, leading a dun cow and too tipsy to realize what he was doing.

"Dick and Devil and dun cow faght
Dick thrashed Devil, and dun cow laught."

Sporting characters are more to their liking. Richard Tattersall who founded 'Tatts' learned to know a good horse when a lad at Hurstwood; he bought a tinker's nag for a song but later he bought Highflyer from Lord Bolingbroke for £2,500; fanciers who met at the 'Fighting Cocks' at Mereclough, cockfighting landlords—

like Cunliffe of Wycoller—who died happy, shouting on their gamebirds in bedside combat.

They still breed gamecocks in Lancashire and show them at Holcombe each New Years Day. Cliviger has its own show, in Autumn, for the Lonk sheep, a very hardy Pennine breed, none better for our climate.

From Cliviger through Rossendale

Cliviger was always a definite cleavage; life north and south developed in totally different ways. The hard and the soft in the Lancashire landscape and character are contrasted north through Trawden, south through Rossendale. You still find descendants of the forest dwellers living here—the old surnames persist down the centuries into the 1970s' telephone directory—Ashworths, Deardens, Cleggs, Hayworths and Haworths, Rawsthornes and Ramsbottoms among them. They continued farming, producing wool, weaving on their handlooms, long after kings had lost interest in the hunt, remaining to provide labour for the water-driven and later for the steam-powered mills, sprouting not only in the side valleys or 'deans' but mushrooming along the Calder and Irwell. When the industrial upheavals demanded it they moved down to the growing towns. More fortunate than workers within Manchester's orbit, Rossendale's millworkers remained countrymen at heart; and many never left the country. Early each morning, lanterns swinging and clog irons clattering on stony ways, they descended to valley mills, and back in the evening to high-flung cottages with lamps welcoming them home—and cool airs blowing from the dark moors.

One of the greatest surprises to strangers is to find thriving Women's Institutes, and women dedicated to the fostering of love of country and improving the lot of countrywomen, not in completely rural settings but in the heart of what many class as 'darkest Lancashire'—Lumb and Loveclough among them. Their's is a changing landscape, old industry departed and Rossendale's valleys filling up with new houses for commuters. Only the wild stark moorlands remain inviolate.

Travel here 'goes with the grain' of the land, north-south on parallel routes through the heart of the Forest—by young Irwell through Weir and Broadclough to Bacup, by Water and White-

Liverpool: the Roman Catholic Cathedral

well Bottoms to Lumb and Newchurch, or from Clow Bridge, Love Clough, Goodshaw and Crawshaw Booth and Constable Lee—ancient names from Rossendale's past—into The Valley. As elsewhere, where for a century and a half "factory chimneys have been grown instead of trees", the narrow 'bottoms' are dense with towns, mills and works—industry covering spinning, printing, bleachworks, felt and slipper making. As Newbiggin wrote a century ago, "Nature denying a fruitful soil" compensated on the other hand by giving Rossendale "abundant supply of coal, almost inexhaustible mines of excellent stone—numberless streams that travel down the hillsides to the bosom of the ample valley below". So blessed, her manufacturing prosperity was assured.

Also its folk were endowed with sweet voices and love of music. Lancashire is a 'singing county' and this is at the heart of it.

In the last century the 'Deyne Layrocks', larks of Dean sang at their looms, their oratorios they practised well unto the night, and their chapel walls on the Sabbath threatened to fall outwards like the walls of Jericho with the gale of music. Once I heard the Rawtenstall Male Voice Choir sing their hearts out and win the covetted trophy at Llangollen. Rossendale has the Irwell Springs Band, the Brittannia Coconut Dancers. . . . This is home ground for singing and music, and as the Bury black pudding maker believes there is everywhere a deep love of beauty, a deep rooted trait in the Lancashire man.

How they revere the memory of Edwin Waugh, the Rochdale-born poet, who lived among them, expressed in verse their joys, and the sorrows of the Cotton Famine, which they felt but could not voice themselves. He was able to popularize in his native speech, the simple Doric of the dialect which has in it so much of the mother element of the English language and which—until he so surely brought out its tenderness and feeling, others had thought fit only for the lower orders and labouring classes.

On a July afternoon of muted colours and stray patches of sunshine, many hundreds of Waugh devotees converged from Edenfield, Clough Fold, Waterfoot, Turn and all parts of South-east Lancashire upon a bare hillside for the unveiling of a bronze head at the well called after him. It was 1966— a century after the friends who dedicated the spring to him had shared convivial meetings on the same spot. At that period Waugh began to frequent the moorland ways below Dirn and Whittle Pike, above

The University, Bailrigg, Lancaster

Plunge and Cowpe, and found constant inspiration for his muse. And little wonder. There is untold majesty in these moors which roll away mile after mile to the west, their moods changing rapidly. They can be "wild, lonely and stern" as at the unveiling, tender and dreamlike on April days under veils of sunshine showers and rainbow bridges, dramatic in deep, purple shade with sunset and dark clouds massed above them. Inspiration here is equal to anything the Lakeland poets felt around Grasmere and Derwentwater—at least, for Pennine lovers.

"But oh the wild hills that look up to the skies,
Where the green bracken wave to the wind as it flies!
Sing, hey for the moorland!"

The wind chases the clouds, and the clouds race after the sun-like life and its ups and downs, "A marlock wi' sun and wi shade", wrote Waugh. And following the soaring lark in its flight—his philosophy,

"But as pleasur's sometimes a misfortin',
An' trouble some-times a good thing—
Though we livin' o'th' floor same as layrocks.
We'n go up, like layrocks, to sing!"

This is the kind of immense loneliness Lancashire's hill walkers love best. One hears of old time characters who walked the land, like Ralph Rooney of Hawkshaw near Holcombe, who covered forty miles a day, playing his concertina, children following him Pied Piper-like where ever he went. To Land's End he went and north to John o' Groats, not singing but playing for his supper, and bed and breakfast, 'Rimington' his favourite tune.

I met a nonegenarian who as a lad at Bury set off with his friend, three-day excursion tickets to Blackpool in their pockets—not on the train but, because the morning was fine, 'walking it'. The friend was a farmer's son. There was a cattle auction at Ormskirk, said he, "Let's go round that way". So they did, the roundabout walk of forty miles taking from 5 a.m. to 8 'at neet'. They used the tickets for the return journey!

Folk still know how to walk, octagenarians and youngsters joining in the Rossendale Boundary Walk in June, and strenuous walking it is, high above the young Irwell on wild watersheds. And every child grows up knowing the way to Waugh's Well.

Wild tales fit the landscape. Witches riding the night sky at

Brandwood, Old Nick at Hell Clough and watching Sunday football at Crawshaw Booth.

Considering 't' Chapel' in Rossendale was so great an influence for good, a lot of folk kept clear of it! All those distillers of whisky carrying on in secret places—and sure of ready markets locally! The railway navvies tunneling through Sough near Entwistle hid their stills in the lowest workings; excise men, heavily disguised, were allowed down a shaft but never repeated the search after a thorough 'possing' in the mud. Police discovered twenty-gallon fermenting tubs beneath a weaver's loomshop floor on Haslingden Grains, and accosted a moorland farmer with five full bottles on his person which he insisted were "rubbing bottles for rheumatism" an old woman said would cure him.

To produce whisky is very simple. All you need is "potatoes, treacle, sugar and barm—and apple peelings, turnip tops, owt you've got handy", as a hill farmer told me. Cut up small, everything is allowed to ferment in a barrel with water, for a few days. The resulting 'wash' is heated in a tin over a fire, a long length of copper tubing with one end in this wash and the other in a second barrel, the steam passing through it condensing as pure whisky, drop by drop, a slow business. Contrivances to cover up traces were carried to a fine art, cunning flues devised to minimize discovery. It was retailed in bladders, or carried in special 'waistcoats' each holding two to three gallons, whilst much was carried brazenly in water buckets, as though from the well, to thirsty miners and quarrymen in pit and delph.

In 1858 the local newspapers were full of the story of a Haslingden farmer called Morris, who after several visits and lengthy search by the local police was well and truly caught. When they first called he was reading his bible and swore himself innocent as a babe newborn. They came again and patiently searched for three days; their reward—all the tackle of his trade securely concealed below ground in a secret still which had functioned effectively fifty years before, through his father's lifetime. He could not keep up his pretence when one hundred gallons of whisky came to light. All his gear was smashed. He was hauled away and at his trial fined £200, enough to swallow up all his little farm, Pike Lowe; and the rest unpaid, he was in prison during Her Majesty's pleasure.

Highway robbery was rife in the Pennine highways and byways

throughout the years when clothiers and weavers carried their merchandise by slow transport to the Cloth Halls of Colne or Halifax. Cloth thieves were a despicable lot, preying on the unaccompanied weaver and waiting half-way up a steep brow for the small horsedrawn cart loaded with bolts of cloth. At Weir an old woman related an incident of her parent's childhood; prior to setting out over the moors to Colne her grandfather tested the edge of his wood chopper carefully, then set it down on the cart, ready to hand, explaining, "If them cloth thieves steal up behind and reach out for t' cloth as we're slowing down going uphill!" Suspicious characters with fingers missing were recognized for what they were four generations ago. Trade was often on a credit basis to avoid loss of money if attacked on the roads.

You need not stray far from the busy Hebden Bridge-Burnley highroad to discover high level lanes, lonely farms, gloomy ravines where so many of the wilder deeds of the past were enacted. Ask about the Money Spinners around Heptonstall—in Yorkshire, of course—and the Minions of the Moon who lurked in secret hides between here and Blackstone Edge—where Robin Hood and his men also preyed upon the wealthiest travellers of King John's days. Possibly you will hear also of benign creatures—not the unpredictable boggarts who could be particularly nasty when they had a mind, but of ghost hounds who saw unprotected mill lasses safely home on dark nights.

Calder Valley Families

A century ago no valley in the north was fairer than Calder, for from Holme on one branch, and from Wycoller and Emmott Hall on the other, was a chain of spacious parks and great halls within them. Industry and growing towns swamped some; their old families moved away, but Towneleys remained at Towneley.

What a treasure house it is, a family history enshrined in a hall which began as a hunting lodge, was enlarged in Tudor times, and when religious persecution had died and the family had recovered from losses as Stuart and Jacobite supporters, it was able to change with the times as a great Georgian mansion. It housed Charles Towneley's Greek and Roman collection, now in the British Museum; Burnley has filled the rooms with other treasures, rich and varied.

Shuttleworths, their neighbours at the pele watching the Calder ford downriver, were of equal importance, especially when in 1599 three brothers carried out their plan to enlarge the fourteenth-century stone tower into the tall Tudor Hall of Gawthorpe. Wrapped around by screening trees it adorns Calder banks most beautifully—though a new estate is at its gate. Forward in council, prominent in Government, generations of Shuttleworths were high in esteem when the Towneleys—as staunch Papists, Royalists and Jacobites—were constantly in trouble and unable to control local affairs. Richard Shuttleworth in 1642 failed to bring about a round table talk, hoping to avert a civil war; the Parliament prevented him. Soon he and all his sons were organizing the Calder and Pendle anti-Royalists from Gawthorpe as military headquarters. For some years old friends and neighbours were on opposing sides.

It was strange Fate should decide that Shuttleworths who had never been military minded or professional soldiers should be caught up in so many wars and so many sons should through the centuries be called on to pay the highest sacrifices.

Towneley Hall is a town's proud possession: hall, park, museum, art gallery. Gawthorpe Hall handed to the National Trust a few years ago found a tenant in the Lancashire County Council in 1965, and for a peppercorn rent they are now set to make the most of Lord Shuttleworth's rare and precious gift. Perhaps its destiny is to become known as the finest source of inspiration among all the great houses in the North-west; a college, formally opened in 1971, where the arts and crafts, all that men create with 'heart, head and hand' can be seen, handled, studied.

Gawthorpe has had a very rich past; kings and queens, great thinkers, politicians and literary figures—like Charlotte Brontë—have been guests. But now the great dining-hall with its minstrel gallery, the beautiful drawing-room with splendid carving and plasterwork, have become lecture rooms, exhibitions of exquisite, workmanship now fill the upper period rooms and the Long Gallery. Possibly the coach houses and capacious stables and outbuildings may become 'working museums', housing the wheels, looms and all the tools with which men have perfected their handiwork, and made the north pre-eminent in the world of textiles.

Thanks to the late Hon. Rachel Kay-Shuttleworth in whom

past and present met and whose dreams for the future are now realized, Gawthorpe is to mean even more to future generations, and to a far wider world. Many alterations have been made internally and far more are planned.

Wherever you see the stork as badge, the Stork on inn signs, and liberal applications of turkey red paint on property you are in Huntroyd land. The Starkies have been Gawthorpe's next-door neighbours from the fourteenth-fifteenth century when early Shuttleworths were protecting the Calder ford from king's enemies, robbers and rebellious pillaging Lancashire families. Huntroyd Desmesne also adjoins the Park of Read, seat of the Nowells who certainly made their name known in Elizabethan days. Three brothers rose high in the Church: Alexander Nowell was early Head of Westminster School, Dean of St. Paul's and active among the scholars who devised our Church of England prayer book; a notable angler too and discoverer—accidentally—of the bottling of beer! Roger, of a later generation, was the J.P. who swore he would eradicate witchcraft in his territory, and with the 1612 pack haled off to Lancaster, was successful.

The Parks of Towneley, Gawthorpe, Huntroyd and Read made of mid-Calderdale a place of great dignity and 'arboreal' beauty. Smaller halls continued down the river, Portfield of the Bradylls who forsook the Calder when one wed a wealthy heiress, Sarah Dodding of Conishead Priory. Simonstone Hall of the Whitakers and, over the river, Martholme of the Fyttons and later of the Hesketh—a fair moated house with imposing arched gateway—hobnobbed with the Banastres of Altham Hall, though they were a belligerent lot. Overlooking Calder bottoms—Clerk Hill of the Whalleys, and occupying the river flats, Moreton Hall of the Taylors—all 'houses of character' when the valley was still rural.

Calder Valley Survey: From Cliviger to Colne

Now for a north-going series of ancient highways de-graded to unclassified byways, the best of scenic routes for surveying the whole of the Calder valley, from a safe distance. Just as Lancashire tends to lost itself in the dense linked towns from Manchester to Middleton and Rochdale, so do Padiham, Burnley, Nelson and Colne with their perimeter developments appear much of a muchness and need distance to bring back enchantment. And enchantment there is, or rather wonder at the men who created during the late eighteenth and nineteenth centuries that fantastic patterning of factories, streets and road links thrown over what seems to be impossibly difficult terrain. No brow is too steep to halt their upward progress; terraced houses cling crazily to sheer hillsides and roads appear to be heading heavenwards, cars like flies climbing vertically, bonnets tilted to the sky.

We pass quarries from which they were built, like the great Catlow delph part of which—with the swing of the pendulum of change—is now being filled by a continuous flow of lorries carrying the rubble from the 'unbuilding' of the very same towns.

How comely and permanent the old cottages and farms; how flimsy and 'fly away Peter' the pretty new bungalows scattered like children's gay-coloured building efforts on windswept heights on the upper edges of each town. One day as I admired the pleasant old houses, in neighbourly rows at Hill Lane above Haggate, the owners looked dubiously at the brand new little boxes alien to this grim countryside and said with feeling, "Nay, they should give us better improvement grants to do up our houses. They'll last a sight longer than them flimsy bungalows, and a lot warmer."

Starting north a mile beyond Holme-in-Cliviger, climbing from Mereclough to Worsthorne—with a diversion to Hurstwood—and back again to continue past Bottin, Swinden Water, Halstead and Haggate, the road passes many an interesting old homestead which has successfully weathered three or four centuries and has memories of families whose histories go back far longer than that. Above and below Catlow too, and at Southfield and along Thursden Water, and back by the up and down, twisting and turning lanes, are equally substantial buildings bridging every architectural period, one sheltered in each dip, one sturdily facing the elements at every hilltop.

Turning eastwards, away from the 'civilized' and humanized landscape the Pennine scene is as it always was, hardbitten, unfruitful country breeding none but fighters. Men here waged war against the elements, fought for a bare living, and being above all independent, sticklers for what they believed right, they fought for ideas and ideals. Many of them, to survive, needed what is known as Lancashire grit.

First among them were men of prehistory who hunted across Black Hambleden, above Gorple, Swinden and Thursden, leaving as their signs tumulus, camp, cairn or circle in many an upland acre. Celts cultivated terraced fields at Lenches and maybe Lidgett Anglian settlers 'bedded in' more comfortably in the hospitable 'dens'—scores of them, each a wooded valley sheltered from the wild. A few infiltrating Norsemen arrived from Earby way and Barnoldswick; tough material.

All the high land we look on was forest in the eleventh to fourteenth centuries, and being within the Honor of Clitheroe was controlled by De Lacys whose castle was there. They soon decided to increase revenues by encouraging the 'natives' to bring in 'waste' for cultivation to pay rent and become small farmers. It was not easy husbandry but the farmers put their backs into it, expecting no rewards but as fruit of hard labour. And how they held on to their 'starveacre' holdings. Like Lancastrian hill men of future centuries they never expected 'summat for nowt' or to have any 'brass' but what was earned by the sweat of the brow. Money so hard won is thought of highly and disposed of reluctantly.

They were still hanging on just as tenaciously when the forests were dis-afforested, when the abbots and monks who had had quite a say in local affairs were no longer at Whalley Abbey. This was the time many former forest tenants rose to prominence; there was good stuff among local stock. From late Tudor to Stuart times most of the old halls continued to prosper; proud builders saw that their initials and the date of entering into their homes were recorded on stone tablets over lintel or porch.

Look for Tattersall's Tenement, Spenser's Cottage and the fine and beautifully modernized Hall which make Hurstwood a perfect pocket of Old Lancashire. Worsthorne's seventeenth-century hall has disappeared but not pleasant 'Wall Streams'.

Only a dated doorway and no dwelling remains of the Parker's New House above Thursden, but their other hall stands—as a bleak, weatherbeaten farm gripping the upper edge of the 'den' at Extwistle. Another place on our lane where history concentrates —Catlow, a charming nook where singing birds make music regardless on the most blustery March days, and from the hushed stillness of the Bottoms you can hear, loud and clear, skylarks carolling high above.

'Of Catlow' were Radcliffes and Sagars. One, Stephen Sagar, last abbot of that once glorious abbey of Hailes, near Winchcombe in the Cotswolds, when deprived sought his brother's vicarage at Warmfield in Yorkshire to live out his days. Neighbours in Tudor times were the Blakeys of Southfield, who as 'stubborn Papists' had to endure years of utmost privation and punishment for refusing to conform.

I said the local hillmen were made of uncompromising material. For generations they grumbled at tithe paying to the abbots, and just as much at payment by money. When the abbeys were dissolved and the new order was in time introduced to Colne parish church, many held doggedly to the Old Faith—like the Blakeys; and how they suffered. In the Civil War a large proportion chose the side of Parliament but parishioners loyal to their old parson would have shot the Cromwellian troops who dragged him from his desk. With the appearance of the first 'Friend of Truth and Light', and when John Wesley stood up to preach, they were equally ready to rise in protest and anger; but Quakers were as willing to endure hardships and kicks as the Methodists who came later.

Prominent Quakers like the Eckroyds were prosperous traders in wool, cloth merchants and employers of local labour. The well set up farms of the eighteenth century were homes of farmers who combined their activities as clothiers with land work; with their pack ponies they travelled the same lanes doling out raw flax or wool, or thread spun by local spinsters, to the handloomers, later collecting the cloth to take to Colne Piece Hall. All roads descend at last upon Colne—only to rise again, for bonnie Colne is very high on its hill. East-west roads make over the Pennines to Halifax, the other great centre for trade in woollens. The weavers' cottages at the wayside stand in twos and threes, stone walled, stone flagged roofs and by now, unless new owners with money to spend on modernization have treated them with love and care, they are sinking back into mother earth with their burden of years.

Though our ten-mile route is well above the upper limit of modern industry, it was well within it just before the industrial revolution changed the pattern of life; it also was 'throng' when early mills grew up in the upper dens, dependent on water power. Old folk of Worsthorne whose parents and grandparents were handloomers tell of the Extwistle Mill by Swinden Water, now demolished, where they were employed; when their cloth was ready they had to shoulder it and carry it down the steep paths to Heasandford. Other mills have disappeared—we notice their cleared sites—and at Colne the oldest are being swept away. Between the gaps, Colne Water which for generations had not seen the light, is exposed to the sun.

If you walk, as I did, there will be plenty of gossip with others who walk, and old tales remembered as we stand surveying Calder dale from many a breezy viewpoint.

Six ruddy-faced 'pensioners' met me at Haggate, marching into an icy wind. They are not the sort to sit and watch the passing; if any passing is to be done, they do it. "Grand day", they say. "Just reet for walking. Can't be beat onnyweer i' England." I think they referred to the views. Always the wide landscape, the ups and downs of the coiling lane before and behind, the Pennines east, the valley west and slopes hidden beneath stones and brick, shining roads, silvery roofs, but fewer smoking chimneys. Now smokeless zones, electrified works, are cutting down the air pollution. Watching and giving no secrets away, Pendle heaves its bulk into the sky.

On the raised earthwork of Castercliffe, near my journey's end, I met a man of Colne who in pointing out the skyline features of his town, the wriggling roads and dizzy brows, the cleared sites and ruined mills, waxed so eloquent about history recently obliterated, that I was amazed. More so when he confessed he had just read his first book—"Now I'm on mi pension, time hangs heavy so I've started going to t' Library". It was all about the history of Colne. He had his roots here; now he was beginning to dig down.

Colne Lane, said he, was once main road to Halifax; most trade went that way, centuries of trade. Down below was England's Mill and away downstream Greenfield, where a young lass who had seen first cotton brought into Colne on a canal boat, told everyone about it, and the Englands hearing of it were interested, contacted the men who wished to introduce the new fibre—"and that was beginning of the cotton weaving in Colne".

Around us was nothing but Roman and pre-history. "They say Roman soldiers had a sort of labour camp up here," he volunteered. Below, was little but the nineteenth and twentieth centuries, six sizeable towns stretching along the valley and 150,000 people in them, and all so bound up with their ancestral background and so loyal to it, they have little desire to drift south or anywhere else; not they! They are so accustomed to trudging uphill and down;

steep gradients, like the one I must descend, bother them not at all. Nature has endowed them with strong constitutions and good wind, and the weak-kneed and feeble-hearted recoil and flee. Wild weather? They take it in their stride and when they reach the tops and meet the strong north-easter they welcome the loud moist smack of it as readily as the poet's tender "kiss of the wind".

Colne has a splendid position and its ancient church the proudest site, to which it has been anchored firmly from the twelfth century; it was a chapel before that, dependent on Whalley; and its 1515 rebuilding left it as it is today. The priors of Pontefract and the abbots of Whalley in turn held the church with Whalley monks as priests in its three chantries, five in all serving the very widely scattered parishioners. All its working life the town's chief concern has been cloth, weaving native wool, fulling it in a Colne Water mill, and willing to acquire further skills from immigrant Flemish weavers in Edward III's days.

Every cottager had the wherewithal to weave for his family's wants, and more to dispose of to local chapmen, middlemen, and merchants, who did their rounds with packponies. Fustians, kerseys, serges and worsteds, shalloons and calimancoes were Colne's 'lines', sold at its own Piece Hall, at Halifax Cloth Hall or taken to Kildwick; some went to York or London.

The first new 'aid' Lancashire handloomers welcomed was Kay's fly shuttle, an invention to help cottage industry; production increased. The next, a carding 'engine' to supplant tedious child labour was seized upon by the clothiers who installed them in their mills; a fillip to the spinning.

But James Hargraves was really the man who changed Lancashire's industry. His spinning jenny which was sprung upon unwilling spinners in 1764 was recognized by the manufacturers as a step in the right direction, "several spindles—at first eight, afterwards eighty, made to whirl by one fly-wheel". The death knell of the cottage spinning wheel—and eventual end of the small loom-shop—had been sounded.

A vital period in the county history followed, but so fully has it been dealt with in other books I shall use no pages over it. The Industrial Revolution was 'on', and along the byways from Cliviger to Colne the course is evident: near at hand the old industrial set-up, down the dens and along the Calder the full picture of what the next two centuries achieved.

Take a look at Lidgett just north of Colne; a companiable group of houses, the tall Georgian clothier-type dwelling with adjoining humble cottages which would have their wheels and a hand loom. The neighbouring houses with many-lighted mullion windows looked out on pack horse trains, but the flat-fronted Victorian house knew only heavy laden wagons, carrier's carts, stage coach and mail coach passing by—the Invincible, daily bound for Bradford.

For picking up threads of the past try Laneshaw Bridge or Colne Waterside, their old mills typical of many. Wool merchants and cotton traders in turn frequented the Emmott Arms. Carriers Row explains itself. For a picture of pre-Industrial Revolution Lancashire walk the hollowed flagstones paths and field ways to Wycoller where silent cottages remember the clacketty-clack of handlooms. Better still take the wriggling uphill lanes to Winewall or Trawden, old communities holding on by the skin of their teeth—reminding me of Alpine villages, only their skies are different! From here came the labour for the mills in the growing towns.

Each place has its own special flavour, each small community different from its neighbour and totally different from Colne.

Why, there was a time when Trawden lads believing themselves equals, if not superiors, of Colne's youth challenged them to trials of strength and Christmas Day football, village to town, free for all combat. Every window was firmly shuttered that day!

Though for two centuries Trawden had its fair share of church and chapels it retained old beliefs. Superstition died hard in all the Lancashire forest regions, none of them affected by influences from more enlightened outsiders. Local witches got up to their tricks, adopting animal forms to evade detection. Once some lads tied a vicious squint-eyed feline into a ball; when they bounced it there was a blinding flash and away hobbled 'T'Owd Witch, grasping a broken arm. Witches infected the stock with their evil; calves ran up the cowshed walls and cows danced jigs round and round in their stalls.

Trawden is a lively spot compared with old Wycoller down below which is dying on its feet, but with a glimmer of hope of returning life if Water Board staff can be encouraged to take over the silent cottages. What changes since I first knew it twenty odd years ago!

"We'd have put carpets down if we'd known you were coming", was the welcome of a cheery old man near Dene farm as we picked our way, over shoe-tops in mud, down the ancient sunken lane from Emmott. We looked ruefully at our footgear, and plodded on. We found the handloom weavers' cottages derelict, barn roofs collapsed, once well-kept gardens overgrown. The old hall of the Cunliffes was sad, in ruin, the paved floors deep in tangled vegetation, drifts of leaves scurrying through the roofless rooms, and for cushions the stone benches around the vast hearth—a fire round which in olden times you could sit, and roast yourself—had a deep covering of last Autumn's leaves. This was the house the Brontës knew when the last of the Cunliffes, Henry Owen, had died childless in 1818. Charlotte remembered attached to it the story of "a madwoman having set it on fire"; this has always been considered the Ferndean of *Jane Eyre*.

During later visits we saw the care lavished on the Hall and village by the Friends of Wycoller, how they made safe the tottering masonry, cleared the nettle beds and a century's accumulation of debris. Cottages made teas, happy families picknicked and children paddled and scrambled under and over the old bridges, an outstanding feature of the old place.

Dereliction had won by the 1970s, silence reigned. Calder Water Board would not sell or change anything. But greater interest was roused in '72, opportunity for the L.C.C. to buy and with the Government's seventy-five per cent improvement grant a chance to restore the village for the public good—as an 'amenity'! Restoration in 1976–77 goes on apace.

Rollicking ghosts shatter Wycoller's midnight silence—so they say, but what spirits benign or otherwise walk the deserted gardens and empty rooms of Emmott Hall? The Emmotts proudly traced their ancestry to one who came here in the thirteenth century, but it was a Duc de Emmott, a follower of the Conqueror, who first put the family on the Lancastrian map they insisted. 'Eamot' signifies the meeting of waters, and two streams come together above Laneshaw, so I have my doubts about the Norman origin.

Border country now, Yorkshire advancing to Watersheddles Cross on the Haworth road, over Reedshaw Moss on Cowling Moors and waiting to take over just beyond Foulridge. I know someone who lived by County Brook; no arguing with that boundary over which, in the days before piped water, she had to cross to an ebbing and flowing well, fill her bucket and back into Lancashire again. Admergill on the Gisburn highway, and Ings Beck near Twiston, show what a very determined inroad Yorkshire has made into Pendle's northernmost flanks—and this our favourite, well-loved-above-all-other, Lancashire landmark.

Pendle Portrayed

Pendle, the pen, 'The Hill' to the Celts and Romans, standing out and inescapable from which ever way you look, once was listed with our highest mountains.

> "Pendle Hill, Ingleborough and Penyghent,
> Highest hills between Scotland and Trent."

We know it is a mere 1,831 feet high but the knowledge has never lowered it in our estimation. A two-sided hill: scowling to the Pennines into the teeth of the bitter east winds; smiling in kindlier mood upon Ribblesdale and Clitheroe—hence my prejudice. The eastern side, over-looking the Forest had dark moods. Its bare brown slopes, where a few battered old thorns crouch low before the blast like witches scurrying to an unholy sabbath, are riven by 'boggart' cloughs which are like boiling cauldrons manufacturing mists, or worse mischief, 'witchcraft places' as a town child once described them. Hard grits and brittle shales made this landscape—and 'for miles underground run seams of coal', as Calder folk tell us.

Limestone replaces the gritstone on the west side giving the pastures a brighter green, the landscape gentler contours; dark walls are replaced by white, fields defined by green hedges.

Pendle is worth considering without its witches, though the notoriety of its Demdikes and Chattoxes put it in the news in 1612 and 1633. Now that the tendency is to find natural causes for all diabolical practices we might find Pendle's witch cult began long before. Scholars say that the pagan custom of 'beating' the farm buildings where stock was housed with riding poles in October—the rutting season—was part of a fertility rite. Naturally the church frowned on such, but in lonely forest regions the folk, instead of riding around on poles, took up the innocent besom—the witch's broomstick—and rode astride on that; away on their 'cock-horses' to forbidden fertility 'covens'.

In a book on black magic in circulation in Tudor times new members of the many cults were told how to prepare for broomstick jaunts. They should anoint themselves with lanoline—or the grease of a stillborn child—to keep out the cold when naked, cover the body with grime for invisibility, and drink an infusion of aconite which doubtless induced a feeling of airborne exhilaration.

Pendle is girdled by some pleasant villages. Downham came fifth in a nationwide beautiful village competition, whilst Barley and Newchurch—grown from primitive booths of forest days into most attractive places, each totally dissimilar—have won in turn the first award for Lancashire's best kept smaller villages.

Starting from Whalley, through Wiswell to Pendleton—what more unlike its namesake near Manchester?—and by leafy lanes follow Pendle's western foothills into the coral limestone reef region. Herein snuggle Worston and Downham, the under Pendle farms of Gerna, Hollins, Hecklin, Ravensholme, and Twiston. You come to close quarters with a Lancashire which can hold its own with any part of England's green and pleasant land. You wander across the fields to find sixteenth and seventeenth-century halls, now farmhouses, each backed by its own tree-filled clough and looking upon its wide pastures full of the happy medley of plovers screaming, lambs' bleating and curlews crying on Spring days; each farm has its brook at the door and waterfalls behind where kingfishers nest and dippers flirt and bob over trout-filled pools. Little Mearley Hall possesses the Abbot of Sawley's fine bay window and a sixteenth-century dated back door; through its sheep fold starts the path to Pendle top.

In the past Pendle suffered from water-bursts or 'gill brasts' when the hill opened and water gushing forth tore like a stampede of wild horses down to the farms and hamlets, destroying all in its way. Such opened up Brast Clough behind Hookcliffe, and north of Mearley.

In 1669, "the water gushed out near the top of the hill in such quantities and so suddenly it made a breast a yard high and continued running for about two hours. It grew unfordable—the houses in Worston two miles from the point of eruption were completely inundated."

The farms between the 'lion's paws'—under the crouching beast which Pendle appears to be from under the Big End—look over an enchanting landscape, to wooded ridges, green dales and far blue sun-touched or blue-shadowed fells and mountains.

Ravensholme's great beeches wave above a tiny grave of a Quaker child. This is a countryside where eighteenth-century Friends were strong, the Bulcocks chief among them. At the lane edge above Twiston, in the Red Sike Quaker Sepulchre, is the grave of James Whipp, husbandman, who in 1668 was first of the local followers of George Fox to be fined. In 1652 Fox stood on Pendle, "and was moved to sound the day of the Lord and the Lord let me see in what places he had great people to be gathered". Within twenty years they were certainly gathering in and around Pendle, constables on the look out and indomitable men being sent to Lancaster "for conscience sake".

At Annel Cross four hill roads meet, a wild and lonely spot in mid-Winter, just the setting for witches' rendezvous, Pendle darkly brooding. A hungry landscape of turf fields, broken gritstone walls and any farms well hidden out of the wind; from these homesteads in 1612 issued Bulcocks, Hargreaves, and comates of the Demdikes and Chattoxes and the Pendle witches, heading for Malkin Tower.

To search for this place, so infamous in the past, is unrewarding,

> "A small cottage where caitiff witches met
> To swear their homage to the devil
> And contrive the deaths of men and beast,"

it was destroyed after the last meeting. Its site is uncertain but the Malkin Fields at Newchurch give a possible clue.

Barley Booth clusters by Pendle Water, borrowing what shelter it can; at first glance a rural community it conceals downstream a most interesting pocket of industry, the Narrowgates Mill, excellent example of early factory and workers' cottages in closest proximity. Keep to the brookside through the mill yard for Whitehough, a Tudor hall typical of those built when forest officials became landowners—the royal arms, a scriptural text "Except the Lord thus hous do make", the date MDXC III, and "Builded by Christofer Bullcocke and Jenet his wife", over its porch.

Pendle Water flows through tranquil scenes these days. Witches, no more. "What chance would they have with their spells," comments a native, "and all them youth hostellers at Whiteho', that

Stonyhurst College

Camp School behind, and caravanners and campers at Lido and Palm Beach?" This is today's Happy Valley. Even Rough Lee looks benign, smiling towards its rock-shadowed stream, and the Hall from which Mistress Alice Nutter went out to her trial and hanging in 1612 is not at all grim. Now schoolboys weekend in the Hall's east wing, and large modern houses fill the field in front.

From Rough Lee Booth, forest tenants climbed a steep hill to Goldshaw Booth, renamed Newchurch in later years but usually called Kirk. Many tracks and lanes make for the village, centre for forest business and religious life long ago, and not one on the level. Its neighbours are 'nook shotten' and tucked into corners, but not Newchurch. It was flung out on the hillside cold as charity and stayed there to ride out the storms like a ship on the high seas. No witches here, except those you buy in the souvenir shops. An unusual oval carving on the church tower is understood to be the watching Eye of God. Folk believed the table-topped tomb by the porch was the grave of Alice Nutter; the Nutter name is on it, but not the witch's. It has other unusual associations. The district was once troubled by thieves known as the Kirk Gang who attacked outlying farms, stole what they could and disposed of their loot in this very secure hide.

Not only do lanes hurl skywards and tumble into hollows but they wriggle and twist alarmingly, especially those heading for Sabden Great Hall, Black Hill, Sabden village, the Nick of Pendle, —circuitous routes halved by walkers cutting across country. On foot, you may meditate on the spot at Bullhole where Old Demdike 'witched' the Nutter's cow so that it died, imagine dark and midnight hags lurking at the doors of the Great Hall, Lowerhouses and Deane. Somewhere between Newchurch and Great Hall, "nigh to a stonepit in Goldshey", a young woman, Elizabeth Southernes, met a spirit or devil at 'daylight gate', sold her soul and became the founder-president of the Pendle witch group, her alias Old Demdike. At Deane farm by Sabden Brook the inscription tells that it was built in 1574 "by Hugh Moore son of Chrestover Moore and Letis Hugh wyf", but not that Old Chattox and Hugh fell out about cattle, that she "did curse and worry him so that he fell sick, languished and died".

Pendle is a completely reformed character these days, not a hint of old superstition or diablerie. Or so we think, until reminded by 'natives' that the old days are not so far behind us. I, myself, was

Hornby Castle by Lune

told by an octagenarian that his grandmother saw an intricate patterning of pottery mould on the Rough Lee Hall hearthstone—"to keep witches from entering down the chimney!" Another villager had seen two old dames from Barrowford lay annual tribute of wreaths on the witch's grave at Newchurch. A barn behind Huntroyd was pointed out as chosen by a man 'witcht' to hang himself 'wi' his galluses'. And there is a field corner above Barley, tangled with rank vegetation, "never mown because long since witches fouled it and grass would poison the cattle".

The last word came from an old cottager at Newchurch who from his highbacked chair wagged his finger at us when we made light of superstitious fears.

"You should have met my grandmother," said he. "She believed in 'em, and i' witches. She used to say, you've got to believe i' 'em when you've seen an old witch look at you, yourself, wi' her evil eye'."

As a town child exclaimed, looking on Pendle under its head covering of ink-black clouds, working up to a thunderstorm, "It looks like a witchcraft sort of place".

As I have written elsewhere (in Chapter VIII) there is no spot so enchanting as Pendle on a Midsummer morning. And no hilltop more worth-while for surveying large tracts of Lancashire, work-worn eastwards under the Pennine background, rural contentment westwards where "Lancashire Without Chimneys" takes over, where the pattern of life predates the Industrial Revolution, and its face is clean and bright.

Some of the most friendly, honest-to-goodness communities in the country are here—close against the Pennines. Where an influx of Manchester commuters has not swamped the old indigenous folk the native characteristics are obvious. They are a race who have strong local loyalties—witness the opposition to being taken away in '74 and 'put into' new districts with which they had no long-standing allegiance. They have a deep-rooted love for their countryside, bold, bare and strangely beautiful as the pictures show; among them are stalwart walkers.

V

LANCASHIRE—WITHOUT CHIMNEYS

LANCASHIRE, so much of it given up to dairy farming, egg producing and growing of greens, can leave fresh milk on a million doorsteps, send everyone out to work on a egg—and plenty over—and keep salad lovers content all the year round. If a time ever came when the populace drifted south leaving the county to continue as an agricultural area we would do pretty well supplying the United Kingdom with milk, eggs and greens; our climate is so congenial!

We could also put ourselves back where we were as producers of the best beef cattle; in the past Lancashire 'beef' bulls were supreme. Did not James I in 1612 knight a loin of Lancashire beef at Hoghton Tower?

Does it come as a surprise to learn that meat, pig and bacon prices, grain, potato and tomato growing are as much the concern of Lancashire farmers as in counties which do nothing else but grow food?

Where are the best equipped and most modern farms in the land? On Her Majesty's Duchy estates, especially those in the Fylde—thousands of acres and the profits 'ploughed back'. Probably the most satisfied tenant farmers have the Queen for landlord.

Countrygoers know that the most restricted countryside for freedom of movement is where all is arable farming. Our farms are mostly meadow, pasture and hill grazing. A network of public footpaths criss-crosses them and—until he is troubled by ill-behaved folk 'who bring town ways into the country' and treat his private land as if a public playground—the farmer rarely objects to walkers wandering around.

As a matter of fact a public footpath is merely a right to walk from one point to another across a field—not to stray, and certainly *not* to put up tents, set out table, chairs and all the impedimenta of what the affluent think is necessary for a picnic nowadays, nor to let dogs run wild, leave gates open—and strew the greensward with litter. All my life I have wandered and never encountered a farmer who objected; true nature lovers, bird watchers, botanisers, always welcomed. Now hundreds of green and white signs mark public footpaths and bridle paths, county-wide.

Friends have often been amazed at our access to so much country, mile after mile of grassy paths, stiles, gates, and in and out of farm yards and none to say 'Nay'. How I hope the ill-mannered are not going to spoil it for others.

I can see both sides of the matter. When I read of the National Farmers' Union legal and parliamentary representative suggesting at the 1966 meeting in Manchester that footpaths are archaic, that they are merely cartographical fiction marked on maps and, as nobody walks any more, no longer of any relevance, my Lancastrian and north country blood boils. Perhaps in the south, I think, remembering how people from whom we inquired the way in Devon, Cornwall and Somerset, constantly directed us to the road, because "No one walks any more. We all have cars. The farmer has blocked the stiles!" But take precious footpaths from northerners; no!

'Lakeland Lancashire' in the late '50s pioneered in providing footpath signs—because of walkers and tourists, and the L.C.C. in the '60s required local councils to undertake waymarking from all main roads, of public rights of way. In our parish scores of posts were erected, distances given—but vandals did their work! Now local rambling associations are defining the lines of pleasant footpaths along their course—yellow arrows on fence, gate or wall where necessary so that no walker need lose the way or trespass unwittingly. Here the farmers would do well to cooperate for mutual benefit.

Footpaths do matter. Fewer are walking for pleasure than formerly, but as roads become more impossible to travel, is it not likely coming generations will seek the field ways again, in sheer desperation? For them the old paths *must* be kept open. And new paths made.

And farmers must be protected from the inconsiderate and irresponsible. If every townsman before being let loose in the country could be taught that: (a) the country is the farmer's workshop and the field his factory floor; (b) the footpath allows him to cross from gate to stile, but if he hankers to do more than walk through, then 'he can always ask', as every country woman tells her child; (c) strange though it may seem, no land is No Man's Land, every piece of field is someone's property, and if for generations folk have picnicked, bathed, idled away the livelong day on riverside banks where a footpath ran, only by the courtesy of the owners and farmer have they enjoyed that privilege. So, courtesy on both sides and Lancashire will still be the most pleasant county for the country lover. The Lancashire countryman is so fair minded. He says, "When we go into towns we expect amenities, so why shouldn't the townsfolk expect them when they come into the country? Fair's fair!"

After many generations of conditioning to towns, the Lancastrian is a rebel and fighter for his cherished rights, on occasion. Everyone appreciates the dogged determination of Darwen's Fight For Freedom of the Moors in 1878 when the Lord of the Manor, to preserve game, tried to bar walkers from rights of way, then becoming disused, to old pits and stone quarries. Five men took up the struggle alone when the town was lacking in interest and after a Sunday stroll on the moors writs were served against them. Their spokesman raised his train fare to London, borrowing the coal money!—and won the case; twenty-nine miles of hill paths and fifty-five acres of moorland declared free for innocent enjoyment. Twenty years later Darwen Moors were freed completely for the people to use for the recreation of themselves and their children 'for ever'. Which is really why the Tower is there, raised in celebration at the time of Victoria's Jubilee.

In 1905 evening strollers along the reservoir embankment called The Razzy—between Bury and Radcliffe—by tearing down fences and battering down barriers put to deny them access, started a long struggle for their old right of way. Eight leaders and a partisan lawyer appeared at Manchester Assizes in defence of their free access—and won. The Great Trespass Case ended amicably in true north country style—or is it really English?—at a celebration dinner to which the L. and Y. Railway officials were invited, accepted and most cordially bowed to the toast in their honour. They actually gave one of the officials a pair of binoculars. To spy out trespassers, or for bird watching?

Men of such spirit are needed more nowadays with so many lovely places being 'developed', lakes taken over for city water, green hills levelled for sand or lime, and most picturesque cottages demolished to make bigger car parks for village pubs. The most vulnerable spots are near towns which Big Business says complacently, 'are spoiled to begin with'. Thousands spring to defence of Lakeland, everybody's heritage; the less known local beauty spots are now defended by watchful village societies if endangered.

So I am hopeful of the future. By the 1980s I hope the image of grime and gloom so convincingly presented by northern writers, and perpetuated on radio and screen, will be outdated. By the 1990s this picture—preserved in archives doubtless—will be regarded as we now look on child labour in mine and mill, the Cotton Famine, Love on the Dole and the slump of the 1930s—as ancient history, never to be again. My hope is that life in towns, and where people live and work, will be so pleasant that the escape into the country bordering on hysteria, now a weekly occurrence, will be needless. Then the countryside left to milk, meat and vegetable producing will be safe—and the beauty we seek there, unspoilt.

The great headache of the future is of course what to do if the twenty-six million cars it is estimated will be on the English roads by 1980, all decide to fan out from town into country at the same time. One tenth of them could be Lancashire escapists heading for Lancashire coast and country. The planners decide, "Let there be country parks for them; allow in the crowds cars and all, so car parks to scale". You just cannot divert a thousand people into a park and say, "Now go on, enjoy it". They might not like it, turn tail and say, "Oh, let's go back to Blackpool". Why not make the Blackpools bigger and better, with quicker roads to them. This has happened: fast roads to the coast, new country parks—Beacon Fell east of Brock the first, Lever Park near Bolton, Jumbles at Turton, Witton Park near Blackburn, Darwen planning to use its fine moors and wild countryside—nature trails, wild life sanctuaries; in the '70s folk begin to care.

By Douglas and Yarrow

Two little rivers, the Douglas and the Yarrow, rise on the same moorland between the Belmont road (Manchester, Bolton to Blackpool) and the Bolton, Chorley, Preston highway and A6.

Their beginnings share wild moors, their middle courses are through large towns but, having done their duty as handmaids to the industries of Horwich, Wigan and Chorley, they take diverse and roundabout courses to meet once again near Bretherton and A59; thereafter to the Ribble estuary and the rolling tide. What charming countryside they share in middle life, rolling green hills with cornfields on their lower sunny slopes and carpetted with golden gorse and blue bells, heather, and banks of brambles and whinberries—according to season.

Thousands leaving Liverpool and Manchester, on highway or motorway have between them these low hills for backdrop. The steep escarpment of Billinge Stump, Ashurst Beacon, Parbold Bottle, High Moor and Harrock Hill face the western plains, their sweeping gradual slopes turn towards the east. Under the scarpline agriculturally-minded villages like Parbold, Burscough and Rufford and unexpectedly charming places like Newburgh, not concerned at all with coal or cotton but corn and cattle, and the rich produce of that large reclaimed region of moss, swamp and mere which extends mile upon mile to the hinterland of Formby, Crosby and Southport.

What a view over this wonderfully patterned market garden landscape from any one of the scarp landmarks!

Quite the best viewpoint is Ashhurst Beacon where natives promise you 'sixteen counties' in one encircling panorama. They were enjoying it, 'the pleasantest place, the most gallant prospect', in the 1760s and, if the New Town Planners of Skelmersdale keep their promise to reserve the hill foot for open spaces and school sports fields, it should still be worth coming here in the 2060s.

Douglas, below the hill, and Yarrow farther north, can claim some of the prettiest villages. Eccleston has been the Best Kept, and each midsummer is a renewal of community effort to keep or win back the trophy; its church and churchyard and Yarrow side fields make a picture of most peaceful England. So does Croston on Yarrow, with water-side rows of cottages, and Church Street framing the out-of-line tower of St. Michael and All Angels, so old a foundation no wonder it leans! Mother church of a large area of South-west Lancashire it was founded in 651. Its manorial lords date from Norman days, markets and fairs were held after 1283, John o' Gaunt licensed its grammar school in the fourteenth century—a long and honourable history, and a natural tendency for old ideas to die hard and traditions to be remembered.

Mawdesley, hide-away in a network of wandering lanes, is a friendly homespun place, once you find it. It has a village inn called Hell Hob—scene of wild behaviour 'long sin' and with a poker clamped by the fire large enough to use on a hearth in Hades; its Sunday-best name no one ever uses. Long famous for willow basketry, the old craftsmen, Cobham's and Mawdesleys, are gone but the Coates' sons carry on, making 'quality' baskets from willow grown in Somerset, using the local—as we may see waving in the red willow fields near Clyde and on the road to Rufford—for rougher potato swills. Mawdesley natives plus enthusiastic incomers pool their 'know-how' for the public weal. There is "nothing wrong wi' Mawdsla'!"

Interested in museums? Then look for the wheeled-in field near Croston, a collection here of coaches, carriages and everything that runs on wheels. At Carr House near Bretherton was a fascinating doll museum, in a seventeenth-century homestead where Horrocks the star-gazing curate of Much Hoole watched the Transit of Venus in 1639, an outstanding astronomical event.

Douglas meets Yarrow not far away. The lowland west-wards, "benign and sunny—where to leave lanes leads to mystification in bypaths, sensations of lostness in ploughed fields and quaint replies to inquiries at farms" according to a writer of a century ago—is dead flat, like Holland. Free wandering is here discouraged. The richest land in the county, every yard is valuable.

Ribble, Hodder—and New Ribble Valley District

The Ribble, flowing in wide horseshoe windings, each with an ancient hall-cum-farmhouse on its rich alluvial acres, is Lancashire's for its last forty-five miles, a mature river of quiet dignity and complete serenity. The old farms are tranquil too, though their founders, the Langtons and Southworths, Osbaldestons and Talbots, Walmesleys, Baileys and Sherburnes, Hothersalls and Bradylls playing their part in local history, sharing the bad patches and, if fortunate, survived to enjoy the good. Their ancestral homes—none occupied by the original families—being at river edge, by ford and ferry for bridges are few and far apart, are now at dead ends, therefore as one must walk to see them, peace is inviolate.

Only one, Samlesbury Hall, is open to the public, the home of Southworths from the fourteenth century when they transplanted themselves, after the Bruce's firing of their original Ribbleside hall to a fair—and safer—site among green woodlands. It is a fine timber built hall, black and white work facing inwards and mellow Flemish brick and Whalley Abbey stonework in its outer walls, abutting on the busy road A59. A White Lady ghost occasionally disrupts traffic, so they say. As the family were Roman Catholics, under a cloud in Tudor times and harboured priests, the ghost stories were possibly invented to allay suspicions and scare investigators from secret rooms and equally secret approaches.

Other halls interesting for their architecture and family histories, views of which may be enjoyed from lane or gate, are at Osbaldeston and Oxendale Hall, Dutton and Dinckley, Hacking and Little Mitton. Others too, have fascinating interiors, the outsides giving little clue.

The Ribble is everybody's river. In fact, many an industrial town claims it and uses it as an inducement to draw new business and new interests northwards. Angler's meditate by its rushing waters, angered when canoeists, who also claim a right to it, flurry the most peaceful stretches. There are bathing places—hot summer days, and swimmers are chasing the fishes at Cuerdale, Hacking and Brungerley; paddling pools—and children with nets and jam-jars; and for walkers who love idling at the river's brink, well away from the Little Blackpools like Edisford where too many take too many cars to look at the water, miles of happy wandering.

"Earth, sweet earth, sweet landscape, with leaves throng", so wrote Gerard Manley Hopkins of the Ribble. Landscape with figures, landscape with villages, and countryfolk going about their own rural business.

Ribchester is an honest to goodness village which welcomes but makes no undue fuss of visitors. It got used to strangers nineteen centuries ago when Julius Agricola crossed the Ribble fords with his road makers, made the best of them for three centuries and adapted itself to changes with Anglian invaders, and all that followed.

"We've had all sooarts here," a local wisebeard says with hints at Celts in coracles, Irish pirates, Scots raiders—and Picts and Scots who burnt down the fort the Romans had evacuated in the fifth century. All sorts, but nowadays they are a community so closely knit that "If you slap one on the backside they all turn round".

Roman occupation brought all sorts 'all colours and creeds' so that Bremetanacum had temples for the worship of seven deities, including Mithras, Mars "the peace bringer" and Minerva whose shrine lies somewhere beneath the parish church.

The chance of Roman finds brought a constant stream of antiquaries to Ribchester in the eighteenth century. After bad floods the Ribble was busy changing its course so that, "rapid and sonorous, running over numerous Roman antiquities", many treasures came to view. One was the perfect bronze ceremonial helmet kicked about by a truanting boy in 1796; the very good Museum of Roman Remains—its site near the H.Q. or Praetorium—owns a replica as the original is in the British Museum.

Doing history can be fun at Ribchester. Not only in the Museum but tracking down Roman stones round about; after undermining its own banks the Ribble uncovered stone pillars once the supports of pediment and roofs of Bremetanacum buildings and these were hauled through the village to become part of the White Bull porch, almshouse balcony at Stydd, and—chiselled smooth, to hold up the church's new musician's gallery in 1736. Between church and Museum, hypocaust, granaries and sections of north wall and gateway are uncovered too.

Stand where you will near church and river and beneath your feet is ancient history still to be unearthed. The churchyard sundial —"I am a Shadow. So Art Thou. I Mark Time. Dost Thou"— covers a corner of the fort's treasury. An altar dedicated to the Emperor Marcus Aurelius Severus Antoninus the Pious was discovered near by.

Is there anywhere a better-kept churchyard; or a church more full of beautiful things, austere in its lines, restrained in its furnishings? The fourteenth and fifteenth century Dutton and Hoghton chapel screens have a warm gold patina; the Jacobean pulpit, ornately carved, is restored from many coats of paint to its original colour. The St. Christopher mural was hidden for centuries under many layers of whitewash and plaster; five centuries ago travellers bound for the Ribble ferries invoked the blessing of the saint. The chancel arch carries thirteenth-century masons marks; in the north wall, a so-called lepers' window, most probably the opening through which a ringer watched for the signal to pull the sanctus bell, and stone grave lids which covered the graves of Knights Hospitallers of St. John of Jerusalem whose house was a mile away in the fields at Stydd.

A church in the meadows, so small it might be overlooked as a barn, is all that remains now at Stydd. The Knights Hospitallers who had accompanied Crusaders to Jerusalem were disbanded after the last pilgrims had returned and this community at The Stede was dissolved too. It is an 'architect's' church with dog-tooth decoration over a Norman door, transitional window tracery and a south doorway with carving so delicate it was given a porch for protection over three centuries ago.

The seventeenth and eighteenth century almshouses on the lane from Ribchester to Stydd have had more than a face lift recently but the balconied façade with a sweeping staircase approach and the draw well—now a picturesque bygone—remain to delight passers-by; as I was delighted when I used to visit one of its residents to hear of ghostly visitants, chairs that rocked and no one in them, and tales of a childhood way back in the 1860s.

Ribchester has modern mills, and a mill shop for bargains! By every stream which runs to the Ribble, are thickly wooded cloughs with paths losing their way among beeches and bluebells, and unexpected discoveries. Ruined walls, choked mill ponds and pretty cottages in deep dells, like those in Dilworth Bottoms and Hurst Green Dean, tell of the early days of the Industrial Revolution. The first phase left less permanent disfigurement than what was to follow. Nature has healed old scars—and no eyesores remain.

Hurst Green, deep in its Dean, or flung high on a breezy hillside, from Macadam's dignified new road of 1822 to the park gate of Stonyhurst, shows a pleasant face to all comers. But a great invasion—that of Cromwell and his Model Army of Ironsides in August 1648—it did not welcome. Nor did the Royalist Sherburnes at the Hall whose reception of the intruders was so frigid, Cromwell, fearing the worst, slept on a hard table, pistols to hand and men on guard. His 'bed', now in the college refectory, is said in schoolboy parlance to 'stink of Cromwell'!

The next day the army marched away to overcome Lancashire Royalist opposition at 'Langridge Chapel' and an overwhelming victory at Preston by Walton Bridge.

Stonyhurst was then 'a half house', incomplete because great plans of three generations of Sherburnes were held up during years of fines, imprisonment and near-poverty, in the penal days. Following the Civil War they were involved in further troubles, during Stuart plots and conspiracies. The Sir Richard who founded the almshouses on Kemple End—now rebuilt as estate workers cottages near the Park gates in Hurst Green—left it to his son Nicholas to finish. Nicholas in marrying a very wealthy heiress took over the task of completing what was begun by his great-grandfather. He had the best men to design and build—the two Stantons from 1690 to 1717—who with Nost the artist created statuary to adorn the new gardens, and Henry Wise, a royal gardener who designed that perfect approach, the drives and two long canals in which the whole is now so enchantingly reflected.

The same team of artists left their handiwork in the Sherburne Chapel (1594) in Mitton Church. Few churches have a more complete family history, wrought in alabaster, marble and stone, than this. The most appealing mural memorial is one to a child showing him wept over by cherubs; he was the heir of Nicholas, tragically poisoned in 1702 by eating yew berries in the park. His death ended his father's most cherished ambitions. Work already begun was completed; no more.

Had fate decided otherwise Stonyhurst would now rank as a stately home. Instead, the Welds to whom the Sherburne possessions passed, allowed priests and scholars from their old school, St. Omer's—where Jesuits had taught the sons of English Roman Catholic families from Elizabethan times—to occupy the vacant hall when they were forced to flee from Flanders during the French Revolution.

They said these were temporary quarters. They are still there. Stonyhurst has world-wide fame as a great Roman Catholic public school and seminary. Here too the best architects, Hansom and Dunn, and modern names are associated with the 'new' Stonyhurst.

Many pleasant and historic places come within Clitheroe's very wide scattered rural district, a compact of sylvan and pastoral and entirely beautiful countryside. A lifetime's affection for it, and for my birthplace Clitheroe, has gone into many of my books to which I refer any who want to enjoy, through me, its rich past and satisfying present. All the lovely tranquil landscape seen from Jeffrey Hill or Kemple End, from the Bowland Fells and Vale of Chipping, the whole of Ribblesdale from Ribchester northwards, to the brooding Pendle foothills and Sabden Valley,

Longridge Town and Clitheroe Borough, from April '74 comes under the Ribble Valley Authority; all predominantly rural, much desired by townsfolk hankering for that 'place in the country', the natural wandering ground for walkers and town motorists on afternoons out.

All will indeed be Lancashire in '74, waiting to surprise the stranger even more, as Chipping's pleasant face, a comely place, architecturally satisfying, full of visual delights—"not a bit like Lancashire!" exclaims the delighted visitor. The village is one of our best kept and most beautiful, half as old as Time, yet keeping up to date in its well concealed modern factories, making cheese, and chairs.

On no account fail to introduce the visitors to that enchanting limestone region of Little Bowland and its fairy-haunted nooks, Dinkling Green, Whitmore and Lickhurst (two feet required); this is Lancashire's seven square miles of the erstwhile royal hunting forest, so long cut off and preserved from outside interference it seems somehow wrong to trespass therein now.

So to Clitheroe, its castle a far-seen landmark as the Norman De Lacys, who built it in the twelfth century, intended. Being rather short of castles in the county we are very proud of this, that is what was left standing after Cromwell's orders had it battered down in 1649. It might still be a royal castle—like Lancaster's—but Charles II in 1660 gave it and the Honor of Clitheroe to General Monk the former Parliamentary leader, who put in so much hard work in bringing about the Restoration.

The site is exciting and in some lights as dramatic as Buck's eighteenth-century engraving of it, highly romanticized. What a view from the ramparts, a comprehensive sweep five eighths of which—south-west, south and east—takes in green and pleasant Lancastrian land. The sheltering heights, Pendle, Longridge and the moorlands south, have changed little down the centuries. Clitheroe though outgrowing its old medieval bounds has kept its figure and still is more the country market than commercially minded town.

Dig anywhere under Clitheroe and you hit bedrock limestone; coral limestone reef knolls, the two most southerly in a chain, provided sites for castle and parish church and streets linking them. Lime, Law and Latin—the old borough claimed pre-eminence in these from Elizabethan times; now much of its prosperity rests on lime, and cement works. The limestone belt from Ribble to Pendle foot is a mile broad, and very thick.

Names outstanding in the borough's history? We know little about Orm the Englishman except that the Normans turned him out. Roger de Poictou, Williams' head man in the north-west, was expected to lick the local English into shape and defend the northern borders; he chose Clitheroe as one strong point. After him, the De Lacys were in possession of the Honor (a large number of manors and estates passed to their underlings). Ilbert built the castle on the rock; he did not like the natives and they had no love for him. In 1137 the Clitheroe English made common cause—for the first time—with the Norman garrison in attempting to stop the advance of Scots raiders under William FitzDuncan. They fought by a Ribble crossing at Edisford but were defeated. Being henceforth on much better terms with their overlord a few years later he granted their first charter, exact date uncertain, but the borough, to make sure, celebrated its eighth centenary in 1948! Another De Lacy in 1283 repeated its contents in another charter confirming "the Villeins in their houses, tenements, customs, and liberties" such as Chester's citizens enjoyed. They had to pay for the benefits—ten marks annually on the Feast of St. Michael.

This De Lacy, most powerful of his family, married the daughter of William Longspée, son of Henry III and Fair Rosamund. His only daughter Alice became the wife of Thomas Earl of Lancaster, and as his sole heir, all the family possessions eventually became her husband's, and because of his rebellion, passed to the Crown. Henry had 'willed' the parish of Whalley to the monks of Stanlaw, Cistercians already richly endowed by their De Lacy patrons and others with lands in Lancashire. They willingly moved in, the site in 'Calder-botham' infinitely preferable to that by the Mersey. In 1310 Henry de Lacy was buried near the High Altar. Whalley and Clitheroe have long been linked by more than highways. Both won a measure of quiet in January 1971 with the opening of the bypass, a pleasant sweep over limestone pastures west of Pendle.

Clitheroe castle grounds and the surrounding gardens are the escape for one; and for the other, peace untroubled in church and abbey precincts, on the ancient lanes climbing the Nab—or by Calder side, and where the rushing water flows over the sill of what was the abbey mill dam.

In 627 St. Paulinus, or his missioners, full of zeal after the conversion of Northumbria and its king, preached to the Calder valley natives not far from the riverside and later in a clear pool baptized them; the founding of the mother church. It is not impossible that similar deep Calder pools near the weir were used for trial by water, King James' sure test for witches; read about what could have happened in Harrison Ainsworth's *Lancashire Witches*.

That bridge spanning the Calder; it replaced an early ford in 1316 when stone for its building was given to the abbot who recognized urgent need for a safe crossing. Trade and traffic was increasing now the abbey was settling in and considerable activity enlivened all roads converging here; Whalley was the new hub in this part of Lancashire. The De Lacys disappeared for ever from the local scene. The Crown for over three-and-a-half centuries was in possession.

Whalley church is perfect for parish history and architecture. Look at it as a book with many chapters, each a century; nineteen hundred years if we begin with the stone quern and Roman altar in the north aisle, thirteen if we start with the arrival of the Paulinus missionaries—and a few decades longer if we date Christianity from St. Augustine. The pre-Norman churchyard crosses span three periods, Anglo-Celtic, Anglian, Anglo-Norse. Of the wooden church nothing is left, but of the first stone building, "the White church under the lea", a few carved fragments, built into the outer south wall of the chancel. The priest's door with the head of the old knocker—maybe for sanctuary—is coeval with the twelfth-century chancel. The thirteenth and fourteenth centuries saw the nave lengthened, then aisles added, and in the mid-fifteenth century, with the addition of the belfry tower and nave roof raised to take inset clerestory windows, the fabric was completed.

Always growing, like the best things in English villages, craftsmen in wood came next to add beautiful screens, pews—one a veritable 'cage'—all wrought for the greater glory of God. The same men who worked for the abbot laboured on the church. When the monks left Whalley their misericords from the abbey choir were brought to the 'church next door'.

No museum, this, but a living and lively church.

The parish boundaries have become more restricted than they were in the thirteenth century. Then among Whalley's neighbours were the parishes of Mitton, Gisburn, Barnoldswick, Kildwick, Rochdale. As time passed its daughter churches were many, those who pleaded for chapels in remote places—as Goldshaw Booth which finally had its Newchurch-in-Pendle, and Rossendale which had to wait for its new church until 1511 when Henry VII heard their petition, a very piteous one it was complaining with some reason of 'foul painful and hillous' ways dividing them from the castle chapel at Clitheroe.

Why is it so many people flock to see a ruin yet pass an even more venerable building which by good fortune remains intact and unimpaired? Hundreds converge each year upon Whalley Abbey, not a 'first class' ruin as are Fountains, Tintern and Furness abbeys, but of considerable extent and beautifully set among trees in a sheltered valley—just the place to while away a summer afternoon in drowsy sunshine among butterflies and bees, blossom and flowers; then it is enchanting—and even more so at the edge of dusk when birds sing their hearts out in long sweet vespers, their bills cocked at the sunset.

It takes far more money to keep ruins, as ruins, safe for children to scramble among and saunterers to wander through, than to preserve buildings which are roofed and defended from the weather. Whalley Abbey began its life as a ruin in the 1540s when its masonry was for sale, and snapped up by numerous local builders. Then the abbot's house became the Assheton's mansion, with late Tudor addition in the form of Long Gallery and kitchens; where the brethren had paced with sacerdotal tread they and their guests walked and talked. The towering walls of the abbey church cut out the light. Being very much a white elephant in their garden, orders were given in the 1660s to raze it to the ground. A great pity, but as it had never played any part in village life no one missed it.

When we walk the terrace which makes a high wall north of the precincts, there is much abbey masonry under our feet; one way of disposing of vast quantities of masonry and rubble!

Where the high altar of the Cistercians stood, a new one is raised; here is held the open air Whitsuntide communion service. In the June floralia, move the Bishop's garden-party guests. Thousands of children from the wideflung Blackburn Diocese gathered here for the great Ascension Day Pilgrimage in 1965. At quieter times students and church workers stay at the abbot's

Gawthorpe Hall, Lord Shuttleworth's gift to the nation

house, now a conference house, work, study, discuss, and gather for worship in a very beautiful and completely modern chapel.

Whalley Church is part of past and present. Whalley Abbey is playing an increasingly important part in Lancashire's present too.

Age-old tranquility, settled peace, architectural beauty in a setting equal to it, gracious living as in a Georgian Age, complete rurality on the rim of what is one of the most industrialized parts of Britain; where else could this be but Downham?

When it is realized that coral limestone hundreds of feet thick underlies and encloses the Downham hollow—of the same series of rock which is removed by the thousand tons from quarries not so far away between Chatburn and Clitheroe—and that new towns cry out for it to build their giant concrete skyscrapers and modern developments, we wonder how long before this precious plot is seized upon. With less devoted owners it might have been swept away before. Not if the Asshetons, owners who have loved and cared for this green and lovely countryside continuously from 1559, continue to have a say in their own desmesnes.

"When we decided to come to Downham, doctors said my husband had no more than a year or two to live. We've been here twelve years in May," an 'offcomed' villager once told me.

That is what Downham does, gives a new lease of life. According to two elderly visitors who looked around one sunny day when it looked more than usually enchanting it was a demi-paradise. Said one, "Some folk has their heaven on earth". For their own sakes I hope St. Peter is not going to bar out all from Downham!

There is nothing 'precious' about this village. In a British Travel and Holidays Association competition to choose Britain's prettiest village Castle Combe, Milton Abbas, Dunster and Finchingfield were placed at the head of the list. Downham came fifth, and was very modest about it. As for the Best Kept Village competition, it does not compete, having enough admiration, quite enough to cope with, already.

Like the best villages it is centred around farming and wrapt up in the land—no mere dormitory for town workers. How many recognize the large building in its enclosure in the centre of the village as a cow shed for one of the best Ayrshire herds in the north? And who would guess, poles, wires and cables bēing absent

Hall i' th' Wood, Lord Leverhulme's gift to Bolton

from the scene, that Downham has long enjoyed the full blessings of modern light, heating and communications? I doubt if many who say, "Oh how beautiful", realize why it is so.

How can perfect harmony as this be achieved? Partly because for four hundred years there has been single ownership and the owners have been at great pains to keep 'uglification' at bay. No two cottages or houses are alike, yet notice how windows and white painted glazing bars are the unifying element—even the new Village Hall, the best of its kind in my opinion, has windows and white paint like the dwellings round the green and up the brow.

Look in vain for placards, notices and the like which hide the best features of many a village. If the villagers have their way one will search in vain for litter too.

Looking at Downham with the eye of a judge of Best Kept Villages I would find it difficult to find a single fault in the care taken to keep it neat and trim—ignoring its *natural* advantages of comely dwellings and attractive setting.

Looking at it as one who loves what is old and good; as a period piece I find it equally perfect, with its Anglian village plan—facing to street and brook and ring o' roses round the green—ancient grouping of church hard by the hall, and inn conveniently near both, and a fascinating assortment of Tudor, Jacobean and Georgian houses with handloom weavers' cottages and humbler homes at the 'town head'.

For one of the happiest pictures of Downham and its setting among coral limestone reef knolls, climb one of them, Worsa Hill—which played its part in "Whistle Down The Wind". For an even wider prospect, of Pendle and the Ribble country, where the river, "an alien known to be, from Yorkshire dares intrude", or in modern idiom 'comes over the border', take your stand on the green ridge behind the village inn.

There was no 'Dunum' when the Romans came marching this way; when they buried two soldiers who died by the roadside theirs was a lonely grave. Two centuries ago, when the Asshetons were erecting a new high wall along the Chatburn lane, under a boulder the burial place was unearthed. The stone was replaced and the wall built over it; look for it protruding like a footing stone, a little beyond the Hall gates.

River Scenes—Wyresdale and Lonsdale

Unless you know where to look for them the rivers running down from the high hills of Amounderness prove most elusive. Brock and Calder play hide and seek through some delicious woodlands, so does the Wyre in its middle reaches, whilst two hardly known rivers, Cocker and Conder, make hardly a splash to attract attention on their way from Clougha and Quernmore to the lowlands. The motorway passes over each in turn, but anyone who wants to get to know them is like a window gazer who can look at but not touch the goods displayed.

Never were so many baffling lanes thrown hither and thither for the express purpose of confusing the stranger. Nor, where lanes peter out, are more tantalizing alternatives ever waiting for walkers. East of A6 and M6 is Lancashire unspoilt, virtually unknown except by local country lovers. M6 will keep it so. Those who survey the four points of the compass from the top of the Forton Observation Tower will dwell longest—distances being clear—on the faraway Lake Lancashire skylines. But in the near 'sights' what is more exciting than the east, fells reaching away into the clouds, and between them mystery—and invitation in every opening dale. That is the Brock and Calder, Wyre and Conder country; unapproachable for motorwayfarers!

From A6 see what happens by turning 'inland' at the Roebuck, Bilsborrow, and following fingerposts to Inglewhite, Bleasdale or Chipping. Or try the next right turn with possibilities of reaching Chipping via Claughton (Cliton), the Brock and Bleasdale. Or keeping to north-going lanes, discover Grizedale, Caldervale, Oakenclough, where you take your choice from windswept fell country dominated by Parlick Pike or the equally windraked heights of Harrisend Fell which reach over to Wyresdale. The same remote regions may be entered from the Brockholes Arms and from the east-turning road just south of Garstang; or north of Garstang from lanes signposted to Scorton. Galgate is gateway to the main Wyresdale road; try the offshoots—preferably on foot—to peace-making retreats like Lentworth with Quaker school and farms, or to the head of the Tarnbrook Wyre, a cul-de-sac cradled in tranquility.

This was the Wyresdale Forest of the Norman and Plantagenet kings which soon changed its role from deer preserve to rich dairy farming, each township later known as a Vaccary. The landscaping and reclamation of Mr. Fenton-Cawthorne made beauty at the dale head of the Marshaw Wyre early in the 1800s; the lime kiln near the Trough Stone provided the lime which was used to turn 1,500 acres of waste into green pastures and at lower level, near the farms, into rich grasslands, nowhere else so bright an emerald. His treeplanting transformed a wild, bare clough into the 'highland glen' with tall conifers throwing bars of shade on the soft turf-clad banks, so attractive for day-out motorists and picnickers.

Later landscaping was the work of the Earls of Sefton who in 1885 purchased the Abbeystead estates, 13,000 acres of field and fell, created a large park around their new hunting lodge, made grouse moors of the surrounding dale head fells and rebuilt—most attractively—scores of broken-down farms and cottages.

Lancaster also took a hand when they acquired the gathering grounds and water rights. Abbeystead lake was impounded to provide enough compensation water for the many mills needing power from the Wyre to turn their wheels; none has wheels in use now—they are ruinous or turned to other needs. The lake is a sheet of untroubled water, haunt of wild fowl and wintering migrants.

Nether Wyresdale and the Fylde, where all rivers slow down and are given artificial floodbanks to safeguard the agricultural land on either hand, will come into my chapter "Lancashire Coastwise", the Lancashire of the estuaries, the sea verge and the bays. So, still in search of rural Lancashire, north to Lune, the health-giving god, Lon, its watery deity.

This queen of rivers named Loncastre of the English and later Lancaster-shire, the county. "Sing hey for Lon, and hey for Lancashire." The Lune rises in Westmorland, rollicks through the most westerly parts of Yorkshire but takes her time once she comes into 'Lancastrian land', doubling her necessary journey by winding and horseshoe bending all over the valley floor.

History has been channelled along the Lune. There is ample evidence in the Roman milestones in Lancaster Museum, in the carved Anglian cross fragments in the priory church, and in Halton's tall churchyard crosses and the 'loaves and fishes' stone at Hornby.

Norse men must have suggested that Sigurd appeared on the

Halton Cross. They were Christian Lonsdalians in the eleventh century, their yarls, Ulf, Orme, Torfin and Tunwulf, the élite among the landowners of the Wapentake. Hardly a name but was of their giving and Norse was more commonly heard than Northumbrian English.

Before the Conquest, Lonsdale was royal land. After 1066 what was Edward's—or Tostigs—was now William's, and when his thugs had finished with the dalesmen the whole of this territory was so devastated—like so much in the north, it was 'waste' and fit for nothing but forest. The Conqueror included all this in the estates handed to his kinsman, Roger the Poictevin, who saw the site above the Lune at Loncastre as eminently suited for a strong-point. This was the only really formidable castle the Normans raised in the county, the only one now whole, complete. Other castles there were up and down the dale, but no more than mottes and baileys, thrown up at strategic points by ferry or ford.

The Montbegons were the only barons whose castle became more than a temporary castlet within a stockade; Hornby they chose to keep watch over wide Lonsdale lands.

The Forest played the most important part in medieval times, its foresters the most powerful officials, and as the suppliers of hawks for royal sport, honoured above all.

Prince John made himself popular hereabouts by granting to his thanes and freeholders in the Honor of Lancaster—at the bargain price of £500 weight of silver—"the liberty to sell and give their underwoods, build houses, to own dogs and hunt the hare and fox and all other beasts except hart, hind, wild boar and goat". They paid up an additional £200 and ten chargers when this was ratified on John becoming king.

The dalesfolk bore the brunt as second line of defence against invasion from the north during all Scots raids, from the incursions of William FitzDuncan in 1137 to the dreadful times following the English defeat at Bannockburn. Lonsdale parents for generations used the names of the Bruce, Black Douglas and the Earl of Moray to frighten naughty children. 1322 was a year long to be remembered for the Scots left Lonsdale wasted—as in 1065 and 1067—desolation in their wake and Lancaster town in flames, though the Priory was spared. The men chalked up the casualties to be remembered till a later date; their descendants paid out all old scores at Flodden, after nearly two centuries waiting. They were among the four thousand fierce men who went north behind Stanley's banner.

> "Every bairn had on his breast broidered with gold
> A foot of the fairest fowl that ever flew on wing,
> With their crowns full clear, all of pure gold.
> It was a seemly sight to see them so together
> Fourteen thousand eagle-feet, fettled in array."

No occasion in Lancashire history so set the ballad and song writers to work, perpetuating the bravery of our lads.

The Scots king bade his herald tell whose was the banner and who the men; Stanley's eagle and Stanley's tenants. Edward Stanley of Hornby was there and men of Lonsdale behind him, and his brother the Bishop of Ely, and Derby's folk from south Lancashire with many others.

> "Lo, how he batters and beats, the bird with his wings!
> We are feared of yon fowl so furiously he fareth!"

> "Lancashire lads like lions laden them aboute.
> All had been lost, by our Lorde! had not those lads been!"

Lonsdale men,

> "All such as Tatham fells had bred,
> With such as Botton Banks did hide;
> From Wharemore unto Whittington
> And all to Wenning water side."

were in the rearward, the left wing under Edward Stanley, which brought final victory. The Scots King James IV was killed.

> "There by the hand of God he was prostrate.
> By the help of the eagle with her swaddled child."

Edward Stanley was rewarded by his grateful stepbrother, Henry VII, took the title Lord Monteagle and, retiring to his Wenningside castle, erected thereon the tower with the eagle surmounting it. His memorial, the octagonal tower at the west end of Hornby church, has a terse inscription befitting a man of action —"Edward Stanly Ld. Monteagle, a soldier, caused me to be made". What a soldier. " 'On, Stanley, on', was the last cry of Marmion."

The castle appears unbelievably romantic from approaching

roads, more so than in its original form. It was demolished by Parliamentary orders after the siege in 1643 but later the walls were raised once more. Finally, embellishments were added by Colonel Charteris 'the infamous' who by questionable means acquired a large fortune—"said to be worth £200,000" according to a newspaper in 1730.

Some rich and varied stories colour Lonsdale landscapes. I enjoy talking to the villagers and hearing such surprising comments as "Down there is Flodden Field", with my attention drawn to a Lune side pasture. It is too: one of Monteagle's followers was given the field on his return from the fight and called it after the place of the great victory.

The villages are a mixed bag, some like Caton and Halton growing far outside their old limits but encompassed by green fields and pleasant prospects, fieldpaths wandering off to the sort of secluded nooks where one wishes it was always summer weather and right for idling away the hours. Not a chimney in sight; nothing but sweet rurality.

Near Caton turn towards Eskowbeck and the drive through the Gresgarth parkland, perfect peace and quiet charm, with the hall —medieval core concealed within a romantic neo-Gothic exterior —against a white froth of cherry blossom or a blaze of June's rhodoes and azaleas, spanning the centuries, cherished by one long established family. The drive curves away into the gentle pastoral hollow of Quernmore; nothing but green serenity yet the wild fells are very near, and upper Wyresdale and the Trough of Bowland highway. On foot, turn left and follow the fingerposts over Cheese Banks—best grazing for cows producing milk for cheese-making, they used to say—into Littledale which is still as near to the gates of Faery as when I first knew it twenty-five years ago.

From Brookhouse also—full of pretty bits and odd nooks—you may discover Littledale or, hankering for headier heights, make for Winder, a lonely farm facing all the winds that blow, an outpost of Roeburndale. Paths in plenty cross the broad shoulders of Barkin, crossing tiny gills merry with bouncing becks and little falls. Or we take little-used paths meandering over acres of bracken, sweetly scented as the fronds unfurl in June, treading flower-spangled turf or warm moss, cushion-soft. Keep high, or drop low to the dale; all the eye looks on is fair.

Claughton (Claffton) possesses in its road-edge church the

oldest dated bell in England; 1296. Neighbouring is a seventeenth-century farmhouse, a mere half hall, the south-east wing being transplanted some years ago, at great cost, to a high level site far up the Gill—just for the view! For views even wider climb to the sheepwash in Kirkby Gill and beyond to Moorcock house by the moor top quarries. "Behold mine eyes have caught new pleasures" —the best of North-West England in the superb spread.

There are some spectacular viewpoints in North Lancashire—from the Trough Stone, from Jubilee Tower above Abbeystead and Quernmore, from the head of both Roeburn and Hindburn valleys at their watershed—but this 'cannot be bet' as a farmer remarked. Just the place to put final irrevocable, indisputable conviction on any claim that Lancashire is not what she is thought to be?

More lovely landscapes for the collection? Admire the river scenery from the Crook of Lune, considered a *must* for travellers from the eighteenth century. Follow up with silent meditation from an embrasure in Loyne bridge between Hornby and Gressingham, with green willows glinting silvery as winds stir their tresses and swans gliding by. Then upriver—by riverside path preferable—to the waters' meeting at Arkholme, the most peace-making spot I know, polished water, flowery meads and dreamy distances, adding up to perfect tranquility.

Away from the great river, to smaller streams. Udale Beck meets Artle Beck at an enchanting spot near Littledale Hall few ever see. Roeburn, leaving the bare defile of Mallowdale, disappears into such mysterious dark depths at Backsbotton, very near Wray, I was reminded of Styx and sacred rivers running "through caverns measureless to man", to emerge with relief once more into sunlight and warm air. Hindburn, Roeburn's twin sister, has fewer dark and secret moods; her dale floor below Lowgill and Ivah spangled with flowers. These dales suffered appalling flood damage in August '67.

You might think the countryside was constantly having a spring clean so bright and shining its face. The beautiful freestone quarried locally, gives the farms and cottages, most of them with seventeenth or eighteenth century date stones, a new look in old age. Winder, Swans, and old farms around Wray and Lowgill are of this pale grey stone.

Each old house has its share of traditions too. In *Countrygoer's*

North I wrote of Blands, a rare puzzle of a place with its Pict's House, Twelve Apostles Seats, Norman undercroft and stone passages; and of Robert Hall the ancient fortified dwelling of Harringtons and Cantsfields, with more than its share of old tales.

The other day a farmer drew my attention to the venerable group of farms at Outhwaite, a mile above Wray, where he remembered whipping post and stocks in a paddock, and the 'hungering house'. What was this? "Well," said he, "monks used to come here and them as'd done owt wrang were hungered to death. Building's got narrow slits in t' walls."

So, with history at every turn and tradition filling in any gaps Lonsdale is 'more than a pretty face'.

Here is the Lowood country of *Jane Eyre*, with 'Brocklebridge' church at Tunstall, the school at Cowan Bridge, and the Rectory of the Rev. W. Carus-Wilson at Whittington, a most pleasant place where in the 1820s the Wilson family formulated plans for a "Clerical school so that poor clergy unable to bestow on their Female Offspring that to which their rank in Society entitles them could have them educated"—the Bronte sisters were early pupils.

It is also the Classic Ground where many came after Camden's visit to study Veritable Antiquity at Roman sites like Overborough. Burrow Hall, much visited by antiquarians long ago, is beautifully placed.

Almost a neighbour of Cowan Bridge and Leck, a border outpost, is Ireby-with-Leck, another hide-away spot with a gracious hall to which Lord Shuttleworth came with his family after he had handed over Gawthorpe, his ancestral home, to the nation.

Ireby hamlet has a Rip Van Winkle air, asleep and not too eager to rouse itself; nothing but flower-covered cottages and smiling farms flanking the beck; birdsong, rural interruptions involving cows, sheep, barking dogs and crowing cocks, nothing more. Upstream the Old Hall, a pleasant farmhouse, was part of local history, Scots soldiers, probably Hamilton's in 1648, and Jacobites of the '15 and '45 being overnight guests in the barns. The sixteenth to seventeenth century building, incorporating an earlier battlemented tower possesses a great hall once the manorial Courtroom, narrow oak benches along its side walls, a vast inglenook fireplace filling one wall together with flanking doorways each with mason marks on the jambs; the roof timbers are unceiled.

The side wings would be 'unhandily' cut off one from the other did not a wrought iron balcony link the upper floors of each.

And here we had better leave Lancashire's completely rural dales, backward glances at homespun villages like Wray where I once watched oak splitters, swill makers and clog block makers at their craft, at Thurland Castle where the stainless knight Sir Brian Tunstall lived—a moated hall within a tree shadowed parkland—and the 'linked sweetness long drawn out' of Arkholme, Whittington and Gressingham.

There are some lovely places near our border with Westmorland, like the perfect little village round a green, Borwick, with the gracious Hall of the Tudor Bindlosses—who made their money as merchants in Kendal cloth—a dream of a house in gardens as enchanting. The Lancashire Association of Youth Clubs is tenant.

The Kellets are down to earth villages tied up with the limestone and limeworks near the Lancaster Bypass and the new motorway, but ignoring both. From their upland pastures—the coast, the Bay, the sea are a bright shining world like a child's morning face upturned to the sun.

All these communities 'without chimneys' are the rural and unspoilt subjects of my book *Lancashire Villages*. Joining these in '74 is a group of my best-beloved, from Craven and Bowland of my forefathers, part of Yorkshire's West Riding but with closest associations with Clitheroe from the 1830s. Among the nineteen Yorkshire townships in the Clitheroe union in the last century are Gisburn, Rimington, and Sawley, Bolton-by-Bowland, Grindleton, West Bradford and Waddington, small communities like Mitton, Bashall and Browsholme, Whitewell and Dunsop, and attractive villages like Newton and Slaidburn. All their Women's Institutes, showing good sense, have chosen to be in the Lancashire Federation. So to join with the Borough of Clitheroe and other Lancashire Ribble Valley rural areas will be no revolution—a natural affiliation?

Ribble and Hodder, county borders for eight centuries, were always bridged or fordable allowing the neighbouring villages to fraternise.

VI

LANCASHIRE'S MARITIME WEST

Lancashire — Coastwise

A Portrait of Lancashire without its seaside resorts would be unthinkable. The holiday coast is enjoyed by millions—153,000 enter Blackpool alone on a normal summer weekday—and increasingly so since the motorway has shown the way north more swiftly. They come for the sea, bracing breezes, fun and friendliness and everything the gregarious can desire. Commuters come too, to live in the modern flats, or pretty bungalows peeping at Morecambe Bay from wood and copse; and more and more retired people. 'Over 60s' are one in four of the coast's population.

When Operation Neptune was launched in 1965 we looked in vain for the inclusion of our Lancashire coastline. Considering we are a maritime county this exclusion seemed odd. Later, Lancashire was asked to give support to the scheme at a national level; we had no share in the operation, except as enjoyers of other counties' shores!

The hundreds of thousands who pour into our coastal resorts and bathe in our briny are not asking for the seclusion of select Cornish coves nor for the towering cliffs of the Channel coast; their pleasure is in proximity, their cliffs manmade as Blackpool's. But where, as the County Planners see it, in 1980 with an estimated thirteen million living within two hours travelling time of these resorts? They will be living there, having fun there. Blackpool and Southport, Fleetwood, Morecambe and Grange, each different from the others, catering for widely different tastes, must expand. But how, if the fine natural features are not to disappear?—Two National Nature Reserves to be protected; two wild fowl refuges, as well as 'scenic beauty round Formby, St. Anne's; parts of the Ribble estuary; the Wyre/Lune marshes; Morecambe Bay and the coastal plain of the Duddon estuary' which must be safeguarded.

What of the Ribble estuary with its mud flats, salt marshes grazed by sheep and cattle, its wild-fowling and reclaimed marshes under intensive arable farming. So much has already been disfigured by power stations, chemical installations—and who knows what nuclear power or atomic plants in the future, if and when the barrage schemes materialise? Small wonder folk who love the coast from Mersey to Duddon Sands, and enjoy the sea-washed shores of Leven, Kent and Keer, are fearful.

The future uncertain, what of the past?

Not a very eventful history, our sea verge having few good ports or harbours in early days. In Roman times the Ribble was tidal; shallow bottomed galleys sailed up to Ribchester—and so did troublesome hit-and-run Irish pirates. In a Heysham creek St. Patrick came ashore, and a century later more Irish missionaries, in impossibly frail coracles, came up the Wyre. The monks of Lindisfarne sought our lonely shores in their years of journeying out of the way of pagan Danes, carrying the body of St. Cuthbert. Norsemen grounded their longboats up Keer and Lune, Ribble and Mersey in the tenth and eleventh centuries.

King John saw in Liverpool a valuable embarkation point for Ireland and put the place on the map. Now it is landfall for Irishmen who gaze on the Mersey front and the spectacular skyline as though it is the gate to Eldorado. So do West Indians, with one-way tickets, descendants of the Africans bought into slavery by cheap trading stuff from the holds of Liverpool ships manned and provisioned by Liverpool investors who expected, and received, good dividends.

Incidents in local history?

I have heard no traditions of bells ringing beneath the waves as at Aberdovey, but lost churches there were and villages 'whelmed' by the sea or hidden by drifting sands. Old Singleton, Kilgrimol, Argamels and Ard-grimol—they existed in the dim past, as 'they say' did Old Aldingham by Leven Sands.

One of the fleeing Armada galleons was grounded off Rossall Point and its cannon fire has resounded down the ages. The loyal Stuarts, the Tyldesleys of Fox Hall, prepared a shelter for James II in 1690 should he return to the Fylde coast from Northern Ireland; news arrived about the Battle of the Boyne, but no king came!

Incidents long remembered: a Jacobite ship with ammunitions for the use of Lancaster rebels intercepted by King George's men in 1715; in the Lune estuary, launching of sailing ships and return with rich cargoes from Africa and mahogany from South America; sailing of Lune-built ships fully armed for skirmish with privateersmen, and return with prizes and the honours of war; by Morecambe Bay shores, stories of high tides undermining the grazing land by Keer and Kent, one parish deprived, another gaining acres cast up by the sea; and tragedies in crossing the sand, a daily occurrence so that only near relatives were overcome by grief.

The Mersey Estuary

Fords, ferries, and no less than six bridges at the lowest bridgeable point at Warrington were needed to link north-south and age-old routes across the Mersey. What a barrier it was, a twenty-mile 'arm of the sea', and inland, woodlands south into Cheshire, mosses northwards. Little wonder activity in dangerous times concentrated on Warrington and its bridges fought for, deliberately put out of use, or damaged by war. Cromwell's statue has a strategic position—overseeing the Mersey bridge, where he put 'finis' to his overcoming of the Scots and English Royalists in August 1648.

No traveller entering Lancashire today from the south but must perforce cross the Mersey, four great highways converging on Warrington Bridge, the M6 crossing to the east, and more roads making for the new Runcorn-Widnes bridge which replaced the old 'transporter' in 1961.

In the past the Butlers of Bewsey ran their own ferry; the monks of Stanlaw ferried their own boat, and Norrises of Speke could ride across at low tide to safety in Wirral when their recusancy brought danger. Birkenhead Priory's ferry was busiest of all.

Speke Hall, in spite of the ever encroaching airport—one of the most modern in Europe—is a Mersey-side pocket of quiet. The city leases the Hall from the National Trust; we may wander in the rooms Tudor Norrises panelled with loot from Holyroodhouse, and indulge all our latent interest in such excitements as priest's hides, escape routes most cunningly contrived, for the family being Roman Catholic, and later Royalist, were constantly on the run. Standing by the river we look across to the low blue Wirral hills. The intervening channels, shallow possible fording places in the Norris's days, are now dredged out of existence. Large boats move by, up to Eastham and the Ship Canal which makes a busy inland port of Manchester.

Mersey Banks have for so long made themselves useful we find it difficult to believe that in the 1860s Widnes was still "a quiet industrial village"; Hale, "a gem set in the Garden of Lancashire with rows of snow white cottages embowered in roses, jessamines and stately 'holyoaks' "; and Oglet, "a hamlet where the last ancient fishermen live catching shrimps in abundance". Where chemical factories and scores of chimneys poured dense volumes of smoke to blast green vegetation, folk said smugly; "If damage has been done, did the works not extend commerce and make land values to increase? Are not thousands employed, and necessaries for public good reduced in price?"

Such works must exist—"and Mersey might as well have the benefit". Towns having tender consciences are now trying hard to make amends, the Otterspool Promenade is Liverpool's gift to its people and Widnes is valiantly reclaiming Hale Bank for a riverside park.

> "The Mersey,—a perfect sea for twenty mile or more—which poole is formed by a point of land that runs almost around the entrance from the sea, being narrow and hazardous for strangers to sail in the winter, the mouth of the river by reason of the sands and rocks is a gate to the river; this I ferried over and was a mile and a half in the passage, it's of great breadth—the waves toss and the great rocks all round it and is as dangerous as the sea."

That was Mrs. Celia Fiennes on her impressions of the Mersey in the 1690s. The history of the river is that of its crossings. The best pictures are from the pens of early travellers. Daniel Defoe also put Mersey and Liverpool on the literary map by describing how he arrived in the ferry boat; then "the traveller must complete his way on foot—or ride through the water not on horseback but on the shoulders of some Lancashire clown who comes knee deep to the boat side to truss you up and then runs away with you as nimbly as you desire to ride". Mrs. Fiennes thought the town handsome, the many people well and fashionably dressed, "London in miniature as much as ever I saw".

Defoe recognized the town in 1680 as "one of the wonders of Britain". In 1690 it was twice as big, on his third visit had again more than doubled its size, "and what it may grow to in time, I know not". He wrote of the stirring spectacle of King William's fleet in 1690 riding on "the roads of Hoylake" waiting a rendezvous with transports from the Mersey and Dee with men and ammunition, then away to the conquest of Ireland.

Very different was the gathering of little ships I saw at the Pier Head in that eventful first week of September '39: incoming boats of the Yarmouth fishing fleet; convoys arriving; more and more trawlers, drifters, and big ships like the *Accra* anchored in mid-river, 'waiting for orders'. It seemed the river could hold no more.

The Mersey grew in importance during eighteenth-century wars, for her north-west approaches remained open when the south-east channels were under enemy surveillance; so during 1939–45, though the enemy kept watch too. In the Picton library, what a formidable collection there is of German aerial photographs of the complete dock system!

From my Liverpool wartime diaries:

> May '40—drawn irresistibly to Pier Head. Venus rising bright in a circle of barrage balloons, and balloons like golden galleons caught in the criss-crossed beams of searchlights as they raked the skies for intruders. Hospital ships in river. Swedish cargo ships. City streets today filled with wounded men, their white armlets with red crosses upon them. Heinkels chased away last night. News of Dunkirk. Thousands of men from the Forces crowd the city, every street fluttering with flags and buntings. Crowds welcoming weary men pouring through the barriers at Lime Street station. Barricades put up round a tented refugee reception area at Aintree racecourse. Processions of French matelots, red pom-poms on their berets, ambling down Scotland Road; trestle tables laden with food—how, on rations!—for any hungry man to help himself. On the Midland Adelphi steps coming and going of distinguished looking men in operatic uniforms, leaders of overrun countries. And Mersey crammed with ships of all nations and half the French navy in port.

The next May, '41—a different picture:

> A succession of perfect days, and moonlight nights, mild as milk, and bright as day with exploding shells, bursting bombs, seven nights of hell when Liverpool people slept out in the fields and the city went up in flames—one with Troy and Tyre and Ninevah. Yet each morning the Pier Head skyline looked the same—and the cathedral on the mount, though all below was in ruins.

A second blitz, selective in its destruction, goes on now on

300 acres of old obsolete docks and the waterfront from the Pool to Seaforth and beyond—ripe for commercial development—and the new docks, the best the modern age can make, are to continue downriver towards Crosby.

Nothing is standstill about the Mersey. Nature—or Neptune?—has sent tides racing through the narrow bottleneck, scouring out the channel and making the open basin anything but a calm anchorage. Man made the wet docks to harbour shipping, and dredgers and hopper barges cut deeper channels, suck up sand and silt; and, to secure the wide, buoyed, approach channel, eighteen miles of limestone 'embankment' have been built above low water level to show the tides wherein to flow.

For two centuries Mersey has been improving passage and anchorage. Early last century when "gales and fogs stopped transit and seas lashed into storms made it extremely dangerous for small craft", it was suggested, "a subway would obviate these mischances". In good time the Mersey Tunnel was engineered.

Mersey to Ribble

Long ago, shorefolk tell you, a ship was wrecked off Formby and 'earth apples' were washed up—the first potatoes, and here the first were grown: an Irish vessel, in 1565—to be more precise.

'*Rich, Formbie Hic Jacet*'—so read a stone brought in 1840 after the fire of York Minster to Formby old church. Richard was Henry IV's arms bearer. Old tales.

One of the earliest 'traveller's tales' of Lancashire was on this coast. A clergyman called Richard James was listening on the seashore at Meols to the wisdom of an old ex-navy man—who fought at 'Cales':

"Welcome gentlemen"
He said, and more. "You gentlemen at ease
Who money have, and go where e'er you please
Are never quiet; weary of ye day
You now come hither to drive time away.
Must time be driven? Longest day with us
Shuts in too soon, as never tedious
Unto our business, making, mending nets,
Preparing hook and baits wherewith to get
Cod, whiting, upon ye sandy shelves
Wherewith to feed ye market and ourselves."

Hodder Valley border country

The poor and humble were always with us. William Blundell in 1684, fifty years later, met a woman on the road near Crosby. He asked her how many children she had.

"Six," she replied.

"Here," he said, "is sixpence for them."

"No, sire," she said most simply, "I will not sell my children."

It needs old letters and diaries such as his to bring the past to life most vividly.

In the present, the Formby and Ainsdale coastline are recognized for their wild life and rare plants. Freshfield sand-dunes—what an expanse of sunbathed beaches and, behind, miles of Sahara-like sandscapes for children to play desert Arabs in striped bathing towels on the way home, and dim pine woods, deliciously aromatic airs, fairy tale mystery within them, and butterflies like summer flowers on wings in the clearings.

Ainsdale is for the nature lover, 1,216 acres of foreshore, dunes, slacks and pinewood, a protected Reserve with a bird population of over two hundred types, breeding grounds for seabirds, with many rare flowers; and evidence of man's long fight to hold back drifting sands by planting the marram and star grasses. Red squirrels wait for you, pheasants wander about unconcerned; and Natterjack toads—about the highest number in the U.K.! Lads come poaching with sacks to supply the demands of collectors! And schoolchildren, in study groups, learn to know better.

When did the civilizing hand of progress change South-west Lancashire, its meres and mossland? When local landowners decided to try out similar drainage and reclamation schemes to those which had proved successful in places like the Bedford levels and the Sussex marshes. News travelled north. In 1692 Mr. Fleetwood of Bank Hall—where Douglas and Yarrow combined to become the Asland—set about his drainage schemes. At great expense and with gangs of 2,000 men he drained, trenched, and raised banks with floodgates to hold back the tidal waters; he failed because drifting sands blocked the inlets/outlets. His land remained 'marsh and moorish' and hardly ready for tillage. Bog lights still flickered on dark nights, rheumatic bones creaked, and women continued swingling and pulling hemp and flax as for centuries past. Success came in stages. Eccleston of Scarisbrick, by effective floodgates fitted with paddles which kept the mud and sand at the tidal outflow from choking them, diverting bog water

Cartmel fells and dales from Bigland

into miles of sluices so that during the 'war years' of the 1790s new won land was waving with oats and barley and fattening prime beef cattle. The Hesketh too had their efforts crowned with success. Their embankments kept back the tides, winning extensive game preserves south of the Ribble estuary—providing high jinks for local poachers! With more high banking, by the 1890s a belt one-and-a-half miles deep was added to that already won from tide and swamp.

Nature would continue winning back, alone, if man did not keep up the fight. Most land for five miles behind Southport is below high tide level. Farmers tended to lose a great deal by flooding—£200,000 in 1956—but now the pumping station, where the River Crossens is natural outlet for the old Martin Moss 'basin', keeps working day, and all night, after high tides and heavy rains. Pumps dealing with two million tons of water daily make it possible for local agriculturalists to sleep sound in bed o'nights.

As the land was tamed so were the natives 'civilized'. It is often said that the Banks fisherfolk are 'descended from Vikings'. In the past like all the shore dwellers they were wreckers and smugglers when opportunity knocked.

To carry coal from Wigan's pits, the Douglas was canalized; barges heavy laden were a common sight along the Ribble estuary, watched by curious fisherfolk of North Meols and the farmers of South Hawes. By 1774 a new canal carrying trade from Liverpool to Wigan curved across country, bringing the first outsiders and visitors to the primitive coastal hamlets. They must have enjoyed the seashore, the sea breezes and watching the simple fisherfolk—who were perhaps not quite so simple as they looked—at their reed gathering, basket making, fishing and shrimping, and trudging down to the salt marshes to bring in their cattle before the oncoming tide.

The wind of change was blowing strong; progress was in the air.

Southport is Born

Churchtown had always been the most important place on these shores. Its church was an ancient foundation (rebuilt in the 1730s); here was a grammar school, and inns named from the landowning Hesketh and Bolds. By 1759 the surrounding estates had come into the hands of Bolds-Fleetwoods-Hesketh through marriage of heiresses—the son of Hesketh of Meols Hall with the heiress of Rossall and Penwortham, and their son, Fleetwood-Hesketh, with the Bold heiress.

A Churchtown innkeeper called Sutton had an eye for the main chance. A flow of visitors hankered after sea bathing, and the best bathing place was at South Hawes. There visitors were conveyed by 'local transport'. But once there they found no shelter, no privacy. Horse-drawn carts carried bathers into deep water.

Along came Sutton, tidying up the timber from wrecks which littered the shore. Up went the first bathing hut, and what might be called the first refreshment kiosk. Southport was about to be born. Mrs. Sally Walmesley thought 'taking in lodgers' might pay, and Sutton on a plot he leased near his hut erected the first seaside hotel. At the house warming in 1798 his friends pondered deeply over a name. An eleven-fathom pool out to sea, the nearest 'port', decided them. It should be the South Hawes port hotel, Southport. They had christened the new resort also.

Sutton earned the nickname 'Old Duke' and his first shelter, 'The Folly'. His grandiose schemes to make of Southport a fine placed failed. His hotel was let for twenty-one years, and he became a guest of the king in Lancaster debtor's prison.

But Southport was set on its course, attracting the more select visitor—its seal for elegance came with royal patronage. William, Duke of Gloucester, as Commander of the North-west Approaches, enjoyed the bathing and waited for the French invasion in 1803, whilst in 1815 Prince Louis Philippe, later King of France, after sporting at Ince found himself relishing the Southport air. One up on Blackpool!

Development was from the start firmly controlled. Neat 'marine residences' were allowed, with fronting gardens; many lawns were adorned with ships' figureheads, sea gods, mermaidens with ogling eyes and tritons with tridents. Visitors called in at a 'Repository of Conchological varieties'—worth seeing in the 1810s. A garden lay-out—with Nature providing along a series of peat bog, dips and hollows, the site for Lord Street—followed, surely one of the most attractive modern features of the town. Victorian Southport was pleasant, tidy, respectable and a perfect setting for promenades and carriage rides, for crinolines and parasols.

The first serious set-back came with the sea's withdrawal during the 1860s. To chase it a pier was built, its termination in the high tide and a tram to take the visitor to look at the sea! From the pier one could embark on trips to the Isle of Man, Blackpool or Piel Island. But still the tides were reluctant, finally drawing back until any mention of Southport as a seaside place provoked mirth. Then in the 1880s the Marine Lake was created, gardens designed and the right to call it 'seaside' continued.

Now we visit Southport for other reasons than to see the sea; for leisurely shopping; idling as on the Boulevards of Paris—if less gay, though at times the posters do come to life; for flowers everywhere; and shows, and shrimps. We buy our shrimps from Banks families—Rimmers and Balls who for generations have 'stood' our markets. Descended from the Vikings, it is whispered, like Flookburgh fisherfolk, they live at Marsh Side and Crossens, and their boats are drawn up on the channels and inlets.

A century ago, Hesketh Banks—on a hill fifty-eight feet above the Asland—had a share of seaside visitors who came for the bathing, the salmon fishing and flounders at the river mouth. Then it was cultivating the seven hundred reclaimed Hesketh acres, so rich in marine deposits they were more fertile than any manure could make them. Today Hesketh Banks is intensively farmed, with miles of vegetables growing in rows converging to infinity, with acres of glass and every day some form of field work in progress.

As Dutch or East Anglian landscape in Lancashire it has a certain charm, dead flat under billowy skies and rimmed by the sea. I travelled across the bare landscape in March, between vast unfenced market gardens, miles of wind-raked, black peaty ground beyond, with but an occasional plantation to break the sweep of it, and along the mile long drains pollarded willows and sallows with golden haze upon them; in each cultivator's land, dark tar-felted huts; here and there a lonely field worker bowed over the furrows and a scarlet tractor let me know this was no still life.

The people are warm, friendly, nothing secretive about them, as open as the clear skies above them. Bright eyes, clear skins, jolly voices—these we find among the folk who toil in the fields by day and tend their productive gardens on summer evenings. How they must have changed in two hundred years from the marsh folk who were resentful of strangers, suspicious of incomers, isolated and 'impervious to the regular influences of civilization'.

Ribble Estuary

Until I made a Midsummer night crossing of the Irish Sea on the transport ferry, the *Ionic*, little did I realize how lovely the Ribble estuary could be. Down the flood tide we moved smoothly leaving Preston's chimneys, spires and the rigging of scores of ships in the docks, in a soft blue haze. Our pilot boats fanned out before us and the flotilla going decorously ahead, in single file, seemed to be heading into the sunset.

I cannot recall a more tranquil evening, golden as a Flemish angelus painting. We kept intimate touch with land too, children waving from farm walls, courting couples looking on, haymakers from Lea downing forks for a moment to watch our passing, and a boy and dog leaping away from our following wash. Not until well beyond Warton Brows and Hesketh Out Marsh, where the estuary widens into a funnel, did the shores begin to recede.

Blue dusk filled in when the sunset glow paled, and lights began to prick the low shores of Southport and Lytham, outlining promenade and pier. A last thin sliver of darkened land, a church tower, a slim spire—and the pilots turned, leaving us to proceed alone into the open, heaving sea. How the last buoys danced as we passed and shorelights flickered like fireflies. Blackpool's lights disappeared and Lancashire melted into the night.

Preston's are our newest docks—dug from the Ribble's north bank in the 1890s, and touch and go for years whether it would make money for the town or be a drain on the rates. Doubts about its future continue.

As for the transport ferry, the idea was tried soon after the war when a tank landing ship was taken on for the ferrying of vehicles to Ulster; very different from our superbly fitted *Ionic*, and the *Bardic*, which were the pleasantest crossings to Ireland in the sixties.

Digging the basins in the 1890s brought to light hunting grounds of prehistoric man, and the giant urus-animals with seven-foot horn span, and red deer they had killed. Neolithic man left stone axes and arrowheads littering ancient shores, buried deep in the bed of the docks.

Dredging for the shipping wiped out historic fords—all the banks show where crossings used to be—'Hyroads from Lancaster to Chester'—'Over Ribble Water at Hesketh Banks to ye Fyld', 'Over Ribble Water at Warton'. As late as the 1870s guides met the train at Wrea Green to convey travellers safely across from Warton to Hesketh. Much history lies beneath Ribble's flood tides.

Fylde Coast

The Fylde coast early in the eighteenth century, nothing but bog and swamp on Ice Age boulder clay, only low ridges above marsh level with ancient tracks linking small hamlets—as in early Anglian and Norse days; a few pockets of sand and gravel and along the sea verge fishermen's hovels near breaks in the boulder clay cliffs. Through one creek Marton Mere drained its peaty waters to the sea; the pool, which was brown, was later named Blackpool!

A rural population, concerned with oats, barley and beans, cared little about the world beyond their mosslands; new ideas were held at bay. Like the most important families, the Cliftons who bought the Benedictine priory lands at Lytham in the sixteenth-century—and were rebuilding their fine mansion there in the eighteenth, and the Tyldesleys with their hunting lodge at Fox Hall, many were Roman Catholics, loyal to the Stuarts and well disposed to the Jacobites.

As south of the Ribble, change came with draining of the mosslands and land improvement; with new roads over the marshes came the first visitors.

By the Spen Brook outflow they found a bathing beach, near the pool houses and Fox Hall. When a local innkeeper heard them laughing and splashing inspiration seized him. He acted quickly; first a bathing machine, then, in 1735, the first inn. Cottagers were quick to welcome lodgers. So was Blackpool, as a pleasure resort, launched.

They discovered Lytham too, with two bathing machines waiting and the owner a most delicate 'handler' when the timid ventured on their first dip. On Sunday his machines conveyed the frail to church!

By 1770 inns and lodging houses multiplied but still could not cope at busy times. Then, not a farm, barn or cottage from Kirkham and Poulton to the coast but was also filled to capacity. The new workers in the growing towns—who had never been nearer the sea than the silver glint on their far horizons, arrived. They took the seawater, inside and out. Had not a blind man been cured and a paralytic made a new man by Blackpool's brine?

It was good fun. They walked the two-hundred-yard-long, grass 'promenade' and 'got off'; they danced on the green near the inn to the music of a fiddler and for a play went off to Poulton's tithe barn theatre.

A thousand visitors arrived in 1824—by steamer and daily coaches. "No sea bathing place can be better situated, opening out to the sea, refreshed with a pure and bracing sea air, presenting a fine smooth sand, new modelled by every tide, but always firm, smooth and elastic and admirably fitted both for equestrian and pedestrian exercises as well as for the display of splendid equipages."

If only a branch canal could be brought to Blackpool! The innkeepers looked across the estuary and envied Southport which had such an unfair advantage. Its visitors could arrive by packet boat; it was going to steal all the tourist trade!

The railway age was dawning. With the coming of the trains nothing could hold back Blackpool's progress. In 1840—the Preston-Wyre line reached Poulton, and there carriages were waiting to carry passengers to the sea. The first Sunday trips, on the mill operatives' only free day, were started. In churches preachers referred to the "Safe and Swift Trips to Hell". But to the trippers the train ticket was passport to Paradise. When in 1846 the line was continued to Blackpool, there was never a shadow of doubt that Blackpool was 'made'.

And its neighbours shared its prosperity. Lytham's first trains arrived also in 1846. Thanks to the restraining hand of the Cliftons it grew graciously, its charming Regency and early Victorian houses and side streets setting the seal on how it was to develop. No destroying of the old Wind Mylne for a fun fair, no replacing of the attractive and extensive green by hard promenade concrete. Like Southport, set to attract a more staid and opulent type of visitor, so Lytham appealed to those less inclined to be noisily gregarious. Both have successfully retained quiet dignity and a measure of old-fashioned charm quite lacking in big, bright, bold Blackpool. Without them where would the gregarious go?

Each one is perfect for where it is. So is St. Anne's-on-Sea, born in 1875 when wealthy cotton magnates and those who had made their 'brass' in the towns decided to develop the flat land behind the sand hills, build fine mansions, and either retire here or travel daily to Manchester. St. Anne's is quite different from the others.

Only Blackpool has a Golden Mile, a money making foreshore "fine, smooth sand—always firm, elastic, safe", formed of minute grains from rocks of far away moors and mountains pounded by the sea. Quartz and calcium carbonate, garnet and zirion, tourlamite, apatite and ilmenite are in the sand we shake from our shoes. "New modelled by every tide", but, alas, the Golden Mile is tarnished and not half so gold as it should be, for litter collecting annually devours about three-quarters of its £40,000 revenue from stands and deck-chairs.

Wyre mouth to Lune Deeps

The Wyre estuary where

"She in her crooked course to seaward softly slides
Where Pellin's mighty Mosse and Merton's on her sides
Their boggy breasts outlay."

For some reason the Wyre had far more publicity than Ribble or Mersey mouth.

There was the early tradition of Portus Setantiorum intriguing generations of historians, a Roman sea-port? The Allens of Rossall were deeply involved in its history during Elizabethan times. Especially the Cardinal—"the purple of his hat dyed in the blood of the martyrs he has educated", as the King of Spain said of him—founded the school for the sons of English Papists at Douai in 1568, the first page in Stonyhurst's long story. He was empowered by the Pope—if and when Philip of Spain's Armada landed its troops—"to admonish the Nobility and Gentry in England" to rise and cast Elizabeth from her throne. No wonder his actions were suspect, his house watched, his friends who were known Papists kept under close surveillance. Had he contact with the captain of the grounded galleon off Rossall?

Along Wyre shores, as far inland as Skippool and Rawcliffe, old farms are said to have hides which concealed Allen and his relatives in those highly dangerous times. Mains Hall near Aldwath, was one. But later this was remembered as the place to which Mrs. FitzHerbert retired when George IV, whose morganatic wife she had been, was forced to 'put her aside'.

Local lore is very rich and doggerel couplets many. Some distance off Rossall shore at the edge of a stretch of lost land and where men saw tree stumps of a buried forest, was a route used by travellers from Lytham to Wyre mouth and Cockersand; preferable to the swampy going inland. Half way was an inn, where travellers halted for penny pots of ale, slipping their horse's halters round a large stone at the door. The inn has been washed away but the Penny Stone was seen at low tide, long enough for tales to be spun about it.

"Penny stood; Carling fled
and Red Bank ran away"

And seeing it doubtless "Rossall's wife went on churning"—and the sea off Rossall Point boiling and thundering!

And the warrener snaring his rabbits on the sandhills, earmarked for Fleetwood of the future, registered no interest at all!

In those days fishermen struck rich when they found pearls embedded within Wyre mussels. They called the pearl mussels Hambleton Hookings, "from their manner of taking them, by plucking them from their Skeers, or beds, with hooks".

Hambleton, hanging on to what is old, is most attractive, a place belonging to the sea and fishermen rather than to tourists and commuters. So are the creeks of Wardleys and Skippool, redolent of the past and their heyday when, as small ports with shipping bringing in Baltic trade-timber, grain and the like, they had their share in Lancashire's maritime prosperity; all this was before Glasson stole Lancaster's trade, and Fleetwood ousted Glasson, and Liverpool outstripped them all. There is no scene so pleasant as these creeks with the tide full in, the sky blue above and gay pleasure craft bobbing about like feathered shuttlecocks.

Some days when the sun shines and has warmth in it old salts take up their stands in sheltered places. Small boys gather round and listen; though the old men have no rings in their ears they might well pose for 'The Boyhood of Raleigh'.

From the Fylde's earliest days where did all ridge roads run? From Ribble fords to Wyre, and here to Aldwath and the place later bridged at Shard. What a utilitarian bridge it is, built for toll catching. The 'bus conductor comes round to collect our pennies before we can cross, giving time for us to scan the List of Tolls devised in 1862, when bull, ox and ass must have been harnessed to local transport, and wheeled vehicles now relegated to coach house museums were still in commission.

It is said that in the 1830s the street plan of Hesketh-Fleetwood's new town, between sea and Wyre mouth, was defined across rabbit warren and sandhills by the plough; the beginning of a most impressive piece of town planning.

Fleetwood took its name from the owner of its soil and sand; his family had been at Rossall for centuries, at the hall Sir Peter handed over in 1843 to become a school for sons of gentry and clergy. He foresaw a town and market inland, well away from the noise and confusion of dockyards and fish wharves, a watering place pleasantly situated and workaday Fleetwood 'round the corner' out of sight. He visualized a thriving dock too, and when the railway arrived in 1840 with passengers eager to cross to Belfast or the Furness coast, there seemed every likelihood it was Lancashire's up and coming shipping port.

But it did not work out quite according to plan. By the 1880s as a watering place "it was tolerably well patronized in the summer though its principle prosperity depended on daily steamers to Belfast and in the tourist season to Piel in Furness". For the rest, "the views over the bay were fine, but inland not much to encourage the visitor" and only the H.Q. of the "Government School of Musketry infused a little life into the town".

Liverpool was determined to countenance no rival port—so bang went Fleetwood's pretensions in that direction. But its fishing industry continued and for me a most fascinating spectacle is unloading time at the fish wharves with deep sea trawlers from Iceland, the Faroes and Norwegian waters, disposing of their catch.

One of the first chemists in Fleetwood made a comforting liniment for the exclusive use of trawlermen, to keep out aches and pains when in northern waters; later he made lozenges too, just the thing to have in the mouth when ploughing through the watery main. I had heard of them for years, "J. Lofthouse's Fisherman's Friend", before I tracked down the makers. I was told that the cough lozenges are on demand by sailors on the seven seas and urgent orders for them come from places as far apart as British Columbia and New Zealand. This kind of 'sweet' for prevention and cure of coughs we were always given when going out into a foggy morning.

There are three totally separate parts to Fleetwood. The docks, wharfs, and the jetty from which the fussy Knott End ferry boats make the jolly crossing of the Wyre carrying holiday makers and, all the year round, scores of commuters who work on one bank and choose to live on the other; this in the rather dingy and purely for trade and commerce part. The town centre has done very little to make itself bright and gay like Blackpool; it might well be an old fashioned borough of far longer than a hundred and forty years standing, and we hope it stays so, and keeps its open market which my Fylde friends swear by as "the best in Lancashire". But seaside Fleetwood is a different matter, modern, attractive and out to entertain its visitors in the best possible ways; you may saunter in the Marine Gardens or along colonnades with vistas of flowers and lawns, or sit in the Marine Hall, or listen to music in the Concert Hall, or watch the lovelies on the terraces and sun balconies of the fine open air swimming pool; or just look at the superb prospect over the bay, as they did in 1840.

Any old 'native'—that is one of over fifty years 'sand-grown'—will tell of the Roman quay over which he climbed and played as a boy, and insist that the great stones were shaped and laid there by the Romans—whatever geologists say about natural rock formations. Let them stick to their Portus Setantiorum if it pleases them. And to the tons of sand and gravel which every tide leaves piled against reef and shoreline. Fleetwood is lucky; not a hand's turn, but the willing sea deposits wealth to be shovelled up and carted away, the raw material for this concrete age!

Peninsulas, like islands, have a life of their own, a self-sufficiency, a dislike of change. Between Wyre and Lune, Lancashire has a special flavour. Some changes have entered—new houses, sprawling estates at Knott End and Preesall—but the rest is still a land of waving corn, oats and barley, lonely farms raised on low platforms above old mosslands—and every tree shaven-headed and listing to port. People list to port too, men in the fields, children blown home from school. And the bus rocks too. What a boisterous bracing land!

The foreground could be mistaken for any 'Little Holland'—but wait for it! Over the bay, the Lakeland panorama in full colour!

It was once said the peat was inexhaustible, the Mosses 'bottomless', but where roads, arrow-straight, run high above fields of corn and crops there are the worked out bogs. Those between Hambleton and Pilling were reclaimed by the moss lords who after drainage—the Duke of Hamilton set up tile works to enable hundreds of miles of drains to be laid—turned the bog floor, "cleared of its bleak turfy surface into meadows, pastures and grain fields".

Farmers rarely cut turf for sale these days; it does not pay to set a labourer digging. But for home consumption they greave and stack their 'Round Robins', bringing the 'Rockles' to stand at backdoors for winter fuel. In their grandparents' time turf was fifteen feet thick; now but six feet, and of that only the bottom layers are good for burning, the top fitter for moss litter. They find roots of yew, birch and hazel when digging; occasionally, bog oak hard as iron ('bends a four inch nail') and show pegs and small articles made from it. At Parrox Hall the Elletson's have a fireplace, a case clock and a Mother and Child carved from the oaks of ancient times.

At Pilling, an old place most interested in its past, I have heard of a cord road with oak timbers side by side, secured by pegs like horseshoe nails, laid with great labour for the monks of Cockersand from Aldwath to the Priory. 'Danes' Pad', 'Kate's Pad' they call it, and sometimes 'Roman'.

Tales are remembered of the days when seas at its front door were liable to batter the village and destroy many cottages, as at Christmas 1720; and the Black Lake to the rear likely to heave by tremendous under-the-bog accumulations of water, lifting high all living things upon it, "then with a mighty shudder swallowing all that could not escape".

One Pilling man rode a swaybed and lived to tell the tale. After an upheaval lasting half an hour the gap in the moss was twenty acres.

Pilling reminds me of a small town in County Derry where an enthusiastic schoolteacher encourages the children to bring in 'Finds from Bog and Thatch'. Turf is a fine preserver and who knows what will be turned up next? Local historians are keen.

A fascinating bygone in Harris Museum, Preston, is a large unwieldy wooden frame, one of a set of four-horse pattens worn by animals ploughing the soft ground of reclaimed mosses. Such were worn by men too on turf fields like Pilling's.

Another kind of Pilling Turf, sought after by makers of fine lawns, covers the salt marsh in the raw state, shimmering long and silky as a mermaiden's hair. Nothing hit and miss, it is sown with red fescue, and after fifteen years or so of twice daily washing by the tides, is ripe for further treatment with fertilizers, weed killers. It is grazed close by sheep—good for them too—mown, trimmed and grazed again before the cutters arrive to slice it in thin sods and transport it to customers.

Follow signposts to 'SHORE' to see men at work.—lovely shores in June, blushing pink with sea thrift above which Lakeland's fells look more blue than ever.

I like Pilling; in spite of Pilling Rock for Blackpool coach parties, it is more a place of Pilling Chickens, for which folk came centuries ago; and for the chance of a boiler or roaster shoppers crowd round stalls on Lancashire markets nowadays where Pilling farmers 'stand'. It has new houses, but picturesque old cottages too in a froth of orchard blossom in April; and the old mill, a sail-less giant, "built by one man in twenty-one days", is now having a new lease of life as a round house.

There is the old-fashioned Ship Inn too, and not far from the new church, the old, deserted in a breeze-shaken churchyard, with superb seaward views. Among characters, Pilling's Parson Potter is a legend. A rollicking parson who would bring services to an end when word came of a wreck—"Wait lads for me to get my surplice off—lets start fair!"—off he would go, as eager as his parishioners for the kegs and casks to come into his hands. Contraband, spirits, silks, tobacco were 'Corn in Egypt'; and peat stacks, thatch roofs and hollows under hearthstones were good hides.

Cockerham was as likely to indulge in beachcombing. The sea is not far from the village and the square church tower—the same from which the Devil, confounded, took off when beaten by the schoolmaster?—is battered by sea winds and all trees bow to the east. Sometimes it seems incredible that the rolling Wyresdale skyline bordering on Bowland does not also heave like the sea.

The Cocker is 'a shy nymph' shunning popular applause, as the poet wrote. Cockerham is retiring too, though its few new houses blend with the old.

Ever heard of the Vicar's Tide? Until a few years ago the salmon trapped in the ancient fish baulks, skilfully contrived by the brethren of the Priory to trap salmon at the ebbtide, were still claimed by the Vicar—at the morning tide of new moon and full.

When the tide is low one may walk between the bulrushes to the shore path and Cockersand's lonely site.

Once the shore was less lonely. Leland and Camden saw the

Salt Cotes—"Divers heaps of sands taken off ye salt strandys out of which by often wetting with water they pike out the saltness", in other words, the brine was boiled over turf fires leaving the white salt in the pans which was 'after sodde' or sold!

The Priory I visit for atmosphere—little but atmosphere, and the heart-raising views oversands. It is easy to see why a recluse like Hugh the Hermit chose this place for his cell, on a remote shore cut off from interfering, disturbing elements by marsh and tides. The Abbot of Leicester founded a hospital at this holy spot for the sick and leprous, well away from towns. And in 1190 the White Canons arrived to build for the Norbertines St. Mary-in-the-Marsh. This priory might well have been called St. Mary-in-the-Sea, for from the outset the seas in battering site and walls swallowed up revenues in reparations. When the seaward buildings were undermined and graves washed into the sea, bones left strewn upon the shore, the Pope offered penance relaxation to all who helped Cockersand's fight against the elements.

Approaches from inland were dangerous, tracks across mosses making it necessary for important prelates to have local guides. For those who followed the sea ways the Canons erected a beacon to light the Lune channel approaches. Two small chapels were served by the canons.

In the fifteenth century Cockersand possessed a quay from which men embarked for far away places. In 1430 Sir Guilbert de Launoy set sail to Drogheda to do penance at St. Patrick's Purgatory on Lough Derg.

In spite of revenues from Mitton All Hallows and Churchtown St. Helen's, for which the Priory provided rectors, the canons were constantly in financial difficulties, especially during the period of Scottish wars with damage done by raiders. In the 1530s Henry VIII's axe fell. In 1539 the brethren departed. Stones from the 'abbey' are found in many local barns, farms and halls. So thorough was the plundering only the Chapter House remains intact, because the Daltons of Thurnham who acquired the monastic land made use of it as the family mausoleum. A pleasing picture: the four square buildings, one wind-bowed tree, grazing cattle and masses of scudding clouds. A sorry end for what was ranked among the three greatest abbeys in the county. Furness and Whalley fared better. But they did not have hungry seas ravening on *their* doorsteps.

Until the eighteenth century the Daltons were the chief family by the Conder, but "Now like all the rest of us, all they can claim is six feet in Glasson churchyard", as an old man informed me near the Dalton Arms.

Like their friends, the Butlers of Rawcliffe and Tyldesleys of Myerscough, they were involved in the '15 rebellion, in the ignominious surrender at Preston and after trial at Newgate were found guilty, but later pardoned. Long imprisonment, crippling fines—and John Dalton, free at last, walked all the way from London to Thurnham. Family tales tell that he sought long for his wife, finally discovering her, a beggar woman gathering wood for fuel in their own grounds.

Glasson is a pleasant place, raked by boisterous sea winds but it has sheltered corners, like the sunny side of Tithebarn Hill where seven 'pensioners' told me they had taken root; "sick, lame and lazy, that's us". They had been thinking of taking a walk up the hill, they told me, but now they had stopped thinking. I knew why when I climbed the brow. I had to anchor myself to the seat at the viewpoint. How the landscape rocked, and tears made my eyes grow dim as I looked into a fierce north-west wind, trying to pick out Sunderland Point and Overton, floating like islands cut off from the Lancashire mainland.

I returned to my seven old men, still standing rooted. One remembered the building of Lord Ashton's ship, the *Rylands*, for trade with Cornwall; called *Moby Dick*, and later the *Hispaniola*, the *Treasure Island* ship, fire destroyed it off Morecambe Promenade. He had served his lifetime on ships, taking coal from Glasson to Cornwall and bringing back china clay, and said he, "I've seen all sorts in these basins. Timber and woodpulp from Finland, iron ore from Spain. Place used to be full of foreigners". Canadian timber ships unloaded in the upper basin and pine logs left floating there, roped into rafts, provided thrilling playgrounds for lads playing 'logrolling'.

They had long memories. "Ninety's nothing. You've got to shoot us off i' Glasson".

One had no memories. "I'm nobbut a foreigner. Foreign devils, that's what they ca' us, till you've been here ten year." But he enjoyed the fishing; "Brown trout, sea trout and codlings up to sixteen inches, whitings by the hundred, and fifty flukes on the line in as many minutes!"

From old people I had heard tales of Glasson characters. There was a local 'Miss Havisham' jilted at the altar steps who never went out again in broad daylight and left uncollected her cottage rents. They knew Old Bill Robinson who used to live above his boat in the Old Custom House loft; an old sea-rover, he went alone to sea, one morning bringing in a drowned boy he had caught in his nets.

"Place has gone to sleep," agreed the old men. But at midday, when hundreds of workmen poured from the welding works and oil refinery near the docks, it looked very much alive.

"Glasson's dead," they said. "Nothing but pleasure craft, crowds at weekends, and a few ships from Holland, Sweden—not like it used to be."

When Lancaster merchants financed the building of new docks here, when the Lune had silted up in the 1780s, Glasson became the port of Lancaster. When a straight branch was cut from the Preston-Lancaster canal in 1825, what a fillip it gave. The large new dock, twelve acres of anchorage, admitted ships of 400 tons whilst the second basin could take those of 250 tons which were to continue by waterway to Preston without unloading. That was how Coniston and Duddon slates arrived to roof the miles of roofs of that quickly growing town.

Glasson replaced Lancaster, and Sunderland the 'out port', but Fleetwood and Preston docks were to steal its trade. Now it is a peaceful backwater, haunted by artists, 'just the job' for collectors of colour transparencies.

Land across Lune looks deceptively near. Actually Sunderland and Overton are only a mile away but to reach them involves a long roundabout land journey; Conder Green, Lancaster, Ovangle Salt Ayre and to the Golden Ball at Snatch 'Ems Overton—tide allowing.

Snatch 'Ems, an evocative name? It became a byword in press-ganging days when raids were made upon it and local lads taken. Listen for the land-lord blowing 'Time' on a hunting horn.

Lancaster's oldest inn, the Carpenters Arm's down old Bridge Lane—off China Lane—and formerly near the Brockbank's ship-yards and Skerton bridge, was notorious also for press gangs. Ships' carpenters were its regular customers, but on market and fair days unsuspecting lads were fair game, offered free drink, then carried away confused and incapable of protesting, with the

Lancashire Maritime: 1, *Liverpool Waterfront;* 2, *Barrow-in-Furness, launching a tanker*

METHANE PRINCESS

King's shilling in their pockets. They were hustled into waiting boats, taken down river to where bigger ships anchored, and became men o' war's men.

Lancaster—County Town and City

Lancaster is so rooted in history, you would expect it to ring its bells and put out all its flags as each ceremonial occasion comes up. But no, like a nonegenarian who does not even turn round when the wild beast show goes by, it allows great events to pass almost unnoticed. Too late in 1974 to share much of the old ceremonial with Lancaster forced to shed some of its ancient traditions, centuries-old customs.

Its people never showed much interest in its early history. Hadrian put it on the Roman map when his military experts came north and decided on a fort to watch the Lune. Angle settlers called it Lunecaster and built a church on a basilica site. Norman kings whose forests were controlled from Halton eventually moved their HQ making this their chief Vill, royal residence, fortress, prison, seat of government; history was made here.

The Mayor's secretary took me into the Town Hall strong rooms to see the town's charters, the earliest King John's who, when prince and the Honor of Lancaster in his hands, gave valuable privileges—at a price—to his "knights, thanes and free-holders who dwell in my forest of the Honor". As king, he granted further "liberties", and the townsfolk perambulated the boundaries to make their extent quite clear. They still hold Boundary Ridings, every seven years, the last in June 1970. A grand array of Lancastrians, proudly mounted, set out to the old marks and bounds, riding where horses may go, walking where it is impossible, the leader—whose chief insignia is a leathern apron—ringing his bell, crying "Oyez" and naming each point as it is reached. Lancaster enjoys this particular occasion, being so rare.

King John showed great interest in the town, held Assizes there, and enlarged the inadequate Norman castle with formidable corner towers and curtain walls. Of this early thirteenth-century fortress, the keep, Hadrian's and Well Tower and the lower gateway walls remain. The towering outer walls and most impressive gate, with John o' Gaunt's statue thereon, and the Shire Hall and Law Courts facing the Priory, and the surrounding terrace walk

10

Quiet day at Lune mouth; Seven Mile Sands crossing

most popular with Victorian promenaders, were the work of that erratic architect, Harrison of Chester, whose "most stupendous creation" this was considered. The romantics were not so sure. The modernizing of the feudal pile, they said, was "a violation of the architectural fitness of things, the result neither castle nor jail".

How grim the windowless outer walls, the heavy guarded gate; most unwelcoming. Added deterrent to crime are the rules on the board in the gateway. Once in, how hard to get out! and five years penalty for anyone who "Aids any prisoner in escaping, attempting to escape from a prison or with intent to facilitate escape conveys anything to a prisoner, etc., etc." I stood reading them one day when a van rattled up, out jumped a number of bronzed young men, with warders who had been on guard during their outside labours, and with a great clanging and clattering the castle gate opened. I jumped back!

What a contrast between these strong healthy men and their predecessors held in durance vile. No exercise and sunshine for the witches held in underground dungeons from Easter to August 1612 Assizes; Old Demdike died in her cell, so cheating the gallows. George Fox, man of peace imprisoned for "trying to imbrue the nation in blood", was so broken in health after long confinement in "a lightless, windowless cell, full of smoke coming through wall cracks, rain and muck seeping in", that he had to be lifted on to the sheriff's horse when orders came to change his prison to Scarborough. Of four hundred Jacobites guarded by a regiment of dragoons in 1715–16, bedded on stable straw, fifty died in the castle—perhaps more fortunate than those despatched to the American plantations and their lot preferable to the hanging, drawing and quartering of other rebels.

Castle affairs are county and duchy business. Lancaster has no responsibilities there. The Priory is a different matter, for it was always the parish church from the time of the Norman Prior of St. Martin de Sees and the Brigitine nuns of Syon who took over when foreign orders were dissolved. The Brigitines rebuilt splendidly in the fourteenth and fifteenth centuries, their nave and chancel flooded with light from tall clerestory windows. The Abbess granted John Gardiner of Bailrigg a lease in 1469, for land to be used for a 'free grammar' school of his endowment, free—but 'money offered voluntarily by friends' not refused! Lancaster is justifiably proud of its 'grammar', one of the county's oldest.

What do we expect of a county town as old as this, a city too, dating from George VI's coronation? An atmosphere of more than civic pride, an aura of history past and signs of moving with the times? Certainly pride in its heritage, an observance of traditions and odd, individual, human touches in unexpected places.

Lancaster talks of 'town'. No one refers to 'going into the city'. Few ever hark back to the past. The planners look forward to the future with the 'old town' bypassed, new roads sweeping east by the canal, and modern thoroughfares converging on the civic centre, its modern heart.

Lancaster historic, the planners assure us, will be saved, the old narrow streets freed from through traffic. Even King Street will be at peace, the sidewalks tranquil as Alderman Penny's Hospital courtyard.

A town where only names are old is a disappointment. Here are St. Mary's Gate and St. Leonard's Gate, China Lane and Pudding Lane, Rosemary Lane, Cheapside, Stonewell and Bashful Alley. Also, Horse Shoe Corner with each worn out shoe renewed ever since 'they say' John o' Gaunt's horse cast one at this spot; or as others explain, it marks the place of the old Horse Fairs.

In one matter the town shows spirit; it has hung on to its old street market, cluttered, untidy—but very colourful, and very friendly.

Old buildings delight us. Round Castle Green stand eighteenth-century houses of attorneys and court officials, very dignified—and safe. Humbler, lowlier seventeenth-century dwellings, derelict and depressed, could be used—as coffee houses, workshops or studios for crafts and arts, in keeping with a town wishing to retain its attraction for tourists. The town houses of nobility and gentry of Georgian times are in good shape—and will be passed down to posterity. One by the Town Cross in St. Mary's Gate was the Beaumont's residence until the 1820s—when taken over for the Judge's Lodging—and very fine it is. The other, at the upper end of Church Street with iron railings (saved from salvage during the war), link extinguisher and handsome façade, was the Duke of Hamilton's, entertained Bonnie Prince Charlie in the '45, and is now the Conservative Club, and very handsome after stone cleaning.

The Customs House on St. Georges Quay, a perfect gem of a Palladian building designed by Richard Gillow in 1764 is still—nominally—kingpin in all Port of Lancaster shipping activities, the busy harbour at Heysham coming under this authority just as when ships laden with Jamaican rum, Antigua sugars and American mahogany were able to sail up Lune channel. The local operatic society meets in the sail room where captains and merchants used to foregather. A pity the unique Morton's Tower or Music Pavilion, abandoned among dingy workshops in Sun Street, has reached such a sorry state; behind that ornate Renaissance façade are rooms with fine Italian plaster work, elegantly proportioned, where the élite listened to the music of Vivaldi, Gluck, Haydn and Mozart. When all is demolished around it, maybe it will be transplanted and have a new lease of life on a pleasanter site.

What outstanding public buildings the eighteenth century gave Lancaster. Its 'Mayor's' church, St. John's, is perfect—Harrison's steeple. The Museum is housed in the handsome Old Town Hall (1783). The New Bridge—also designed by Harrison—completed in 1788, was the first 'on the level', quite adequate in stage and mail coach days, but a headache which the motor way has eased but not entirely banished. The "most amazing object" of its time was the canal aqueduct "the largest in the kingdom" and completed in 1797. In addition, there is Harrison's work on castle, Shire Hall and Courts.

All were tourist attractions, as were Mr. Gillow's "extensive ware rooms stored with every article of useful or ornamental mahogany well worth the attention of every stranger". Famous furniture makers for two centuries, Gillows, with their partners, Warings, became a household name. So did two other great Lancaster industrialists who arrived in the town at the same period, James Williamson in the 1840s, James Storey in the 1850s both interested in producing oilcloth, American cloth, leather cloth and table baize. They both did well. James Williamson's son was created Baron Ashton, the vast ninety-acre Lune Mills were developed and as the family prospered lavish gifts were poured upon the town—the Williamson Park, Lune side gardens, and the Town Hall. 'Storeys of Lancaster' from their White Cross mills grew apace too, and Sir Thomas presented the Storey Institute to the town. One might continue listing gifts which Lancaster, the fortunate, received from these two families. What a lifting of burdens from the ratepayers! I could also list the hundreds of Williamson-Nairn and Storey products which are used in every modern home, floorcoverings far removed from the first oilcloths and linos of the past, vinyl in tiles and sheets, vinyl-coated materials, plastic and self-adhesives every do-it-yourself householder knows.

When Lancaster was chosen for a new university in 1961, the city offered the Bailrigg site—remember John Gardiner of Bailrigg and his free grammar school?—and, until the buildings were erected thereon, an assortment of accommodation in the city, including Waring and Gillow's workshops in St. Leonard's Gate. The landladies of Morecambe-Heysham offered rooms—student terms fitting nicely between holiday periods—and so did householders within ten mile radius, from coast to country, as a temporary measure, until the halls of residence were ready. The first intake of 200 was designed to grow to 7,000 in the 1970s and 10,000 by the year 2000.

I visited the University site when building was beginning, in '66, on blue days with cuckoos calling and whistling workmen tanning visibly in the strong sun. On Midsummer Eve the next year, from the highest completed roof level we looked one way to see Snowdon lording it over North Wales; the other, beyond our near Cumbrian mountains to the Kirkcudbrightshire heights of Ben Screel and Criffel. The Isle of Man westwards seemed near enough to pick up in the hand. Beyond, the sunlight was splaying between the deep blue mountains of Mourne. Compare this with Oxbridge's inward look!

Colleges, called Bowland, Fylde, Lonsdale, Cartmel, Furness and County, are sited east and west of a half-mile ridgeway, the Spine, with colonnaded walks (wind funnels!) flanking squares and places for student assembly, concert and lecture halls, coffee bars and a chaplaincy centre.

I knew the University because of attending Parish Council Conferences, through student and staff friends; and County College better after giving the '73 Annual College Lecture. County was Lancashire's gift, and the County Architect its planner wrote of it as "a proud building severe and incapable of compromise—conceivably with some chance of remaining timeless." An old student in a *Gazette* article with a leaven of merry wit, suggested that County with its high walls, lockable portcullis and rather strange round towers had "the air of a Foreign Legion outpost and would make an admirable fortress." County surrounds a great oak tree, a survivor of the giants of old Bailrigg, the high buildings foursquare and so symmetrical "one needs to look out of a window for a landmark to take one's bearings—or must carry a compass!"

Within this University Lancastrians are always welcome to look around.

We were discussing the road north. "Why is it we feel a lifting of the spirits once we get beyond Preston?" asked one. And, I added, "When we come near to Lancaster don't we all want to sing?" The point is very near Bailrigg, where travellers on the motorway to the east of it, and on A6 to the west, suddenly feel with clearer skies above, a brighter light around and bracing prospects ahead, 'the best is at hand'.

"The lake scenery really begins on the south at Lancaster", wrote Ruskin in 1876.

"The air of Lancaster is salubrious, the environs pleasant, the inhabitants wealthy, courteous, hospitable and polite." The city must live up to its reputation earned exactly two centuries ago!

North Lancashire three centuries ago, was equally inviting. According to Fuller in 1662, "the ayre of Lancashire is subtle and piercing and the effects thereof are found in the fair complexions and fine constitutions of the natives therein, whose bodies are as able as their minds, willing for any labourious employment. I believe that the God of nature having given fair complexions to the women of the county, art may save her pains (not to say her sinnes) in endeavouring to better them".

Two Lancashire Outposts—Overton and Sunderland Point

When the tiny fishing village of Poulton-le-Sands grew into a Victorian watering place it adopted the ancient name of the bay, Moricambe. "A pleasant place with its occasional avalanche of excursionists it had advantages Blackpool had not, exceedingly beautiful views of the bay and the Lakeland hills, and equally good supplies of fresh sea breeze", according to a mid-Victorian paper. By 1880 with weekly boats to Portrush, two links with the main railway from the industrial towns, it was rapidly extending. Finally it submerged Bare at one end, Heysham at the other.

But not Overton or Sunderland Point severed from the hinterland twice daily by the inroads of the sea. Overton no longer cut off by the Ovangle tidal hazards, reached by newer roads from Heysham and Middleton, is admitting change. But not Sunderland which for centuries has regulated its life by the tides and wants to continue doing so, content to remain for hours completely isolated.

Overton, where seventh-century Anglian settlers tucked themselves under a green hill for shelter, has the oldest church in the county, once hidden-away on a remote shore, facing west like the ancient churches of West Wales and Ireland. "When Heysham St. Peter's talks of its forthcoming thousandth birthday and asks when we are going to celebrate ours, I tell them a predecessor did so, three hundred years ago," I was told by Overton's Vicar. The church has Anglo-Saxon cornerstones at the west end, a twelfth-century Norman south door and venerable walls with later windows.

But Overton is growing: new houses flow down Bazil Lane and gather around the churchyard wall; workmen's hammers break the stillness rather than seagulls crying. At the heart of a young community it is shaking its old bones and having a new lease of life.

I was in the village on 31st March, the day fishermen were putting final touches of paint to boats, of the 'coble' type, ready for the opening of the salmon season. They told me I would have no trouble in crossing the Causeway to the Point; tides were at their lowest. A comfort to know. Crossing between tides has always the spice of excitement and apprehension. Suppose you miscalculated and had to outrun the inflowing sea? The tide had ebbed away leaving shining wet mudbanks, swift glistening water ran down the channels and an increasing number of birds were lighting to scrabble on the mud for molluscs, jabbing and spearing with sharp beaks, setting up a quarrelsome clamour. 'Long necks' flew over, spring-dizzy plover, redshanks and oyster catchers and the curlew and widgeon which had not yet made up their minds about leaving for their moorland breeding grounds. Packs of little fussy sanderlings let at the channel edge, and sandpipers with honey sweet notes. I saw grey duck, dark on a sand spit, and pairs of handsome shelduck.

Gusts of wind came from nowhere and momentarily the sea birds crying faded away. The hush was filled at once with lark-song, always in the background, never failing.

An Overtonian caught up with me, near the posts which warn of danger. "You'd think motorists would give heed. Not they! On they go in spite of being warned—and before they get to the Point they're up to the bonnet in water. They try to back, skid into wet mud, and land in a deeper dike. Once I saw a couple waving for help out of the car roof."

He saw no reason why Sunderland "should be made to have a motor road". Why should they, when they like it as it is?

The fishermen busy painting boats on the shingle near the 'landing place' were also content to leave well alone. I remember Sunderland Point with a dozen or so cobles kept busy in the salmon fishing season, with shrimping and cockling from autumn, and musseling too.

"There is little of that now," they said. "Mussels never seem to reach any size; not worth gathering." We talked of the inshore fisherman's life. "Trouble is you can't sleep in bed o' nights. And you can't make it up during the day—they're too many jobs to be tackled!"

With bronzed arms wielding their brushes, white boats and sea green piled with orange—red nets, blue sky, turquoise channels and two small girls with jam jars, one in scarlet and one in a blue anorak, prowling on the shingle, it made a colourful picture.

Sunderland's waterfront is something special, the inspiration of Robert Lawson, a Quaker merchant in William III's reign, a trader with the West Indies and Ireland who used his wealth to develop a port here. It has an old quay and anchorage, a beautiful curve with stone posts at each end, three floored warehouses—converted into charming seaside houses, though high tides wash against the walls and storm doors are fitted to throw back the waves—and tying up places where his ships unloaded their cargoes of rum, timber, tobacco, and the cotton bales no one seemed to want.

It is said seeds from this unwanted cargo fell, germinated and thrived. The wind-battered tree by Cotton Tree Cottage, fifty feet high, its topmost branches shaved flat, is no bush, everyone tells you, but a cotton tree grown wild. So much for kapok, poplar and willow!

It is sad to think that the man who built so well over-reached himself, suffered great losses and was forced to abandon his dream island! His spirit must haunt the quiet shores, wander along First Terrace and Second Terrace and away to the far Point to watch for the only shipping of the 1970s making for Glasson Dock.

People who know nothing of Lawson pay their tribute to Black Samboo's memory. The British have a sentimental attachment to those faithful unto death, animal or human. Samboo, the faithful slave, body servant of a merchant from the West Indies who left him here in the care of an innkeeper, believing he was abandoned willed himself to die. They buried him in the corner of a green paddock. And there he lies still, with an epitaph in copper plate engraving, done about 1796, to help locate it. But I have never seen the grave without its simple tributes, children's posies in jam jars, daffodils, bluebells, poppies and corn marigolds. How many graves are still adorned so well 'two centuries after'?

> "Full sixty years the angry Winter's Wave
> Has thundering dashed this bleak and barren Shore
> Since Samboo's Head laid in this lonely grave
> Lies still and ne'er will hear their turmoil more.
> Full many a sandbird chirps upon the Sod
> And many a moonlight elfin round him trips
> Full many a Summer's sunbeam warms the clod
> And many a teeming Cloud upon him drips,
> But still he sleeps—"

The Lune is a river where 'haaf nets' or 'eaves nets' are used by fishermen as I have watched them in the Solway at Port Carlisle.

I saw several leaning against the Cotton Tree barn.

A slender but strong pole eighteen feet long has at each end a three-foot-long projection, the ends in large round corks. In the centre of the long pole is a four-foot-long handle and this the 'hand fisherman' holds firmly when he walks into the river, until he stands waist deep in the channel. His long and voluminous net, jelly bag shaped, is fastened between the short poles. The net he allows to open out on one side as he faces into the flowing current. Down comes a salmon, enters, the haaf net dips and with a most skilful movement is securely enmeshed.

Draw nets are used too, 'old fashioned but effective', a two-handed job needing one man in a boat working with one on shore. Off Cockerham shore men pay out drift nets, three hundred yards long and with scores of floats to mark where salmon enter the lure.

From Heysham Head—Morecambe Bay Viewpoint

The last day of April yet the somnolence of a summer afternoon lies upon Heysham Head. A blackbird sings from St. Patrick's Oratory, a black pony and a white, manes blowing gently in the breeze, crop the green turf around the golden gorse bushes and a little dog barks a warning to his mistress, a golden haired girl in a scarlet swim suit who is sunbathing in the half concealment they provide.

I am sitting on a sun-warmed stone near the cliff edge, lulled into a dream state by the peace of it and the unreal world shimmering below me, pure blue channels and sand spits turned to gold and for backdrop that fairy land across the bay ethereal beneath a shining canopy of feathery tufts of cloud.

Little of the coastline south and north is manmade—only Heysham docks, with ships masts crowded in the harbour and a few tankers waiting for berths, and away to my right, the curve of Morecambe promenade. Half Moon Bay and Red Nab are below, familiar to holidaymakers. Near and Far Naze, Heysham Lake and The Skeers—better known to fishermen. Out of sight below the church, is that narrow creek—with its juke boxes and ice cream stalls in summer, where the first settlers landed in the seventh century and St. Patrick probably struggled ashore nearly two hundred years before that. Heysham is no mere extension of Morecambe. There is more to it, and a thousand years long history.

These cliffs of boulder clay were always at the mercy of the 'capricious sea' which long ago wiped out the wooded islands off shore and left in the deep valley the blue channel, Heysham Lake, from which the salt water never completely ebbs. Trees have been uncovered in the peaty floor of the drowned valley, bog oak, and antlers of giant urus like those discovered in the making of Preston Docks. Prehistoric Lancashire's coastline was obviously a big-game reserve.

The stranger in 440 we later knew as St. Patrick, must have landed on the Skeers, then an island. He waded across to the creek up to the headland and turning to the west wind chose the site for his cell. A pity nothing is known about his short sojourn or his impact on the native Celts. He returned to Armagh; others must have been sent to make a more permanent cell to continue his mission.

A few yards from where I sit is the oldest chapel in the North—St. Patrick's oratory—a roofless ruin with a perfect south door framing a most beautiful Lancashire landscape, sands, sea, mountains and sky. The door lintel is a massive, crudely-shaped single stone, hollowed on its underside to form an arch. The grouting of the wall stones was primitive but lasting; the imperishable mortar was made from crushed sea shells burnt for lime and poured hot in gaps in the rubble.

This was a holy place, venerated locally and, as in Ireland, burial against its walls was sought by the saintly and the great. Around the oratory, graves were hollowed from the bared bedrock with small socket holes at their head for stone crosses. There are burials still concealed under the rough hummocky turf. From those uncovered the bodies have gone, the grave lids too—there is one with raised crutch-shaped cross head lying on the grass of the oratory floor—and the two graves nearest the steps, one a child's little over three feet long, have been worn by passing feet.

A century ago, to see the stone coffins and the chapel was a must for visitors. They were "requested to obtain a penny ticket at the clerk's house near the gate". Possibly to intimidate vandals the cheese press stone—the one I am sitting on?—was used to tether a bull, guardian of the sacred plot! The flat site of the chapel, the gloomy and romantic appearance of the monastic buildings around, hoary ivy-clad walls perched on dark rocks, narrow, stepped passages between crumbling walls were just to the liking of early tourists. We know that in the middle ages pilgrims were coming to St. Patrick's chapel and that St. Patrick's Day meant something, for late in the thirteenth century the Dacres were holding their Manor of Heysham by "an arrow" on the saint's day. 17th March was a local festival, long after the parish church of St. Peter's was built. The Rector (Rev. J. R. H. Royds) used to talk to me of his pride in the link with Armagh. "We are the only English parish to be evangelized by St. Patrick from Armagh," he said, "so we make our annual gift to the Dean for his Cathedral Restoration Fund, from St. Patrick's English Establishment."

Heysham must have been named by seventh-century Anglian settlers, who became Christian and raised their church on the cliff platform below St. Patrick's cell. Three centuries later new blood arrived, Vikings anxious to establish themselves along the Morecambe Bay shores. As Christians they shared the church with the Angles. St. Peter's celebrated its 1,000th anniversary in 1967.

During the tenth century, a very disturbed period, with many outside elements interfering with Northumbria, a Norse warrior slain in battle held in highest local esteem, was interred in the churchyard under a wonderfully carved hogback tomb cover. For centuries it was hidden till in 1800 a workman unearthed it. Now, to save it from further wear and weathering the hogback is in the church, near the south door of the chancel, in good light which picks up the fantastic details of a battle saga carved thereon. No ordinary battle, but conflict in earth and heaven, evil in many forms; a serpent destroying the firmament by darting flames of fire, hell hounds leaping upon the gods of our Norse forbears, Fenris the devil in wolf form, singling out great Woden for destruction; chaos and dark night about to be banished by divine goodness, the hart, representing Christ, belonging at one and the same time to earth and heaven. On the other side Christ is victorious, death is overcome and evil, again in the form of Fenris the wolf, slinks away.

What great event inspired the Anglo-Norse artist to create such a work? Like others of his period how he enjoyed himself carving fantastic beasts, half human, from Norse mythology. Here two cowering creatures like bears hold up the firmament. At Lancaster two hooded figures with birdlike heads and lolling tongues walk on human feet. At Whalley the Norse dog of Berser turns to bite his own tail.

In its time Heysham has had many lords. Tostig, King Harald's brother, was followed by Roger the Norman, then by Gernetts 'of Hessam Hall', Dacres, Harringtons and the Stanleys, which brings us to Lord Monteagle, the Flodden hero.

The Manor, possessed of windmill and water mill, a dove cote, willow grove, salt and fresh marshes, free warren and free fishery, with wreck of the sea, was sold to Bradley of Thornley in the 1580s, just a year before a Spanish galleon, a stray from the defeated Armada was wrecked on the Foul Ground offshore. Is there Spanish blood in Heysham folk? Some account for black hair and flashing eyes to survivors who came ashore and settled down.

The date on Heysham Old Hall is 1598, the initials Robert Edmundson's. His builder contrived a hidden stair and escape route from the west wing to an attic and—they say—hunted men could get away by a passage underground, now blocked. Perhaps they were Papists and harboured priests. There had been Heysham men in the Pilgrimage of Grace who opposed Henry VIII. Later owners of the manor, Leyburnes, lost their Heysham estates as Jacobites in the '15 rebellion.

A century later Dr. Whitaker gave a gloomy picture of local conditions—"no market, no shop, no butcher, no doctor or attorney or school, no seaworthy boat and no manufactory because there was no good water". For centuries Heysham had boasted two holy wells, but according to the Doctor the springs were mere brackish puddles. A body had been thrown in Crime Well, which hardly led to its popularity as a drinking supply!

Not an inviting picture. In 1800 nothing apart from the poor cottages of very humble fisherfolk, a few larger houses which filled in the gaps, and an inn or two; one, the Cat's Nest, had the sign of a swordfish dating from 1824 when a fisherman made this extraordinary find in the fish baulks.

Apart from the Hall—now the hotel—the most interesting bit of bygone Heysham is Greece Cottage, identified by its stone steps—the Rectory in 1737 and doubtless so named from *Gradus*, to show that parson knew Latin. *Gradus* means 'steps'. Teas are served in the garden.

In the 1820s Heysham began to look up. Some of its deficiencies were remedied. Just in time, for Morecambe visitors discovered it taking a walk along the cliff path or along the shore. "A most picturesque little village situated on a wooded rocky promontory—a favourite resort in the summer time", according to an 1880 guide. The sea bathing was most popular; its visitors "more select than numerous"!

A century ago enormous quantities of herrings and mussels were caught in the fisheries adjoining—on The Skeers and in the bay; mussels were so plentiful they were used for fertilizing the land. A pity there is so little evidence of this occupation nowadays. Heysham is the nearest we have to a typical fishing village, and it has lost itself in a welter of picture postcard stands, souvenir shops, ice cream stalls. A pity it chose the wrong role and did not exploit its picturesque shore, narrow creek and the clustered cottages down the hill. Is it too late to clear away the tripperish and garish, and accentuate its good points?

It still makes something of its nettle drink; nettle beer they called it before the authorities became worried about alcohol content!

It is a jolly place in high summer, holiday makers spilling out of Middleton Camp, Morecambe, visitors ambling in from the cliff path—sun hats, ice cream, lollies, swimsuits—and canned music. Will a £150 million nuclear station improve it?

Ask anyone what they enjoy most at Morecambe and the answer from many will be "the wonderful views over the Bay". Walk from Heysham to the Battery, along the front and on to Hest Bank—the most popular scenic saunter along our Lancashire shoreline, comparable to the Grange to Kent's Bank walk, and the same splendid spread of mountains and fells, peninsulas and headlands, estuaries and valleys continues though, losing height, they appear foreshortened and change position as nearer promontories hide the farther, like a fan half shut. At Hest Bank, at shore level, with the oversands traveller's eye view across to Kents Bank, the seven mile sands look deceptively near.

From here, until the 1860s when the new Furness railway line put an end, once and for all, to oversands traffic, according to a writer of 1844, "the coach, the time of which is regulated by low water, first descends upon its amphibious route". From here the long processions of ramblers venture forth on the organized crossings—several during each summer and advertised in advance in local papers; an exciting experience for all active Lancastrians.

For some years Bolton-le-Sands has been voted a most desirable place to live in and retire to. Expansion has been so rapid and so extensive it threatens to overwhelm the old parish. Fortunately the older and higher part, near the church and above the canal, is a village apart and may retain its character, its charming seventeenth-century and Georgian stone-built houses, no two alike, its close-compactness, a sharing of pleasant memories. But the hundreds of little boxes, pretty boxes, between A6 and the railway!

'*World Stretcht Out*'—*from Warton Crag*

Warton Crag, a great upthrust of limestone, where you watch your step lest you stumble on a cave of prehistory or wandering among primroses, violets and cowslips you discover the tumbled limestone walls of some Iron Age fort. Wild roses and honeysuckle gad over Celtic sheep folds and hut circles. On the tops, the natives of Roman times signalled their opposite numbers across the bay called Moricambe, much as men of North Lancashire in the twelfth to fourteenth centuries gave warning by beacon from Furness Abbey's signal hill, Birkrigg and Warton to the rest of the county when the Scots were approaching.

Dreaming shores encompass the Crag now. The Keer inlet in the tenth century floated Viking ships on the high tide, and Thoredus son of Gunnar wintered his longships herein; not so dreamy then, nor when tides of exceptional strength lifted acres of shore, common land, at Keer mouth, burying Cote Stones, the medieval quarry from which the parish church was built, and destroying the grazing of many a farmer.

Down below to the south the tower is standing up to the sea winds; a fifteenth-century Washington built well; the mullets and bars which we know as 'stars and stripes' told posterity of his family, 'ancient and creditable', around Warton.

Under the crag edge Archbishop Hutton founded the first Grammar School. The boys climbed, as we did, from village to crag top to eat their 'victuals' in the sweet clear air on summer days. Whence the sweet perfume? The opening bracken croziers? Farmers gathered brackens from these terraces—to burn for ash rich in salts to mix with lime and tallow for ball soap, to dry as fuel for lime kilns and for stoking the baker's oven.

No one shares the solitude with us today. Maybe the wind is too boisterous and signs of coming rain too obvious to tempt fair weather walkers upwards. What a farflung view, all the Lancashire coastline from the Fylde to Furness and the out riding Piel of Foudrey, with fells and mountains shoving for sky room; a bad sign, looking so near. Ranks of dark-edged clouds come marching across the bay throwing forbidding shadows over land and sea. As they pass over in close formation rain scuds along the Crag skyline. The tide is flowing rapidly, silver scribbles widening into long channels. Friends are planning to join an oversands crossing tomorrow—weather permitting. We scan the watery waste subjectively, recalling what we have read of that former seaway. "Kent and Keer parted mony a man and mare," they used to say. And because of the galloping pace and unpredictable channels of the Keer—"Where the Kent drowned one, Keer drowned five". Or was it nine?

Down there, where the crawling tide nibbles the rocks beyond Jenny Brown Point, Warton folk once took their Whitsun walk to Cartmel Fair, or made for a spot beyond Gibraltar where coaches took up passengers.

Backs to the oncoming rain, we look inland, a lovely tranquil countryside Lucas described as "A Land of Canaan, of hills and dales, pleasant and fruitful". It is two centuries later, very fair, a lovely corner of Lancashire. From the Crag Foot is one of my favourite walks, the tide being out, across the Keer towards the landmark limekiln near Jenny Brown Point, and then in the dim and secret woodlands going towards Silverdale station. Or following the shore round the point to Cow's Mouth and below Lindeth's windy pastures to Silverdale beach, perennial pleasure, at any time of year and not least in midwinter when the marshes are haunts of wintering migrants.

Equally lovely, all the year round, are paths towards Peter Lane and so to Leighton Park, or through Hyning Woods. At Hyning lived the late Earl Peel, descendant of Sir Robert Peel, Lancastrian and Prime Minister. At Leighton Hall are descendants of Richard Gillow whose family were not only importers of mahogany, founders of the famous firm of furniture makers, but produced architects too. Near neighbours at Yealand Manor were the Fords, Liverpool shipowners. All showed excellent taste in choosing this delectable corner of their county to build gracious halls, set in gardens and parkland.

Every approach to Yealand Conyers is a delight and with your mood in tune and perception quickened—as it surely must be—the village will be recognized as bonniest in the shire.

Overlooking it is another of my viewpoint hills, a little nearer Lakeland, with glimpses of mosses, channels and intervening knotts receding in order to far fells and remoter mountains.

A few minutes walk up the green slope within the Park from Yealand Manor gate and up to a skyline gap stile—and there it is, a derelict Georgian gazebo and, all at once with the least effort, the most unexpected reward.

Lancashire from Summer House Hill

A green world, a limestone plateau shared only by sheep yet it

Enjoying Blackpool

was used for village cricket generations ago, crowds gathered for Crag Fair, Georgian 'gentry' partook of alfresco luncheons here—they enjoyed good views with food good. In the dim and distant past herdsmen back to prehistoric times watched their stock grazing between these massive rocks no man has ever attempted to remove.

Eastwards is peace and holy quiet contained in Yealand Conyers and Yealand Redmayne and dreaming peace enfolds the landscape to high-riding Ingleborough and the Pennines. A6 and M6 and the route of the Royal Scot lie between but we are not conscious of them. Look south—light shining on Lancaster city and the heights to the Williamson Monument, away to the Lune and the headlands between Lune and Wyre. Northwards, deep woods take over, wrapped in mystery, though if you penetrate them from the glades of Deepdale or Cringlebarrow you find yourself looking on enchanting far-away landscapes between crag-fast yews and hollies, and Lakeland framed, as it were, for your delight.

But westwards is best. Make for the fringe of trees, open the wicket gate—and wait for it; a completely Lancashire landscape unsurpassed. The gentle slope of Leighton Park falls away below—where the eighteenth-century Middletons kept peacocks to destroy the adders, where Middleon's successors, the Worswicks and Gillows, replaced their fifteenth-century hall by a Walter Scott inspired pseudo-Gothic mansion, all turrets, tower and castellations, most romantic in its lovely setting, with splendid trees for side screens.

Below, the hollow is filled by Leighton Moss. Man has worked most admirably hand in hand with Nature in this landscape but this is one corner of the county where Nature has come out on top. That dreaming mere with willow margins, stands of reed mace and a half submerged causeway with its skilfully contrived 'hides', is a fine National Nature Reserve. All our native water fowl breed here, and a wide variety of migrants choose this for wintering. Bitterns returned some years ago so their Mersey foghorn booms are no rarity. Watchers report the osprey, and winter visitors include the greylag geese, whooper swans, the rarer white smew and whistling widgeon.

From Tawtop Hill

Morecambe Bay is a constant delight from shore level with sixty miles of sea verge from Lunemouth to Duddon Sands where

High tide washes Low Furness shores: Walney Island. From Tawtop Hill—overlooking the 'lost' Lancashire to new Cumbria.

we may allow the waves to nibble our toes. But we have not finished with our irreducible minimum of viewpoints yet. Leaving Silverdale's Pepper Pot Hill, Arnside Knott, just over the Westmorland border but more than half the panorama is Lancashire, we hop, skip and jump over Kent Sands to the Winster valley.

Winster was county boundary, but from 1st April 1974 all north of Arnside is Cumbria's. From Blea Crag, an ancient border bridge, the road to Cartmel makes for Tawtop Hill, a sensational bank up which the road climbs in sharp ziz-zags with gradients up to 1 in 3¾. Small wonder the bride of a Rawlinson of Cark Hall refused to repeat the journey and returned to her parents in Northallerton. This was a compulsory hazard for travellers avoiding the oversands crossing before the new bay edge road was engineered over bog and moss a century ago. Better coming down than up, but what land and seascapes from the road top!

I prefer to trust my own two feet on Tawtop Hill, giving myself an excuse at every bend to stop and admire the view, to gather honeysuckle and smell the wild roses, to pick raspberries and, in August, fat blackberries; cherries too litter the lane from many trees which are flame-red in October—the time when hazel nuts make stopping a pleasure. Sometimes a red squirrel runs along a branch and stares unblinking. Once I saw a red fox melting into the red brown bracken.

The dale floor—its fate uncertain, does Manchester still want it as a reservoir for Windermere's overflow?—was once a vast peat bog, the people cut off from the rest of the world like Cartmel's just over the hill—by fells and thick woods, no passages but clog wheeled cart and pack tracks. They were watched by curious travellers, "sun browned peasantry gathering turf". In the 1750s John Wilkinson, the future iron master, began draining and cutting channels in the valley for the getting of fuel; he was experimenting with methods other than charcoal for iron smelting. At Helton Pool he succeeded in floating the first iron boat. Today, peat is cut commercially near Blea Crag.

The higher we climb the wider the view. The bay views widen, the Pennines rise far away, eastwards, and from the skyline the regions we have travelled, dale to dale, hilltop and headland, recede and grow unreal. Higher mountains are beckoning, over the shoulders of Cartmel Fells.

Nothing more of industry, no obvious signs that men make

money from anything but the land. We stretch tall and feel good and when we go forth, westwards or northwards, we are heading for Paradise.

Let it be understood that I am not completely 'enchanted'. The land maybe as Eden, next door to heaven, but the people are not angels. They have the virtues, and the failings, of the Lancastrian with strong Cumbrian attachments. What they are I leave the visitor to discover for himself.

For the connoisseur of viewpoints; from Tawtop keep north towards Cartmel Fell, a highlevel region scattered with hidden sheep farms, with fine old houses like Hodge Hill, Cowmire Hall, historic buildings like Heights Friends' Meeting House (1677) and a joy—if you can discover its elusive whereabouts—St. Anthony's built in 1504 for the herdsmen and tenants of Cartmel Priory. From this fell-top byway many a track goes off westwards, over lonely, sky-high places to farms like Sow How and over Ravensbarrow to the Gummers How old coach road. What uplifting farseen mountain scapes en route, and better still—if you climb the steeps to Gummers How top—no place better for looking down on Windermere. The view encompassed Lancashire—the southern end of the lake and its far west shores from Newby Bridge to Brathay. What would De Quincey say about the changes? He loved this fairy domain, this precious heritage handed to Lancashire by the "eccentricities of geography". And history!

Beyond Claife hides Esthwaite Water, and west beyond Hawkshead is Coniston Water with its mountain range dividing it from the Duddon and the old Cumberland border.

Across the lake, above Newby Bridge, half concealed by trees, is one of the fanciful erections Georgian landowners delighted in, here a belvedere high-placed for exquisite views. The building of landmarks on high hills pleased our ancestors. They preferred to climb towards a definite object rather than to an unadorned height. Think of Ashhurst Beacon, Rivington Pike, the Peel Monument on Holcombe Hill—how far away they seem now!—and let us on to Hampsfell whereon Mr. Remington of Longlands Hall built his hospice so that others could enjoy at leisure what he enjoyed as a before-breakfast constitutional every morning.

Hampsfell Hospice and a 'prospect rare'

Ascend from Grange, from Slack and Eggerslack woods, or by any of the signposted paths, through cool woodlands floored with violets or bluebells in Spring, from silent glades and clearings where a century ago we would have encountered woodmen tending the coppices wherein grew the raw material for bobbins, hoop making, swills and wickerwork. Finally, above the tree-belt, tread the close-cropped turf, gay with cowslips and purple orchises in May, and heavenly scented with wild thyme in Summer.

A limestone fell, it is stepped with limestone slabs, and paths skirt deeply grooved rock, the sort from which landscape gardeners have for so long riven the fissured stone and cottagers brought down strangely weathered 'heraldic beasts' to decorate their gardens. Up we go, terrace after terrace, the breezes sweeter and keener as we climb. At 729 feet, the skyline and the hospice!

"How fair, how surpassing fair is such a scene—the eye sweeps for miles on every hand over a circuit so comprehensive and varied that little is left to wish for." So wrote an ecstatic tourist in 1850.

Everything is spread out and arranged to please. We stand poised as between two worlds. Seawards—the watery waste of the bay whereon sailed pleasure craft, coal boats and many ships carrying the produce of the High Furness fells and the Low Furness mines and forges, or at ebb tide "people and conveyances so many it had the appearance of a caravan crossing the Arabian desert, oxen, cattle, horsemen, fishers, carriers, chaises, gigs, coaches, all in close succession, wheels and footprints alike making a furrow upon the desert plain". Landwards—the walled-in world of Cartmel and the Vale of Eea, the fine priory queening it below us and the delightful village grouped so perfectly about its walls. Across the green valley and above the park is that tree-crowned hill called Howbarrow, or Mt. St. Bernard, on which, an old tale tells, the brethren who arrived here in 1188 decided to build; a voice bade them seek another site "in a valley between two rivers, one going north and one south". We can see that they obeyed; the two streams are there, east and west of the great church.

The bay, far away 'mainland Lancashire', the long peninsula of Low Furness, the dreaming peace of valleys east and west, the semicircle of great mountains, was ever a climber so well rewarded after a mere 729 feet? But there is still more. Mr. Remington wanted you to enjoy rarer prospects from the roof of his tower, and over a century later a retired railwayman added an indicator for everyone's pleasure. Every feature is named for identification.

Mr. Remington devised admonitory and explanatory couplets

to adorn the walls. "A flight of steps requireth care",—steep and slippery with a gale meeting you at the top! A warning against litter louts "who possess more muscle than brain". A directing hand towards

> "The noble bay and stealthy tides
> That treacherous creep along the sand"

An invitation to let class prejudice fly away on the winds.—

> "And if the rich and poor together meet
> I trust they will each other greet."

He intended after refreshing the mind and spirit the visitor should gather ferns and ling for fuel, light a fire in the corner fire-place within the hospice and with water from the roof (!) "boil his tea kettle and sit around with other of its worshippers" on seats provided. He thought of everything; his love of Lancashire was great and born in him. The Remingtons were associated with many parts of the county, their interests bridging the bay from Melling and Lancaster to Longlands and Cartmel vicarage.

Looking westwards over Cartmel valley we see the heart of the fair land, which was less fair, more cut off from civilization a thousand years ago. Tradition says St. Cuthbert was given "Cartmel and all the Britons in it". In the twelfth century it was William de Mareshal Earl of Pembroke's gift to twenty foreign monks "for the increase of our holy religion", and as an influence for good in country desperately in need of colonizing.

Windermere with Brathay and Leven, and the Winster, were the river boundaries no one could argue with, formerly in the Barony of Kendal. To the west the Abbot of Furness ruled as far as Duddon. Both abbot's and prior's lands were included when Lancashire was created in the twelfth century.

Low Furness from Birkrigg

"By all means return from Furness Abbey through Urswick for the sake of the view from Birkrigg", Wordsworth advised Victorian tourists, just as Father West had told eighteenth-century 'curious travellers' who wanted "the best, most extensive and pleasant views of land, sea and mountains and islands".

A mere 425 feet above Leven Sands, Birkrigg for emotional appeal beats all. The atmosphere is charged with a beauty difficult to put into words.

I was here one afternoon in May, the day just relenting after hours of rain and I was delighted witness of magical weather changes. A sudden wind tore grey clouds to thin shreds, rolled them up like threadbare curtains, revealing shining sands, channels pearly bright in the ebb-tide, then the low green hills of Cartmel shore and, after clearing Holker Mosses and the overhanging Ellerside Heights, hung in dark rolls above them—in suspense. When the sun won through, as suddenly the Sands turned to polished silver, the ridges became glowing tawny-gold. It was only a matter of minutes before the star performers took the open stage: first the Coniston mountains took a bow, whisking away their cloud drapes, advancing in indigo and rich deep blue; west and east more appeared until the far away, pale blue, heart-of-Cumbria pikes and folded fells filled the stage, breathtakingly beautiful.

Delaying until last—as though determined to outdo the rest—Black Combe, a dramatic appearance westwards in blue-black with a whiter than white cloud curling round its flanks.

What is brighter than a world like this, degged and drenched in raindrops, transfigured by a sunbursts? Rubies, emeralds and diamonds trembled on the short turf. Wet limestone slabs and boulders became polished silver. The inverted world of Cartmel, Holme Island and Humphrey Head, Winder, Sandgate and Chapel Island floating upside down in the limpid channels—in melting hints of sky blue, sea green and turquoise—was a mirage, too lovely to be true.

Birkrigg can be the most silent place I know; but out of it can grow the wildest, maddest upsurge of song. Today every lark in heaven was singing. Plover too, seabirds and—from the edge of Sea Wood—a cuckoo.

They say Birkrigg is haunted. Knowing it on summer dawns and autumn evenings 'quenched in mist' I can well believe it. Are the spirits at large those of herdsmen and hunters whose hut circles, cattle folds and burial mounds are scattered over the ridge?

Among the tumbled stones nor far from Sea Wood a number form a clear double circle, Druid, say the locals, but they were probably part of a burial mound raised by Iron Age Furnessians, the same whose ridge top camps were defence against the first wave of Romans who invaded across the sands.

Not an acre but carries some mark of prehistory, if one knows where to look. Foula, an Ancient British village—Iron Age farmers—covers the slope east of Urswick Tarn and Holm Bank. Going one better, archeologically speaking, west of Little Urswick School is one of the most fascinating sites in Lancashire covering acres of limestone pasture. Here are two sites, Iron Age and with signs of Roman connections. The Romans needed iron and the smaller site has a bloomery, iron workings and a primitive smelt-ting hearth outside its enclosured walls; the larger stone-walled enclosure contains the tribal leader's hut, serfs' hut circles and nearby cattle folds.

Maybe these early dwellers in 'industrial Lancashire' walk by night and make one feel their presence! Or do the gentle spirits of the 227 Friends who lie so quietly anonymous beneath the sheep-bitten turf of the Sunbrick Sepulchre, walk the hill? Theirs is the most silent and serene of resting places, sighed over by sea winds in the treetops. One buried here was Margaret, widow of Judge Fell of Swarthmoor and later wife of George Fox. Swarthmoor is only a mile or so north, the lovely Tudor Hall where Fox had the protection, loyalty and all the home comforts the Fell family could provide, over many years of dangers and difficulties.

Prehistorics, Romans, Norse farmers, medieval travellers, Quaker funeral processions, all the activity of Low Furness 'Golden Age' when westwards was 'the Peru of England' and the mineral wealth of Whitriggs, 'the greatest iron mines of England' was carried over and around Birkrigg to the Bardsea shore for trans-shipment—how times have changed!

Victorian travellers wrote of the "red earth, red walls and all things impregnated with iron, universally a deep red", on the Ore Gates which today are quite deserted, and certainly not stained with red ochre. Bardsea shore is quiet too where until a century ago it shared the activity of loading the ore, ships calling, steamers passing down channel. These were laden with the copper and slate from Coniston, pig iron from its forges, charcoal and gunpowder from Low Wood, and cargoes of fine edge tools, spades, bills and axes, the famed products of Newlands, Arrad Foot and Leven shore villages—until the 1850s.

From Birkrigg and the north-west panorama displayed from it—and with thoughts of its "obvious scope for development as a tourist centre", and possibilities of a Leven Barrage, linking Cartmel with Low Furness, down to sea level.

Down by Sea Wood or The Gill—old lanes—to Bardsea, a silver bright village sparkling and clean as though new on the map yesterday, and to the wateredge, and The Skeers. These rocky reefs are excellent for the getting of flukes and dabs when summer suns have warmed the waters. My friends go down on summer mornings knowing unerringly where the fish will be. Their nightlines are baited with sand worms, but flukes enjoy a meal of molluscs too, infant cockles minute as wheat grains and tiny mussels which they crunch, digesting the soft centres and parting with the shell particles—so telling the fisherman where to peg their lines.

I like talking to the shore folk. They know all about the sands, of the shrimpers who go out from Baycliffe and what is happening on the far shore of Cartmel, scene of much more activity. From Birkrigg it is exciting to watch slow moving shrimp carts following the ebb, growing smaller and smaller until horses and carts, almost submerged, seem to be as boats on the water.

Now no shrimp carts are used. Instead, dark objects draw swift silver tracks on the wet sands, racing full speed after the receding tide; these are light caterpillar tractors driven by men whose forbears followed the seas in the old days, harvesting cockles and shrimps laboriously. Now, knowing by inherited instinct where going is firm and safe, they race along to the likely beds, slow down until their nets are filled, then round they turn with a white flurry of churned up water and at 40 m.p.h. make for Sandgate and Flookburgh.

Ann Radcliffe was here in 1795 crossing Leven channel in the morning mist. She wrote of eerie cries of gulls and hoarse croaking of sea geese, unseen. When the mist lifted she saw "fishermen with carts and nets stealing along the margin of the tide", local shrimpers, cocklers and mussel gatherers, Burrows, Butlers and Bensons most likely, ancestors of the fisherfolk of today.

Little wonder the imaginative waxed eloquent on the beauty of the Oversands crossing from Sandgate to Canal Foot—"little gay islands and promontories seeming to hover in the air", and caravans of travellers crossing the flat making a picture "awful, new, magnificent" wading as their guide instructed over the best fording places of each channel.

Now large numbers cross Oversands for fun, putting their trust as always in the marked channel, defined with 'broggs', by the guide who is prepared for them. Guides were in the pay of the Prior of Conishead and the Prior of Cartmel before the Dissolution, and a canon on Chapel Island prayed for Leven Sand wayfarers. After 1530 the duchy took over the care of travellers, provided the guides—and still does so—and saw that a light warned passing ships of dangerous skeers and shallows.

Descend east to the Leven shore from Birkrigg, but drop to the west for Urswick, where the folk, though not web-footed, are known as Ossick Coots. On quiet mornings there are certainly more water fowl than humans in evidence padding round the shores—coots with their tiny chicks more like animated balls of fluff, swans with their grey cygnets and, as the local butcher informed me, this year Little and Great Crested Grebe also.

This Urswick smiling in the sun in its sheltered hollow is, they say, the successor of Old Urswick lying deep and drowned below the iron-tinged waters of the tarn. Unpleasant grumblers, the old villagers, who complained about inadequate water supplies, pestering the vicar 'to do something'. He prayed, marched the women widdershins round the church as he did so, his words almost drowned by their clamour. But water began to flow into the valley, a red-brown flood which angered the women. "Pray again, this time for clean water", they screeched. He order them home to an hour's silent meditation "And it you still want me to pray, open your doors and windows and wave white flags as a signal".

They waved their white flags, the vicar prayed, with astonishing results. Stormwinds rose, snow, hail and an earthquake tremor shook Old Urswick and a flood burst forth—and all, village and people, were drowned.

At the tarn edge is the church of St. Michael and St. Mary—in a churchyard almost circular—maybe a prehistoric site? A Viking Urswickian, Tunwinni, called on Lyl to carve a cross with runes in memory of his lord Torchred. On the west wall of the tower is a beautiful relic of medieval carving, Christ being lowered, drooping from the cross; in the ancient glass of the chancel window—a leering devil from Furness Abbey; in the churchyard, scything grasses, weeding the paths, or tending the verges, or in the church cleaning, polishing—a team of helpers. One was 'Lile Sam', a small man with a white beard, who devoted many hours to the loving care of the old church. At Old Michaelmas the parish keeps up the rushbearing tradition, simple, for its own sake.

From Birkrigg to Barrow

Leaving Birkrigg southwards, from Sunbrick farms old lanes drop between almost white, limestone walls and a welter of flowers to Baycliffe, a fishermen's hamlet with its back to the sea winds, but all the bright new bungalows—thanks to central heating—are able to thumb their noses at the elements and enjoy the view.

Or, with so much choice, one may decide on the lane down to Scales—'Skali' were Norse shelters—a straggling mixed village, very bonny. Still more byways continue south by Lily Mere and the mill stream to Gleaston where considerable ruins are left of the castle the Harringtons built; most romantic. And tucked and folded into this warm red earth and green hedged landscape, where short lanes run up to meet windy skies, are Leece round its half-choked village pond, and Dendron, a leafy place holding tranquillity close to its heart.

And out of sight nearing the tip of the peninsula, the vale of nightshade, Beckansgill, within which hides the most glorious of our north-western abbeys.

Look north from Birkrigg; all we see—to the Coniston mountains and Wrynose Pass beyond—was included in the grant made in 1127 by Stephen, Lord of Furness—and later King—to the monks from Tulketh near Preston. Its vast mineral wealth, flocks, herds and horses were the abbey's and "fellows fierce from Furness Fells" were at the abbot's call when Scots were raiding, greedy of his riches. Twelve hundred tenants, four hundred mounted on nags grazed on the High Furness farms, provided his armed guard, protecting mountain approaches and the Low Furness coast.

Look south along the peninsula; there was wealth of another kind, the valuable iron ore, rich crops, the abbey itself, and in the sheltered channel within the archipelago of islands, anchorage for trading ships which dealt with foreign ports. To keep this safe the abbot built a castle on Foudray; the stark ruins remain of the Piel. Another strong tower they erected at Dalton, the ancient market and business centre for abbey affairs. There was a beacon hill too, above the abbey.

During four centuries the abbots ruled Furness like princes; their abbey is princely in its proportions too. Approach from the rolling hills patched with cornfields and meadows, hedged by close-shaven thorns, a cheerful landscape full in the sun; drop from Roose to the unsuspected concealed solitude at Bow Bridge, a green glade precious to the brethren with protecting Deer Park walls—large sections of which still stand—and you draw in your breath at the magnificence of what comes to view. "Antique, mouldering ruins", maybe, but their green lawns are too green, their stones too warmly glowing to be melancholy.

How well the first monks chose their site. It is said their sanctity was so great that the deadly nightshade which named the vale was rendered harmless. That was in the years of their deep piety, before their abbots turned into businesslike estate organizers, rich merchants, and power—even if for the glory of their church—ruled their actions.

Four centuries was a long period. At a stroke of the pen Henry VIII could 'pluck all down', grant permits to cart away the masonry for the reparation and building of half a dozen churches, dispose of mines, furnaces, deer parks and vast tracts of land in High Furness and Low. But not he, nor another four centuries, could obliterate the hand of abbot or abbey. It is a glowing jewel in the portrait of 'old' Lancashire, north of the sands, a gift to Cumbria.

South of the abbey, lining the tip of the peninsula, spread over islands and growing outwards along the east and west coast—Barrow-in-Furness, a place I was reluctant to know, believing—how very wrongly—that it was an industrial blot, depressed, and depressing.

How wrong can we be? Approach with an open mind, preferably by that ten-miles-long open promenade called the Coast Road built during the 1930s which beginning outside Ulverston runs out to the shores of Leven Sands, within hearing of the pounding waves, white horses galloping and breaking on shore, shingle and skeers. Not one off-moment. At the turn of the tide, hosts of sea birds, clouds of whirring wings, wheel, whistling and calling; at the ebb the shining shores are alive with them—and in lonely places family parties of shelduck, such handsome birds, stand out clearly defined at the water edge.

Each mile, and beauty unfolds—from the Priory at Conishead, Bardsea shore, Sea Wood's shadowy places, sunshine and blue sky over Aldingham. It is said part of it was wiped out by tidal waves 'long ago'. Today high waves wash over the churchyard wall and fine spray waters the grass. Here, they say, St. Cuthbert's body rested. Southwards, a round hump on a green hill—the Moat—is the site of a Norman Castle of Le Flemings. The ancient church, one of the most interesting in Low Furness has been enthusiastically 'adopted' by later Northumbrians, the Durham miners, convalescing at Conishead.

Knowing what the winds and seas in fury can do in anger on this coast old farms like Goadsbarrow crouch low. The full force of Morecambe Bay tides pounds the sea walls, the typhoonlet of May 1966 breaching new defence-works as though they were flimsy brick. Waves going swoosh-swash over the roofs of passing traffic are an ordinary occurrence.

What invigorating air! Live here and one might live for ever! So to Rampside linked to Roa Island by a long causeway once a railroad. Look at the tall house with twelve chimneys on its roof-line. Which two are farthest apart? Then turn to the island, which has a foreign air of a minor channel port, no place in Lancashire like it.

Trinity House pilots lived on Roa, the shepherds of the ships negotiating the ticklish channel between Barrow Island and Walney and the Piel of Foudray. Moores, Charnleys and Rabys were seafaring families here, and later came others to the rows of gaily painted inward facing houses near the 'station'. Quite continental!

May and June are alive with birds, many breeding on the Isle of Foulney, the termination of a long slender spit of land soon submerged by the tide. Yachts waft up channel—Barrovians are boatminded from youth—and the shores are pink with sea thrift.

Piel Island is seen from Morecambe promenade and from Blackpool Tower. Now it is separated from us only by the channel. That feudal pile was watchdog for the abbots whose builders enlarged and strengthened the first castle erected by King Stephen's men. Massive sea-worn boulders built the thick walls, red sandstone like the abbey's—buttresses, jambs and lintels. It was a necessary safeguard for the considerable abbey trading—some from European ports—against pirates and other raiders. There was a ferry in medieval times, and today one may cross too—to find at the end of the 'voyage' just a landing place, the hotel, the ruins impressive in decay, and rather more than a quarter mile of breeze-swept plain. And tales of rather Nordic horseplay once enjoyed at the hotel, the initiation of the Knights of Piel—sponsored by old-time landlords.

I was shown the Visitors Books with entries from the 1850s

which, as Barrow now owns the island, are in the library there.

A century ago scores of ships were constantly pulling into the island and the landlord, its 'acknowledged King', installed any desirous of becoming Knights with due ceremonial—if he was "of good behaviour, steady, and at all times attentive to the opposite sex". He had to vow to aid the King at boat racing, cock fighting, bull baiting and pigeon shooting. To be a Knight had its privileges too, for 'if wrecked or drowned' he was at liberty to demand free lodging, free food and drink at the hotel!

The Books with Knights' signatures and fitting embellishments are highly amusing. Artists amateur left their mark, like a J. M. Mac Laren of 1879 whose faded brown pen and ink drawing shows himself sitting in the old arm chair, elaborate helmet on head, beneath crossed churchwardens' pipes, and enduring the ordeal of christening by beer poured from a brimming tankard; artists professional like Morton, the cartoonist, in 1913 elaborating his sketch of the ceremonial with pot-bellied goblin-like figures familiar to *Punch* readers.

All around, the sea is busy with islands. "The Isle of Walney whose longitude doth swage" the sea's fury, a ten-mile breakwater for the peninsula, the Norse 'Isle of the Killer Whale', is largest. The abbots secured it by dikes, and the folk of the townships of Biggar and North Scales on stated Dike Days did repair work upon it—but still the waves and gales went on battering. Biggar turns inwards as if hiding dark secrets—piracy, smuggling, wrecking?—or to hide from too curious enemies from the sea. They say the black oak timbers of the inn came from a wrecked Spanish galleon, maybe astray in the same gale which grounded two off Rossall Point.

At one end of Walney are marks of islanders from the New Stone Age, relics turned up on the sand dunes of Bronze and Iron Age people, and skulls have been kicked about by Barrow boys in their play. At the other end, not far from the dazzling white, female-staffed lighthouse, the rarest sanctuary for sea birds and breeding ground for thousands—ringed plover, shelduck and the rarer eider duck. Between is a paradise indeed, carpetted with flowers which are the island's own, crimson-cerise cranesbill, deliciously perfumed burnet roses on close creeping bushes, a playground any town must envy, with larksong perpetual blended with the surging sea and the wind's voice.

Barrow and Its People—new Cumbrians

Barrow is a town of enthusiasts. Where has industry such fine scenery, coast and country on its doorstep? Where such an exhilarating climate? What purely industrial town has streets so spacious, avenues so wide, approaches so attractive? And where so many open spaces and squares with founders surveying what they created? H. W. Schneider in 1839 realized how well the local haematite ore could be processed and shipped from here. James Ramsden arriving with the railway builders in 1845 dreamed great things for Barrow and saw they came about. Two dukes, Buccleuch and Devonshire, owners of land and mineral wealth in furthering their own schemes for development of Furness brought prosperity to the new town also

On the small island that gave the town its name, Vikings had buried their dead in barrows "visible to travellers by sea or land". In 1839 there was but one house thereon and only a few hundred people in the nearby farming communities on the mainland. In 1842 it was 325; by 1867, when the great Gladstone himself visited Barrow, the year it became a borough and he opened the great Devonshire dock, the population was 17,000. Ten years later this "youngest child of England's enterprise" was still growing—40,000 living and working here; now, there are above 65,000.

1867 is the date from which families claim to be true Barrovian; a good mixture they are, drawn from all over the kingdom, a new kind of Lancastrian. They live—until development sweeps them away—in the tall balconied tenements called Scotch Houses reminiscent of Glasgow but much brighter and cleaner, with washing like bunting suspended across the streets; in pleasant houses along wide avenues stretching two miles towards the Abbey, and in the Edwardian and modern housing districts which were once townships with their own 'graves' or sheriffs and their annual courts, as at New Barns and Hawcoat, and at Ormsgill and Roose.

There is an alive atmosphere about the new Barrow where the highly skilled technicians, local and 'offcomers', create such a great demand for houses that prices soar to almost London heights. Do as I did one evening at five. I crossed the bridge over to Barrow Island against the tide of workers flowing from the Vickers yards. What a good looking, well dressed crowd they were, the brains and hands behind the ships, the tankers, the nuclear submarines—

one of them, built to fire the Polaris missile, launched in September 1966 by the Queen Mother—passing in their thousands. As many were turning in the other direction to Vickerstown and their island homes.

What constant excitement in the launching of great ships at Barrow. "No other town in the U.K. has so many royal visits," they say, and when a sovereign cannot be present then, as did George VI when a ship of the Orient Line was ready and he in Australia, he pressed a button on the other side of the world and the cheer echoed down the Walney Channel.

I meet the enthusiasts in the home of friends. W. Melville, Vicker's chief designer of great ships, submarines, liners and tankers among the largest now afloat, who in retirement satisfies a lifetime's ambition to probe into the achievements of Furnessian craftsmen of prehistoric times; and keen technicians from 'the Yard' who share my interest in this thrilling corner of the county.

There is a viewpoint hill at Hawcoat, above Bank Lane which drops to Ormsgill. Beyond the houses are green meadow grasses and corn fields rippling before the sea winds and trees bent at right angles, and behind the great slag bank the golden sand dunes of Walney and the open sea with the Isle of Man riding the horizon like an ocean liner. A magnificent prospect, look where you will. Another viewer says it is the best place to see Manxland. "What I like about it, a cross between the Lakes and Scotland. We don't appreciate the Lakes like outsiders; we can go off there any evening after work, you see."

I saw. I scanned Black Combe appearing from thin clouds, the sunshine on Silecroft sands, and the pure enchantment of Duddon Sands with the drama of unfolding mountains northwards, and the peaks far beyond Leven Channel, beckoning. Always there! What a background for the day's work. What lucky people able to have their cobwebs blown away—if ever they accumulate in so bracing a clime—at such exciting back doors.

Ulverston at the north end of the peninsula is lucky, too, and far more ancient, with an Edward I charter, old highways running in by Daltongate and Soutargate, busy with abbey traffic and royal cavalcades and invading and defending armies in the thirteenth to sixteenth centuries and today much torn in two by modern 'improvements'. The last few years have seen many demolitions of the old and new roads cut through the new Ulverston.

From Hoad—Low and High Furness Surveyed

At last we are at the foot of Hoad, that hill which is such an unmistakeable landmark where ever you look from the shore and felltops above Morecambe Bay.

I climbed the Hill from Ulverston on a May evening with an hour to spare between buses; from the town centre along Church Walk and through the parish churchyard, the 'middle path', along a grey walled-in way to the gateway on the open hillside, guarded by two weatherworn limestone slabs, eight feet tall, more like heraldic supporters than any I have seen before, and I was on the open hillside.

There is a short cut, hand over hand almost, direct to the top, and a more sedate path along the hillside gradually gaining height—this I chose. In twenty minutes I was forgetting the hot sun beating down in the town; up here was blowing half a gale. As I climbed I heard a cuckoo, and curlews, gulls screaming and crows cawing but all sounds were blown 'over the hills and far away' on the tops. If there had been waves to batter the foundations of this Eddystone Lighthouse, how they would have thundered!

Why the lighthouse? It was decided upon as a memorial to John Barrow, born in 1764 at the roadside cottage at Dragley Beck on the edge of Ulverston. A bright lad of the Town Bank Grammar School he put his schoolboy interest in mathematics and astronomy to good effect in later years. He travelled far, whaling in Greenland, teaching at Greenwich, and chosen by Lord Macartney as Controller of his Embassy Household in China; he surveyed the Cape of Good Hope as secretary to the new governor, wrote accounts for Pitt, the Prime Minister, and finally, after Arctic exploration, was secretary to the Admiralty, from 1804 until 1839. He was a founder of the Royal Geographical Society. And he worked with Smeaton the designer of lighthouses.

They called Point Barrow, Cape Barrow and Barrow Straits after him, and raised this monument on Hoad—a 'sham' lighthouse but so made it could become a beacon light if ever occasion demanded. When a flag flies, usually on Sundays after Easter and Tuesdays and Thursdays also after 1st June, it signifies that the monument is 'open'; and after a toil to the top by the inner steps there is an even finer view. And you deserve it!

From the sprawl of Ulverston, shining silver grey and a dazzle

High Furness: Beauty revealed—Tarn Hows

in the sun, my eye followed the canal—"deepest, shortest and widest", they say and I believe them—to the Canal Foot where golden spits of sand showed one of the Leven channel crossings. White waves broke on the rocks of Chapel Island, just offshore from Conishead Priory (many neo-Gothic turrets and pinnacles above the trees). Across the sands I looked to Cartmel shores; beyond, in paling greens and golds over Chanon and Raven Winder's little hills, Humphrey Head, Kent Sands, Lune deeps, Glasson Docks gleaming white, and new Lancaster University showing clear against the fells and dim Pennine backdrop.

North and south, nothing but Furness; Low Furness, the 'mother country' of the Cistercian monks and High, the land to be colonized, cleared for sheep breeding, opened out from the waste, imparked for the abbot's game, and looking from Hoad as Camden described it, utterly overcome by its grandeur. All High Furness, he wrote, "mounteth up aloft with high topped hills and huge fells standing thicke together." And so they do, "magnificence in piles".

Just below Hoad, northwards begins a hug-secret world of tumbling hills wherein lie Mansriggs and Osmotherley, Gawthwaite and Subberthwaite and tiny places with more Norse-given names like Nettleslack and Knapperthaw. Beyond them is the mountain-scape highly emotional topographers described as "an awful scene, mountains heaped on mountains in every variety of horrid shape". Awful and horrid had other meanings in the eighteenth century! To our eyes they are inspiring, and the loneliness they promise much to our liking.

Hoad is as good an appetizer as any height, a grandstand to which the mountains of Old Cumbria make their bows.

All this and no one else to enjoy it. The few sheep, towsled like mops, are not interested but merely look up from the turf now and then with ears to the whistle in the wind.

Down again, the strong winds drop, the gulls' cries are loud again, the cuckoo is still shouting and below, a dizzy drop, traffic is speeding along the estuary edge road from Greenodd.

12

High Furness: Beauty concealed—Tilberthwaite

VII

LAKE LANCASHIRE— IN THE NEW CUMBRIA

High Furness—Leven and Brathay

The lovely region of High Furness came within Lancashire in this way. In 1150 William of Lancaster, a most powerful baron of Kendal, together with the Abbot of Furness, owner of newly acquired lands ordered thirty sworn men to beat the bounds of territory too loosely defined. They perambulated the Duddon to Wrynose Pass, the Brathay down to Windermere water head and down the lake and the outflow, the river Leven, to its estuary. A half way line was defined from Little Langdale along Yewdale Beck, through Thurstanmere (Coniston lake), and along the Crake river to Leven channel; east was the abbot's, westwards the lord's land.

By 1196 both parts were in the abbot's hands. He dealt with the King's sheriffs at the courts of Lancaster—his agents using the oversands route—never with Kendal or Westmorland, so what more natural than that into the County that part north of the sands called Lonsdale, in the Wapentake of Furness, should eventually pass. Unbroken for eight centuries, this link with Cartmel and Furness is completely severed in 1974. None are sure what changes the Cumbrian merger will bring.

Within Lancashire have been startling contrasts, Mersey thronged with the world's shipping, and Duddon and Leven Sands troubled by no more than a shrimp cart and the odd inshore fisherman; rivers like Irk and Irwell, Roch and Darwen, handmaids of industry taking long to come clean—too thick to swim in, too thin to plough—and clear mountain streams seeping through bog myrtle, parsley fern and bracken, hurrying their bright waters through rowantree gills to join rivers like Duddon and Lickle, Brathay and Crake.

A far cry from the wild moors above Oldham and from Blackstone Edge above Rochdale, with Classic Ground and Darkest Lancashire below them, to Wrynose Pass and Walna Scar looking over this north-western territory of jagged volcanic rocks breaking down in spills of scree and scatterings of boulders, and the humped ridges of silurian slates and limestones, the stony heart of High Furness. From the Pennines one looks on Lancashire's industrial present; from the fells between Coniston lake and Duddon on Lancashire's industrial past. Here Time and Nature have mantled old mines and quarries, iron ore bloomeries and charcoal burners' hearths, and scores of ancient bobbin mills and ruins of wool and cotton mills, in mountain, coppice and beck side.

The rivers Duddon, the Brathay which helps to fill Windermere and the Leven which empties it, the becks rushing to Coniston lake and the Crake running out of it were Industrial Lancashire —two centuries ago!

The Britons named the Leven from a word meaning 'smooth', and smoothly it slides out of Windermere under Newby Bridge until forgetting itself it leaps towards Backbarrow's one arch bridge and boils in fury in a deep, foaming cauldron.

Later, relieved from tension down it flows to Low Wood, by the old gunpowder works and from Fish House Bridge wanders without haste to wash the edge of Roudsea Woods and merge with the tidal water in Leven Channel.

Leven springs surprises like pockets of industry at Backbarrow. A grim, dark-walled mill, its walls splashed with blue, is the Ultramarine Works, giving this place the distinction of producing red, white and blue hens!—but originally it was a spinning factory of ill fame after sensational disclosures. A hundred young apprentices mostly from London workhouses, bound to the mill owners until twenty-one, worked like slaves, often chained to the machines to stop attempts to escape, often so weary they fell asleep at their work. The owners, when bankruptcy faced them, took their employees in carts as though to return them south; they were abandoned on Leven Sands before the incoming tide.

Old iron works are a blot on the Backbarrow landscape. Machells owned them in the eighteenth century. A cottager used molten iron from these furnaces to make flat irons, a trade his son John followed up, until ambition urged him forward. They say he was born when his mother was in the cart en route for market—a sign that the lad 'would go far'. He did, for John Wilkinson, Iron Master, was a name known across Europe. He perfected haematite ore smelting with peat, made an iron boat which floated, worked with the Darbys of Coalbrookdale on all manner of iron experiments, invented a blast furnace, an Iron Man for boring in pits—and was an Iron Man himself. His iron monument stands high above the highway at Lindale.

At Newby Bridge the Leven turned the Cartmel prior's corn-mill and sent eels into the millers traps. It flowed wide and shallow at two points so that travellers could cross—the lower ford wide and safe if the deep Dog Hole was circumvented, the higher shorter and deeper and forded by mounted travellers passing from Kendal to Ulverston or Dalton markets. Lake steamers which arrived on the scene in 1845—wiping out the fords—were not the first boats on Windermere. Roman supplies were taken up to Borrans fort by barge. The east bank of the lake to Ghyll Head, the western shores all the way to Brathay, are in Lancashire. After crossing the seventeenth-century bridge by the Swan, the byroads pass through the copses which provided the old woodcrafts with their sapling oak and hazel wood, in and out of beech groves, and shadowed by hollies and yew trees.

The century-old bobbin mill at Stott Park has been 'killed' by the textile trade recession and plastic substitutes. Away beyond the coppices an old spot, the clearing of Finn, carried on many old crafts such as swill making and the tying of birch into besoms. Finsthwaite is only one of many Norse settlements later within 'riddings' imparked by Furness abbots.

Late in the eighteenth century a mysterious young lady rented Finsthwaite House. She died young and was buried in the churchyard. Anyone will show the way to the 'Princess's Grave'. The truth about her? She was the daughter of Prince Charles Edward Stuart and the very constant nymph, Clementina Walkinshaw, who followed him into exile where the child was born: her name, Princess Clementina Johannes Sobieski Douglas.

Tempting lanes run away from Graythwaite, hall of the Sandys who became lay owners of former abbey lands, exploited the iron ore of their mines and smelted it in local forges. One way drops into Rusland, Rolf's Land, and others into quiet glades where a roe deer or a red leaping ahead from sunlight into shadow brings a deserted solitude momentarily to life. New footpaths too are a joy, allowing pedestrian progress to be indulged undisturbed by passing traffic; one, near the lake, ends at the ferry.

Enchanting woods, exciting roads—over The Devil's Galop—run down towards Hawkshead, or west over to Grizedale with its Wild Life Park, Nature Trails and the Theatre in the Forest.

Hawkshead—Capital of High Furness

Haukr, a hardy Norseman, named his 'saetr' here before Norman times. His followers and their descendants, Norse-speaking for another two hundred years, herded their sheep and swine in a ring of clearings at Esthwaite and Loanthwaite, in isolated nooks and pockets at Sawrey, Cunsey and Wray, on old tracks at Barngates and Outgates. When the Abbot established full claim to all Furness High in 1196 they became his tenants by military service—defence against the Scots and breeding of nags. Many were allowed to enclose grounds from the waste or hitherto uncultivated land—as at Borwick Ground—bringing yearly more into cultivation, putting it to their own use as abbey rule slackened. At the Dissolution the tenants became full owners. And what was more important, their market, so long dominated by the abbots, was reorganized as they wanted for disposing of their surplus.

Visitors have reacted to Hawkshead in various ways.

"The small market town, surrounded by lofty fells in a warm and sheltered valley," said one, at cross purposes with another who called it "desolate looking, bleak and uncomfortable as if it wanted blankets and counterpanes on winter nights". "Few tourists ever trouble the repose of this little village town—this domestic Calabria, this one paradise of virgin beauty," wrote De Quincey, Manchester born, in 1840. If only he could see it now on a summer weekend! He would see how modern visitors react, not in words but by the mad-happy clicking of camera shutters. Was ever a place so photogenic? Few believed this was Lancashire.

"Evidences of the past meet you in the face and the spirit of the departed is mightier than that of the present"—especially around the fourteenth-century church, benign on its green mound. Beautiful without, unique within. Where else such primitive simplicity in arcading and ponderous supports, their white plaster ornately 'florished' with seventeenth century decorations and

'Sentances of Scripture'. Hawkshead always had a high regard for its importance. The stone seat, part of the east wall, was parliament for wiseacres of this "county town of Lancashire North of the Sands".

Cameras click at the church gates; at Pillar House which recalls markets of past days and weavers displaying their linsey-wolsey and hodden grey beneath the sheltering overhanging first floor; in Flag Street where fascinating light and shade is thrown on the Brathay quarry flagstones which cover the beck; in Vicarage Lane where the 'Wee House' is squeezed between white cottages; at Grandy Neuk, with rough-hewn steps outside and rooms over the deep askew archway—the most photographed corner, if Ann Tyson's Cottage did not win the prize for popularity.

Ann Tyson, like all her neighbours, lodged the Grammar School boys at her cottage, here and, after her widowhood, at Colt House across the valley. So, the three Wordsworth brothers knew this 'township' from two angles. William according to his poems had deep joy in his schooldays, especially in out of school pursuits!

It is quite obvious Hawkshead evolved from no planning. Is there such an in-and-out, hide-and-seek-round-corners place anywhere else? Half its best bits visitors never see, such as the old yards through archways and behind the inns, Red Lion, Queen's Head, and the Brown Cow Yard where, after heavy rain, beckstones rattle under cottage floors. Long ago villagers came this way to the public drying ground, or driving their geese to the green, their animals to the common.

All roads met at Hawkshead during abbey days and after. The ferry was part of the public highway from Kendal, a large boat rowed by strong arms to carry over men, goods, horses. It had its tragedies, none worse than that of October 1635 when the boat "sunck about sunsetting when was drowned 47 persons and 11 horses". No wonder the ghostly caller, the Crier of Claife, haunted these shores howling for the ferryman.

Visitors welcomed a wait at the Ferry Inn for they could then enjoy the pink-fleshed lake trout, the char "very good anywhere but especially to hungry travellers", and how lyrical they were in its praises. They say it is best "caught by golden rings and silver spoons"—not mere whimsy, for the fish is attracted by glittering objects above all. "As delicious as caviare, as delicate as fresh salmon". Ferry House, the Freshwater Biological Association headquarters knows all about char and pike, perch, salmon and trout in Lake Lancashire waters.

Leaving Hawkshead for the Brathay the highway passes Wray, a sham antique castle such as wealthy Victorians hankered after. They built many a mansion by lake and river, one in a gracious sylvan setting. Brathay Hall is a fine outdoor pursuits centre with a little theatre for cultural activities too.

Little Langdale to Duddon Valley

The Brathay, the 'broad river', takes a score of mountain streams into Windermere, collecting the waters of Great Langdale as well as those from the border country of Little Langdale. The high platform of Brathay Church is best for taking in the lower dale and the steeps above Hacket. From the higher places are almost aerial views of Colwith and its waterfall plunging "with the fury of a wild Arab rushing to the plain" into its deep ravine.

The Wordsworths stayed at Betty Yewdale's cottage at High Hackett when the children were avoiding whooping cough at Grasmere.

A notorious rather than distinguished resident in these parts was the prince of whisky distillers, Lanty Slee, who died at Greenbank in 1878 after a long life spent in evading detection at his many stills. He sold his mountain dew at local markets. Customers asked about his "fine crop o' taties"; officially he was a farmer—at Low Colwith, at Low Arnside and Ivy How. The secret places of Little Langdale—and Yewdale—lent themselves to his purpose, and having friends and customers among local magistrates certainly helped. In this part of the world folk were too cut off to let the law bother them unduly.

The dalesmen were individualists too. In building the Slaters Bridge, below the outflow of Little Langdale Tarn, Lancashire and Westmorland masons indulged their own fancy, by arch and slabs on boulders.

Out of Little Langdale the Brathay comes down from Wrynose Pass, a wild and desolate mountain which probably made the first road-engineering Romans quail. The course of their military road is uncertain but it must have run into the cloudwrack where travellers do now, approaching the Three Shire Stone.

Only Lancashire named her territorial boundary at the head of

Reinhals, the Pass of the Stallion. Here Cumberland met Westmorland also, the three counties deliberating half way to heaven much as the Norse jarls did when they came together at the Thing Motte at Fell Foot.

The Duddon, "child of the clouds, nurseling of the mountains", has an impressive start in life, cradled among stark volcanic rocks which break out in pikes and crags and hurl the infant river down rock-walled ravines to the treeless, wind groove called Wrynose Bottoms. "Unfruitful solitudes", Wordsworth called them, a hungry dale head known only to native Celts who clung to Castle How above the swamps at its jaws, approached warily by the Roman troops heading for Hardknott fort.

Unwelcoming perhaps, but the Norsemen took to it, and when King Stephen gave High Furness to the monks their settlements and outback sheep runs, Gaitscales, Birks and Grassguards, Wallabarrow and Stonythwaite, Nettleslack, Thrang and Seathwaite, Norse names all of them, were firm on the map.

Norse farmers followed the dale floor to Dunnerdale and Ulpha, and pastured their swine and summering herds in those hanging valleys left in suspense when the glaciers retreated, the most delightful nooks for any town-weary Lancastrian to penetrate and know he is near his own ground. Like saeters in Norway, their intensely green plots of meadow ground are like 'stationary sunshine', green oases in a welter of tumbled rocks and sea of bracken.

We still think this the most unspoilt dale in Lakeland, though the old rough track over Wrynose was surfaced after war damage and, with its watersplashes and stepping stones done away with, has brought in motor traffic; and bends and bulges in the byroad updale were removed to let in the market-day bus from Ulverston. Electricity has brought light to dark places—at great cost, underground, and sometimes overground when farmers preferred payment for pole sites, "brass being brass and not to be sneezed at". The Hardknott Forest Park has spilled into Duddon too, and a dark mantle is spreading up the slopes—a variety of trees, Sitka, Norway spruce, Scots pines, and European and Japanese larches. To avoid the hard regimentation, which partitioned too rigidly the slopes of Skiddaw and Whinlatter, hardwoods are planted along the forest fringe. Above 1,500 feet Nature holds its own.

Cockley Beck, the first farm, is above the tree line—and, as in

1880, distances have not shrunk; it is still "verra near oot o' t' warld, sebben mile fra a mill, five fra a shop, and aboon fower fra a church and a hard road tull it as you'll have sin". That was Daniel Tyson speaking to Edwin Waugh.

I have had many Tyson friends. One, old Harry Tyson, explained why the poet never referred in his Duddon Sonnets to one of the most enchanting bits of river scenery, where the water "green as liquid emeralds" is forced under Birks Bridge, and through a deep gorge, from shade into trembling sunshine. Said he, "In my father's time—before the 1840s—when men cam ower Harter from Eskdale to Grassguards they crossed water at Troutal ford. There were no Birks Bridge then". So, no meditation nor inspiration for the poet; no bridge, no view!

From Birks down to Wallabarrow is wildest Dunnerdale, where it 'wasn't finished', the river hidden in a gorge choked by fallen rocks. Near the Memorial Bridge are acres of incense-perfumed bog-myrtle coppices and emerald meadows; and a wandering path to Seathwaite, where the church has now no resident vicar, the school no children, the Ulverston bus comes no more to the Newfield Inn door; a changing dale. Tarn Beck, a Duddon feeder, waters this enchanting side valley.

The Hollins backwater is near perfection, a scattering of farms and cottages round the rim of what was in ancient times a lake saucer. A rough track drops into it from Walna Scar, revealing what the poet called "a peaceful retirement" needing no twilight veil to soften or disguise its features. Looking on it Wordsworth's heart "filled with gladsomeness". And so has mine; something of my delight, after wintering, summering and knowing this 'airt' in war and peace, I put into *Off To The Lakes* and *Curious Traveller, Lancaster to Lakeland.* A pity I cannot do so here. It has even greater power now to draw home the heart to quietness; which for the 1970s is saying something.

Of Seathwaite church everyone knows; of the vicarage across the road; and some may know Undercragg, birthplace of that extraordinary clergyman who, with never more than £17 a year, a large family to feed, and all the cares of a parish—and a weakly constitution which made his parents wonder would they ever rear him!—died at ninety-two and left a fortune of £2,000.

How did he do it? By practising small economies, like whist playing by rushlight instead of candle when he was the spectator, dispensing broth to churchgoers, from boiling of the family's weekly joint of mutton, and by brewing his own ale and selling it, 3d. a quart consumed in the road, 4d. indoors. And by augmenting his stipend by teaching the young, advising the old, acting as letter writer and as legal mind; by farming his own glebe, taking his dues from other farmers' hay and fleeces, by spinning and weaving and carrying his own produce on his back to market—or did he indulge in the common North Lancashire side line, smuggling, too? Wonderful, wonderful Walker!

At Ulpha farther downdale is an inn, the Travellers Rest—where too clever university students on holiday asked the 'primitive' innkeeper for their bill in Latin, and received it in Greek. Inn and riverside church, "to the pilgrim's eye welcome as a star", are in Cumberland, but over the bridge we are well and truly back in Lancashire. We join the ancient guardian of the bridge who with long experience keeps an eye on salmon poachers. Large scale poachers have recently used methods very much like the Cockersand salmon baulks I mentioned earlier, effective traps, wedge shaped, of stones and branches from which the fish once in cannot easily escape.

The Ulpha school, newly enlarged to cope with the combined dale 'population explosion', has been an Academy of Learning from 1793. Its early days were Spartan in the extreme, a tarpaulin to keep the rain from the door, heating depending on what fuel each child brought from home, or on local bobbin mill shavings bought with their pennies. On the coldest days the scholars ran uphill and down to restore circulation!

All this is near-Paradise, a last four miles from Whistling Green and Stonestar—above which are thick Celtic settlements on the fell side, to Bank End where the road tumbles down to Duddon Bridge.

A mile away the most attractive Broughton in the United Kingdom every August celebrates with due ceremony the granting of its market charter. The setting is the spacious Georgian Square remodelled by John Gilpin Sawrey of the Tower when he returned from London in 1760, thrilled with the new face of that city. His widow caused to be erected the obelisk on the Square's steps. Farmers' wives displayed their produce within the arcades—now built up—of the old market hall, and the fish stones recently strengthened and protected from the hazards of backing farmer's vans, were formerly used for price fixing of Duddon salmon and selling of large quantities of cockles and mussels from Duddon Sands, 'the best to be had'.

Seawinds batter Broughton's strong walled tower and toss about its churchyard trees. A venerable pile, a fine Norman door and deep grooves in stone jambs made by men sharpening daggers and blades, give a clue to its age. Farther down Duddon estuary the mother church at Kirkby Ireleth is far older. Maybe the body of St. Cuthbert was carried here in 875. This, the 'Cherchebi' of Doomsday Book, has a splendid Norman door with beaked head decoration and inside two of the most battered oak trunks I have ever seen, hollowed out to form chests and considered as old, if not older, than the church itself. Naturally when the Bishop of Man came to Furness in 1547 to consecrate Kirkby's daughter at Broughton so that the dead of the three remoter chapelries could be brought there instead, the older church was very much put out.

What activity the river saw when local slate was transported by barge. Slate quarrying is by no means a thing of the past on Kirkby Moor. "Kirkby slate splitters, they can make stones talk", a local farmer told me with pride. He had filled a cart with waste pieces and was off to do a bit of walling with it. "Best slate anywhere," he said, "and it's going all ower."

So it is. There comes a time when people turn from modern synthetics in all things. Now Kirkby's Burlington slates, a pleasant steel-blue, are coming into their own again, and export orders are arriving from Canada and, surprisingly, from France where English slate roofs are most popular.

For a high spot to survey the Silurian at close quarters and the volcanics from a distance, Kirkby Moor old coach road is splendid. It sweeps up from Lindal and at every rise, one sees more uplifting views, over the Sands—green coast fringe, silvery scribbles of water in turf cuttings, the golden spits and blue channels, showing up the ancient fording places as in an aerial picture—to Black Combe and Cumberland; but best of all, the Duddon Valley unfolding, its high pikes and rocky skylines very different from the whalebacks and heaving moorlands 'nearer home'.

Down on the Duddon shores, Orm the Viking landed in the year 900—ancestor of the Asshetons of Ashton, Middleton, Whalley and now of Downham. On those fords armed men crossed in centuries of warfare. And where the monks had borne the saint's remains, there was kept waiting by unsympathetic 'natives' for several days—John Wesley.

Coniston and The Crake

As Brathay pours its water into Windermere and Leven empties it, so does Yewdale Beck fill Coniston Lake and the Crake decant into the same estuary. In medieval times the Crake marked the limits of lord's and abbot's land and by the end of the twelfth century the folk of Furness Fells, of Norse, Anglian and Celtic stock, all came under abbey control.

Coniston and Colton were isolated pockets of English in a dale almost entirely Norse-speaking. Non-Norse names, which are the exception on the map, were leftovers of the Celtic population. The greatest mountain is still known by its British name Alt Maen, the high stone; Cairns and Borrans are reminders of Britons whose sheep enclosures, hut circles and burial mounds make a walk across country from Torver or Blawith to Woodland, a journey back in Time and a voyage of discovery.

Overlaying the fascinating pattern of prehistory and pre-Norman times is the strong hand of the colonizing abbots who, on becoming outright owners, lost no time in organizing their 'native' tenants in clearing open fell and woodlands for sheep walks; where modern afforestation has not obliterated them the 'parks' can be identified on the Monk Coniston Fells east of the lake—very high level platforms of farmland reduced now to pocket handkerchief size, once the vast 'heafs' of Lawson Park and Park-a-Moor. Between Coniston lake and Windermere the hunting abbots indulged their sport in extensive enclosed deer parks, especially in Rolf's Land appropriated in the fourteenth century by 'bad Abbot Bankes'. Abbot, Oxen and Stott Park—and the Dale Parks within their five mile fence—are in and around Rusland.

It paid the abbey to encourage tenants to improve waste as small farms and to enclose old common pasture—one and a half acres for each, hedged by dike or stone fence was agreed upon. These new farmlands, as round Hawkshead, became Grounds, named after the new owners, as Atkinson and Holme and Dixon Ground. But at dale heads, at Tilberthwaite and Yewdale, life went on in the old way. Even today there is an Old Norse pattern of sheep farming on these remote farms. The Herdwick flocks 'go with' the land.

The gentle Crake valley, from Greenodd to Lowick and Blawith was first to be civilized, with lush holms sheltering woods 'beautifully divided by hanging enclosures and scattered farms'; then the levels from Nibthwaite to Torver Beck where Torfi pastured his kine a thousand years ago, "a highly picturesque township".

East of the mere the fells rose abruptly leaving the narrowest strip along which a modern byroad can just manage to squeeze; no room for lake edge cultivation, but from early times charcoal burners hearths sent up blue smoke by a score of small clearings, and wherever becks slowed down to fan out as deltas on the shingly shore there were ancient bloomeries—look for the black-bubbled clinkers. The lake was main highway in the past; along it passed boats laden with the beautiful green slate from the now abandoned quarries, with copper ore from the derelict mines, and with Low Furness ore to be smelted on its shore and pig iron to be returned to Greenodd for 'export'. The slate quarries now going strong, exploiting the most modern method, at Hodge Close, Moss Rigg and Betsy Crag, transport their produce by road. The Mine of the Three Kings high above Copper Mines Beck, approached by the ladders and galleries in Tilberthwaite Gill, has been abandoned for years; the offices are a youth hostel—the nearest to the mountains—and the copper sheds where boats were unloaded at Nibthwaite, no more.

In the thirteenth century Sir Richard Fleming came from Low Furness to High, erecting his fortified pele and hall on the flat land by Thurstan Mere, planting his men-at-arms on adjoining lands and enlisting from the local 'fellows fierce' of Conyngs-Tun bill-men and archers to aid him in repelling or attacking the Scots. A most enchanting spot—if you can juggle away the caravan site—a dream picture on autumn days; bliss when silvery mists rise at dawn and on summer evenings in a harmony of pure blues and mother-o'-pearl. Small wonder campers wanted to cling as close as possible to this shore edge 'heaven on earth'; but there is a foot-path for others to share the beauty. The National Trust has taken over, so the lovely lake shore is safeguarded.

Coniston is a tourists' Mecca with the usual necessities for its visitors, cafes, souvenirs, etc. If you know where to look there is much more. The Old Hall with its massive cylindrical chimneys is now a farm, but approaching on the old Priest's Stile—the local parson's short cut when enjoying whittlegait, free food, at the Fleming's table—its "air of grandeur and magnificence" seizes upon the imagination. Across the lake are great houses of another age, elegant Georgian villas; and Brantwood, the mansion where Ruskin, the resident genius, lived to a great age.

These are timeless landscapes, as enchanting now as when Father West with his wonted fervour persuaded eighteenth-century tourists to embark upon the bosom of the divine lake—"a noble expanse of transparent water, rural elegance, cultivation and pasturage, waving woods and sloping enclosures, adorned by Nature, improved by Art, stupendous mountains whose airy summits the elevated eye cannot now reach and which almost deny access to mankind".

Far fetched of course, for what is now inaccessible—every crag swarming with climbers, every track to the Old Man alive with walkers among whom but few possess the Victorian sensibility which saw these "moors and precipices as the very wreck of creation and the spoils of the world forgone". As for Yewdale, a "deep and winding chasm the eye cannot pierce nor the imagination fathom", the Coniston-Ambleside road with buses goes through the defile, and for walkers there are exciting new-made paths away from the traffic. Two byways also probe its depths heading for last outposts, Holme Ground and Tilberthwaite, the latter a slice of bygone Lancashire little changed from the days when Norse settlers of Tibba's Beorg cleared the thwaite by Yewdale Beck.

Gripped between the Old Man and Wetherlam and the rocky hows which lie about the Tarns are some glorious bits of High Furness, still lonely and silent when the car parks are crammed and the water side paths streaming with delighted holidaymakers. There is far more to Tarns and Hows than the one road in, the one road out, and the south banks where the thousands congregate. And Tarn Hows being the only nook of its kind reachable by car all the rest is for the pleasure of pedestrians. I know a score of tarns, glades and bog-myrtle-scented hollows within this north-west corner, between Crake, Brathay and Duddon, where never more than two or three are ever gathered together on the sunniest summer Sundays which bring forth motorists in their hundreds and thousands.

The Tarns, Norse for upland pools, and Hows, Norse for nobbly, rocky knolls, are worth looking at. Wordsworth and De Quincey, both connoisseurs of viewpoints, extolled the beauties—"a coup de theâtre without equal", long before Mr. Marshall made three pools into one irregular sheet of water and, as with other tarns he artificially deepened, stocked it with perch and trout and, with an eye for landscape, planted many larches and conifers. The result was most successful, considered by many as better than before, accessible, photogenic and now provided with picnic spots and parking.

Being fortunate in my Furness friends I can look at the Tarns at unfashionable times—November sunsets, summer dawns. I have never see anything as marvellous as Daniel Fleming's witnessing of "a blazing star with a very long tail about the sunsetting" which on 14th December 1680 set the entire neighbourhood praying to their Maker, but I have seen shooting stars, double rainbows trembling over the tarn after storm in October and, with none but myself to watch, every change of colour and mood from daylight to dark. It is fascinating on autumn evenings to see how clouds are filled with light, mountain tops gilded, and rosy flush and orange glow linger southwards—day loathe to depart, whilst twilight hastens towards Yewdale; darkness has already fallen in Tilberthwaite, and night taken hold of the cwms under Helvellyn.

This then is the silence of the Tarns, broken only by the last croaking raven winging over Tom Gill, a chill whisper of wind in dry rushes, and the cool lapping of water. South-west of Coniston are lonelier places: a tiny tarn and numerous blue sky-reflecting pools and that 'away from it all' feeling—under Beacon Fell west of Blawith; and drawing nearer to the past peopled by Celts, anywhere in the solitudes between Beacon Tarn, Woodland and Gawthwaite. This is a land of smooth contoured Silurian slates and limestones, unfenced ways curving upon bracken-clad ridges from which we look on white gulls on the shores of blue tarns, in May and nesting season. As on Birkrigg, haunt of prehistoric Furnessians, this has changed little in two thousand years. Their cairns are located among brackens and boulders; a vast ancient settlement is flung over a windy slope, a place of low walls and turf floored enclosures over which plover and curlews, larks and pipits, and the cuckoo, join in the spring medley. Giant's Grave is at a lower level near track and rushing beck. Here was the hunting ground of Men of the Mist who had only the wolf to dispute their claims to wild swine and native cattle, to the roe deer and the red. They knew the girdle of bleaberry blue mountains which westwards sweep down from Coniston Old Man and Walna Scar to Duddon Sands, with Birker Moor and Black Combe a darker range behind them. Glorious vistas, and perfect peace wrapping us around.

And all was Lancashire for eight centuries! Look on Coniston from Beacon Fell on the west, or from the Carron Road or Lawson Park heights on Monk Coniston Fell to the east—with the Old Man looking you squarely in the eye; or from the skyline on the Walna Scar track with all north-west Lancashire spread out and Cumberland—and the Isle of Man and Ireland, for good measure. Best of all say farewell to the county from the Three Shire Stone where we meet both Cumberland and Westmorland on equal terms, so near to Duddon's source—so far removed from 'every taint of sordid industry'.

Will Three Shire Stone—put up by Lancashire—have no meaning from 1974, or have a deeper significance? A thousand years ago dalesmen who had no county allegiance but called themselves by Celtic, Anglian or Norse names gathered here—or rather at Wrynose foot in Little Langdale—for serious gatherings, at the Thing Mound, a small version of the tribal meeting places in Scandinavia or the Tynwald Hill at St. John's Isle of Man. After A.D. 972 the incoming Norsemen began to outnumber the Celts of Cumbria, and to infiltrate among the Anglian folk of Eden Vale and Stainmore, the West Moringas. It took time for the three peoples to become integrated. For the three countiesless?

Leyland Festival Morris Men
Whit Walk—Tottington

VIII

A LANCASHIRE YEAR

January

'Seeing in the New Year' depends on where you live. We are near enough the border to let 'first footing' play its part; we call it 'bringing in the New Year', take every precaution to ensure the house is well stocked, all bills paid, and encourage the most presentable dark young man we know to be first over our doorstep. Or else! Any disaster could be blamed later in the year on someone of the wrong colour being first through the door.

Being a bellringer's daughter my brightest New Year memories are bound up with bells. Watchnight service—a gloomy affair, I thought, only enlivened, after the solemn tolling of the muffled bells with the old year a-dying, by the promise of the joyful 'shooting' and pealing by the Cathedral ringers as soon as the New Year was born. The ten men were first out of church, to be ready when the midnight strokes had ended. I followed as soon as possible, round and round the spiralling steps, and from the darkness into the blinding light and ear splitting din of the ringing chamber. What a joyful noise unto the Lord; how I revelled in it, crouching tight in my corner away from the swinging rope ends and the pulling arms; nowhere so much energy concentrated into so small a space.

Through a clear glass 'peephole window' Blackburn far below looked remote, unfamiliar, the streets a stage and the tiny people like midget puppets; outside the lighted area the darkness, very dark.

New Years Day. They call it a day for sport. Bolton has its Fair and Dog Show; the Harriers are out round Pendle and Rossendale. In the Holcombe country the Game Cock Show is held, and fanciers gathered from the length and breadth of the United Kingdom exhibit birds of the unsurpassed Old English fighting

13

Old Ceremonial: Mayor's halberd bearer, Clitheroe
Charter Day Ceremony, Broughton-in-Furness

breed—which members are pledged to keep alive. So many cocks are 'entered' that local breeders hold back to allow long distance breeders a good showing. Afterwards prize cocks are transported by air to improve fighting strains overseas.

I never consider January over drear; days are often crisp and cold, but the sky is blue, the sun dazzling, and when night falls the heavens are busy with stars, Orion's jewelled belt and Sirius, the Dog Star at his heels, sending out shafts of blue and silver.

Youngsters are waiting, skates and sledges ready—for snow, for ice. Skis too appear. With good runs on Lakeland and Lonsdale fells and a ski-club at the Nick of Pendle, why go to Switzerland?

Temperature drops, cold increases and reports come of frozen tarns in High Furness. Tarn Hows: by day, the water stilled but the hills ringing with shouts and laughter; by night, skaters weave patterns in and out of the headlight shafts of parked cars. And no one wants to go home.

One day the shout comes in South Lancashire, "T' Cut's frozen', whereupon lads make a concerted movement to ice skimmed canal, park lake and mining flash. The police are there first, smashing the treacherous thin coating; warnings are blared on loudspeakers and schools visited. There was a terrible 'Black Weekend' in 1954 which Lancashire will never forget—so many children drowned.

Temperature still falls. Point duty policemen stand in piled straw foot warmers; waiters stamp about at bus stops, but the patient queueing women outside the Bingo Halls—'doors open at 6, eyes down at 8'—have some inner fire to keep them warm.

I never see the sun until, about 9.45, the red orb pops up over the edge of Fish Hill; quickly the white mist is torn aside, the rime dispersed and, though the weather news reports 20 degrees of frost in the south, this is the north and the world looks very good. A walk by the Ribble is indicated, through the brittle silence of Sale Wheel Woods; the wide wheeling pool is frozen but white gulls, creamy-yellow contrasted with the snow, dip and swoop over open water, and one lone angler stands thigh deep in midriver, motionless as though turned to ice.

Towards the month-end folk remark cheerfully. "We're getting through nicely". They feel winter's back is broken, that we have been spared the worst rigours as during the never-to-be-forgotten 1940, '44, '47 and '63.

The more cautious remind us, "The last weekend in the month brings the worst".

February

February Fill Dike; white or black, each day will be one cock-stride longer, but also, "As days grow longer, cold grows stronger". Life is stirring though slowly, imperceptibly. One morning the moors and the conifer plantations repeat the frosted scenes on Christmas cards, a sugar-coated world, rushes by the reservoir stiff as bronze spearheads, neat prints of claws making purposefully for unfrozen pools. After hours of sunshine flocks of wintering birds enliven the brown pastures, lapwings and those speckled visitors from the far north, fieldfares, and redwings which give away their names by the rusty patches visible in flight. The first lambtail catkins appear on the hazels, and a perky robin reminds us "I'm always here, summer and winter. Remember me",

Come wind, come weather, football supporters muffled to the eyes follow the fortunes of their teams; on windy hills they stamp around the rugger fields, and knots of ramblers assemble at bus termini, a fact which never ceases to amaze those who have forgotten what legs were for. February can prove the best outdoor month.

Each sunny Sunday is inevitably followed by Monday's newspaper headlines of unprecedented traffic queues between towns, coast and country. What frustration A59 traffic pile-ups made before the 1971 bypass was completed. Now Whalley and Clitheroe enjoy a sabbath calm, and on the Nab and moors—all quiet. Thirty magpies take off, one by one, from a Pendleton oak, and a dipper's bell-like notes are heard by Mearley brook. Over the pastures the Downham church clock tells the hour.

A Worston farmer on his tractor rattles over the hard ground, the brittle ice splintering and black ooze spattering. "Winter finished with? Nay, hold your horses. It isn't spring yet by a long road. We've worse to come". Farmers always know! Grit in piles waits by the roadside and a snow plough at the Pendle crossways. Frost warnings are out when dark comes and the heavy salt and gritting machine flashing its blue lights moves along the highways and then up our hilly lane.

Mid month. "We're not doing so badly. What can you expect

of February? This is seasonable weather." First snowdrops in Cartmel gardens and winter aconites too. The birds are much in evidence. Each dowdy hen blackbird has her glossy beau in tow. Every garden and shrubbery is alive with pairing birds paying due regard to St. Valentine.

In the right place we are treated to the nightly miracle of pre-roosting flight of starlings. At the edge of dusk countless 'murmurations' in dark clouds and spiralling skeins take off for our moor-top coppices. Along the shores of Morecambe Bay we watch amazed in the evening quiet at the age-old ritual as, by some arranged signal, the homing starlings move as to some music we cannot hear, an aerial ballet in arabesques, melting away and massing once more, against the sunset sky; then they move away, flock by flock, to their Kent estuary and Leighton Park roosting haunts.

Lancashire has many bird watchers—some serious students and reporters, others like the business men of Barrow who take their daily constitutionals along Walney Island shores, indulging as part of the usual routine. You may join them on Heysham Head or Sunderland Point, on Silverdale or Holker shores, where Duddon, Leven or Kent 'roll their waters to the sea' and where, at the ebb-tide, the sandy spits and skeers are frequented by wild fowl, shelduck, tufted duck and teal. Binoculars are focussed on skeins of geese, necks outstretched, and maybe honking like boat horns, passing overhead, among them the pink-footed or rarer black- or white-fronted. On the Furness archipeligo of islands the brent goose winters, and that odd goose credulous ornithologists of the past believed to be hatched from the barnacles clinging to the rocks and timbers of wrecks of the Isle of Foudrey.

February's Nature Columns in local papers are full of reports on migrants. Whooper swans congregate and bark away like kenneled hounds in sheltered waters around Hawkshead and upper Windermere and Brathay. Man-made inland reservoirs are as much to the liking of wintering birds; from Anglezarke and Rivington, Abbeystead and the lakes below Blackstone Edge bird watchers tell of large numbers of mallard and widgeon, pochard and long tailed duck, and occasionally of the shoveller, the black scoter, and, well away from the tidal channels, his wonted fishing grounds, the cormorant.

The end of February. The ironbound gates of winter unbarred!

Rapid thaw on the moors, roads cleared of the last drifts, hourly the wan streaks thinning on Pendle. Brooks chattering to make up for lost time, the air full of twitterings, bickerings and snatches of song. My first lark of the year, invisible, over Whalley Nab.

March and Shrovetide

March Many Weathers arrives with accompanying gales, infecting children with its madcap spirit; or docile as a lamb, deceptively promising spring.

Have you ever been accosted by high winds round corners taking you unawares and almost off your feet on Liverpool's Water Street? Or battled against wild north-easters on Pendle or Winter Hill? Still you have seen nothing if you have never met the full force of a sea breeze at Blackpool on a March day. A loud roaring from above as the Tower is battered, a noise like twenty bombers' engines thundering in your ears—and the Tower does nothing but shudder and remain erect. With all traffic brought to a standstill along the 'front', Promenade-facing windows barricaded and all entrances barred and secured, Blackpool, Golden Mile, seven mile sands and all, is virtually stormbound. One ventures towards the front to see whence the gales blow; a little way, then clings to a lamp post until rescued by a bold policeman in the role of Sir Galahad helping the helpless into the comparative haven of streets behind the Tower. A man's hat hurtles by and no one laughs; a large parcel wheels down midstreet and the owner—nowhere in sight!

Shrovetides remembered—in the north-east Lancashire of my childhood a jolly holiday, a round of all aunts and well-disposed neighbours for a feast of pancakes and record consumption. The most laggard eater already full to capacity was sent away, face blackened by soot from behind the fire. On farms around Longridge and Beacon Fell the last to finish was wheeled hilariously in the wheelbarrow and tipped protesting into the midden!

The pancake bell was rung by an apprentice from scores of church towers—a long established custom which meant 'down tools and take a holiday'. The engineering apprentices in the big Blackburn foundries claimed it—but now, through lack of encouragement at managerial level, it has died a natural death. Schoolboys claimed it as by right, participating thereupon in pagan practices with the approval of headmaster and local gentry; cocking was the accepted sport of the old established Grammar Schools like Clitheroe's, Lancaster's and Warton's where the master was paid cockpennies and supplied the birds. What school would now countenance 'cock kailing'? This was inhuman slaughtering of birds buried up to the neck feathers in the ground; boys attacked with sticks, the killer claiming the cock. Blood sports for schoolboys died out, but lads still barred out the master and enforced the granting of the holiday.

Between Preston and Lancaster old Shrovetide and Easter customs die hardest. Children still rush from house to house in the Fylde and Garstang area, round Inglewhite and Goosnargh, begging "Please a pancake", and holding out baskets or even pillow cases to be filled—not with pancakes but oranges! One bright lad changed jackets with another after a successful haul and returned to cry "Please a pancake", from the same unwitting housewives. But, when his father overheard his gleeful success story, what a leathering he got!

There was a time when bull-baiting was enforced by law, as the best way of tenderizing the beef, but baiting was also a sport much enjoyed on Shrove Tuesday. My great, great grandfather at Clitheroe supplied bulldogs of his own breeding for baiting at the bullring—still in its stone—on Worston Green.

Today there are pancakes of course, and much lighter with clean snow in the batter (snow is usually to be had at this time); a pancake race on Blackpool promenade for its sprightly landladies; and Rag Days at each of the county's universities, Liverpool, Manchester, Lancaster and colleges of technology.

Football fever rises to a frenzy; shopkeepers barricade themselves against the rowdier visiting teams' supporters. Bingo queues half surround the block an hour before the two sessions' 'eyes down'. Confirmed addicts exchange advice on how 'to put in time between. Since every town has completed its traffic-free shopping precincts, places to sit down are many, pleasant patios, garden areas with flowers, shrubs and fountains playing. I like Bolton's Town Hall Square, Blackburn's Victoria Court, Preston's St. George's Precinct. Nowhere better for friends to meet, for the elderly to wait while the family shops, and lonely folk to find ready ears to hearken to their woes when spring sun shines.

Across the moorland pastures hares spring from their warm forms almost from under our feet, and away, long-legged, to join in family parties playing 'tag' and 'round, around the gorse bushes', with bouts of shadow boxing and ring o' roses in between. March hares are quite dotty, and Lancashire has so many of them.

Nearing the season's end the Holcombe and Pendle Forest Harriers are out twice weekly, streaming across country anywhere between the gentle lowlands of Much Hoole and Heskin to the windswept slopes of Affetside and Lumb-in-Rossendale, from the Ribble valley to the border region shared with the Craven Harriers.

The Holcombe Hunt have been out and about for the sport ever since 1617 when King James I, in high spirits after good hunting with Sir Thomas Barton's deep mouthed hounds brought to Hoghton Tower especially from Quarlton, was graciously pleased to bestow upon them the privilege of wearing his own royal scarlet livery and right to hunt so many days a week 'for ever' in twelve townships within his royal forest. And they have been doing it ever since, not only the gentry, quality and leisured classes but, tagging on behind all the farming folk, townsfolk and working men of Rossendale with a love of the hunt. When the hounds were heard every weaver left his loom; with a meet in the area every schoolmaster shut down school, and when the bearers in the funeral cortege heard the 'View Halloo', what did they do but drop the coffin and join in the chase!

Farther north the Lunesdale and Coniston Foxhounds are out too, not for the fun of it but answering the call of farmers to deal with lamb slaughtering. Lambing begins in late March in the lower dales, in mid-April it is in full swing on the fell farms and by then the Hunts are alerted, calls upon their time arriving thick and fast.

At a friend's farm in High Furness cockerels were killed overnight and ducks had disappeared; the in-fields were grazed by a hundred and more in-lamb ewes. Was the nightly marauder hiding in the boulder spill at the foot of nearby crags, or did he steal down the fells from his den in the next dale? Two young trencher-fed hounds they had raised from puppyhood were nosing at the birch wood edge. Maybe they had picked up a scent. The Hunt was coming in the morning. Get rid of the killer now before lambing! You need to be up before daylight to watch 'the Hunt' arrive. The huntsman and hounds piled into the van at the kennels whilst Lakeland slept. Only the farmer and his wife were up to welcome them. Soon the old grandfather joined them and sleepy-eyed sons determined to have a few hours with the hunt before making a beeline for school at nine.

What follows is dead earnest. Nothing here of the colourful set-up seen on calendars. One huntsman, half a dozen hounds and a farming family with one aim—extermination of a cruel killer; a slow and tedious business, endless patience involved. Often there is no kill, or in the next dale another Hunt will corner the fox harried from here. 'That ald barren vixen' killed in Yewdale could be the cockerel killer, and the rogue dog fox which stole the ducks the one which got away in an Eskdale borrans. There is a live and let live attitude in Furness farmers concerning the depredation of foxes which steal the odd pullet to feed their young, but not for the meaningless worrying and beheading committed by a 'rogue' dog fox, nor for the aged vixen without family who will kill for love of killing and leave her victims strewn about pen and fold.

Out of the Holcombe country from Rawtenstall, a tough little man called Tommy Dobson arrived in Eskdale to found a famous pack and attain local fame akin to that of John Peel around Skiddaw; sixty years, an indefatigable huntsman, 'none better', and his last resting place in the quiet riverside graveyard of Eskdale church.

Spring is a tardy arrival, with many tentative openings of the door before we know 'for sure' it is about to make a bow. Crocuses have followed the snowdrops, tight daffodils seem loathe to burst into flower; honeysuckle and wild rose sprays are greening in hedgerows, but hawthorn pricked with rosy buds shows not a hint of burgeoning. What a clamour from rookeries—'they're building high so we'll have a good summer'—how vibrant the sky with peewits screaming and larks wound up to breaking point. But no curlew are crying yet—the sound which for me opens the door to spring.

Some late March day the overfull fields around Morecambe Bay seem unusually empty, and on the dale head farms pastures have more than doubled their stock overnight. The wintering hoggs have come home. Hoggs? Last year's gimmer lambs, next year's mothers.

On 17th March we recognize our Irish bus conductors—as if we did not already!—by the green in their buttonholes. The church at Heysham, where St. Patrick landed, exchanges greetings with Armagh.

Mid-Lent Sunday was always the recognized holiday when children working away 'went home for the day'—Simnel Sunday in Lancashire, with delicious spicy cakes made for the occasion! This 'original' recipe that the Bury Librarian has on tape, goes back to the 1780s. The amounts appear family-size; but simnel cakes keep, if you let them.

> 5 lb. flour, 4 lb. currants, 1 lb. sugar, 1 lb. (or 2 lb.) butter, ¾ lb. brewers yeast, ½ oz. cinnamon, ¼ oz. nutmeg, ½ lb. almonds (cut fine), ½ lb. candied lemon, 10 eggs, a gill of cream (half-pint, Lancashire).

The ingredients are mixed as a dough and left to rise the day before baking. Then the dough is rolled to make a 'domed' cake, the rolled edge doubled in for 4 inches. When this is pressed down it naturally makes elevations and depressions. The elevations or protuberances are the celebrated 'knobs', the name for a cut piece of simnel cake. When hot from the oven the top is glazed with ¼-inch-thick syrup. Before required for consumption, sprinkle with powdered sugar.

The third to fourth week in March is cram full of dates—Lady Day, Mothers Day derived from Mothering Sunday, putting forward of the clock for Summer Time, and—what mattered most to me when young as it does to all children nowadays within reach of Clitheroe, the March Fair. Like all such events, cattle, sheep and horses are relegated to a back place though the medieval charter was for buying and selling of livestock. The Pleasure Fair is The Thing.

In Lancashire for Leisure and Pleasure, by coast and in the country, visitors' names are adding up in the booking lists and a spate of spring cleaning, whitewashing, painting and decorating sweeps through seaside town and lakeland resort. Riveredge willows are gold dusted, hedges are growing green and "green spray showers lightly down the cascade of the larch".

Watch for Winter's come-back! Sunny weekends bring forth wanderers, and ill-clad, unseasoned hill walkers are caught unprepared in sudden snowstorms. Coniston crags are alive with climbers; ice has widened chinks, rocks are loosened, hand and foot holds fail—and young lives are lost.

Like the eager pigeons flirting with death between the wheels of traffic in Manchester as they collect building straw, winging side ways between buses and up to stone cornice and parapet—we are incurable optimists at the first breath of spring.

April—and Eastertide

April, when lusty spring 'takes in all beauty with an easy span'. We have walked the plateaux above the Loire on fields of cloth o' gold, been wakened by sweet song in the orchards of Poictiers and Tours where birds must have sipped the dews of Paradise, and welcomed the first cuckoo of the year in the vineyards of Vouvray—and returned home to watch the laggard steps of our north-country spring; to pick the first primrose, catch sight of the first swallow. At the month end the first Lancashire cuckoo shouts and we can plant one foot on five daisies. Then we know 'for sure' our north country spring has arrived.

Daily, louder the larksong, more assertive the territorial challenge of the curlew. "Open the door and the spring seems to rush in they shout so loud," says the moorland farmer. Mad happy the seabirds on Kent and Leven sands, their cries blown about the sky.

Gaiety tugs at you in town streets where almond and cherry blossom rains over new market precincts and green buds burgeon where none have appeared for years in the dark hearts of industrial towns. Sun picks out the brilliance of flowers in angles of St. Anne's church and Cross Street chapel in Manchester, on flower seller's stalls and barrow boy's carts. No need now to travel into the country to search for spring; the new landscaped civic centres welcome her as surely. But Nature, slap-happy in the un-landscaped countryside, gives the best showing, always, each day better than the last.

April is a full month for 'events', with football teams battling towards top of the League or the Cup, Point to Point meetings of the two hunts, Holcombe and Pendle Forest which for its steeplechase combines with the Yorkshire Craven Harriers, and a bag full of 'traditions'.

The First of April fooling is no mere childish hoaxing—'You have a hole in your stocking', 'Your shoelace is untied'—but in the older Grammar Schools every variation wit can devise is tried out on the staff; until noon, three hours of licenced foolery and with the 12 o'clock bell, deep sighs of regret! Reason must return!

Once, Holy Week was observed by Pace or Pasch Egging when small children cried at every door 'God's sake, a pace egg', and men patrolled the streets in fantastic garb, masked, singing, dancing to drum and fife—as in old Blackburn.

Pace egging is by no means a Lancashire byegone, though gangs no more collect eggs by extortion, rival parties indulging in street fights, 'jealous of each other's prosperity', after performances of the mumming play of St. George and the Champion.

> "A pace egg, a pace egg, and if you don't gie us a pace egg, then your hens will all lay addled eggs and all your cocks a stone."

The Low Furness mummers who enact the old play on village greens, one which "dates back to medieval times and symbolizes the rebirth of life", make no such threats. Very popular they are, with bystanders always ready to prompt the 'jolly boys' if words are forgotten.

Pace eggs are such beautiful things, wrapped in onion skins, boiled hard and the multicoloured shells polished until too pretty to break at the egg rolling. Children range them on cottage window ledges, count them and gloat on them. On Easter Monday the 'traditional' fields are thronged with youngsters. Avenham Park at Preston; the 'Easter Field' called Giant Axe at Lancaster—where originally Easter Day, the day when the stone was rolled away from the Sepulchre, was the occasion for the rolling. Jeremiah Wane in 1828 thought hilarity wrong on a holy day so cunningly tempted the youngsters to a Monday meeting by hiring a field, a band and offering books to all pace eggers who turned up. The Amphitheatre Field at Furness Abbey is another egg rolling slope, and on many a green hill the children gather. There is no sign of interest dwindling.

Good Friday is opening day for the hill climber's and rambler's year, parties issuing forth from every town with a hill in its sights. Pendle is what the papers call a 'popular venue', welcoming in sun or more likely to be draped in clouds, and every village within miles prepared to feed the visitors. In the past every chapel and Sunday school room was ready with gargantuan spreads for rambling parties from the towns. Goosnargh, expecting a mighty influx of Prestonians, used to bake ten thousand of its toothsome 'cakes' in readiness.

From Horwich, Chorley and Bolton the hundreds mount Rivington Pike for the annual Pike Fair, come wind, come weather, and usually it blows half a gale, doing its best to whip away the stalls with their gaudy fairings, ('twice the price you'd pay for 'em down in Horridge'), thinning the addicts round the Bingo Booth and making hot dogs preferable to ice cream. Over bog, rocks, boulders, up and down deep gullies, in and out of cloud wrack—that is the Pike Race, a gruelling course but a field of sixty or so runners—sixteen minutes with good going, Lever Park to Pike and hurtling down again.

On the Saturday the Nutters, the Brittannia Coconut Dancers, come to town, dancing at Bacup centre, performing ritualistic leaping and whippings at the four boundary road ends; what a lively clacking as of castanets with the half coconuts at hands, knees and on black leather belts. No one quite knows how the outlandish costume originated—white headgear, red banded white skirts, and pullovers and breeches in black—and with faces blackened too, more than a hint of tribal African about it. Some say the dance was brought from Morocco in the seventeenth or eighteenth century, and that, as in the ancient Rossendale rush-bearings, it harks back to half-religious, half-pagan rites which banished evil by whipping.

Strange that south-east Lancashire taken over by industry, lock, stock and barrel, should indulge in such bygones! Ashton's Riding of the Black Lad on Easter Monday had all the necessary ingredients of age-old springtime ritual, Old Winter driven out and destroyed with great joy by an entire community. For centuries the manor stewards paid town's money for making a Black Lad effigy to be mounted, ridden round the town, thrown down ignominiously, and burnt with shouts and jeers at the Old Cross. Ashton folk say he was the 'wicked Ralph Assheton' who punished the townsfolk for not destroying corn marigolds in the fields—a noxious weed—but one Assheton hero after 1346, when he bore away the Scots king's standard in triumph after Neville's Cross battle was knighted, and left his black suit, coat of mail and helmet for dressing the Lad—the Black Knight? Or was it another Assheton, he who gave to Middleton church the armour and sword he won from the Scots king's standard bearer on Flodden Field, who is remembered? The Winter overcome by Spring theory seems most credible.

Another Easter custom, not practised today but occasion for much hilarity in the past, was the Monday 'lifting' of lasses by lads and the lasses retaliating the next day.

"When James and Thomas and Jack and Peter came to 'lift' Ellen, hoo punched, and hoo scrat, and hoo nipped; and hoo kicked James, and hoo basted Peter, and hoo lugged Thomas, and hoo stamped on t' floor and shouted 'Murder'." Some lass!

The eve of May Day in my father's boyhood was observed as Mischief Night—gate lifting, wheel removing, hiding of tools, etc. May Bough Night was the opportunity to make game of neighbours and plant at doors twigs and branches with 'inner meaning': a wicken (rowan)—my dear chicken; plum bough in bloom—to be married and soon; a briar—a liar. Harmless fun.

The Month of May—Festivities, Ceremonial and Whitsuntide

May, a merry month with Old Winter officially banished on the 12th, Old May Day. This is a date when the songs and poems of May mean something in Lancashire; we need the extra twelve days for the full flush of May.

A pity May morning is not what it was!

Until the early 1800s Manchester and all its neighbours welcomed in May with song and dance. In came the May-ers, with flute or fiddle singing before the houses,

"God bless your house and harbour, your riches and your store,
For the summer springs so fresh, so green and gay
We hope the Lord will prosper you both now and evermore,
Drawing near the merry month of May."

How pleasant when Manchester folk heard under their windows. "Rise up the fair maid of this house, put on your gay, gold ring".

Beauty treatment is easily come by. "Wake and call me early", it used to be, with every girl up bright and early to dabble in the wet grass. As a Furness farmer's wife told me, "It's dabbling in the dew makes the milkmaid fair". The pinkest rose petal complexion I have ever seen, was on the cheeks of two old ladies at a Chipping valley Women's Institute meeting, who confessed to 'may-dewing' every year on Longridge Fell, as girls!

What a fine sight on the First it used to be, when milkmen's horses, and the heavy brewer's drays were all bedecked with shining brasses, paper flowers and coloured ribbons plaited into manes and tails. An overdressed girl it was said, "Was got up like a May horse!"

How many remember tripping around with the maypole dancers—as they still do in the side streets of Burnley? The queen, draped in lace window curtain—now in nylon or terylene—carries her stool from place to place, her confederates trooping behind. Their finery was usually a matter of pink, yellow and white tissue or crinkled paper, wings and bows—now replaced by plastic flowers and the like. But the words are the same, passed down in slightly garbled versions from generations of big sisters to little. The first week in May in open spaces, street corners—

"Round around the maypole, merrily we go
Tripping, tripping lightly, dancing to and fro,
All the happy pastimes, round the village green,
Hurrah, hurrah, for our May Queen.

"Can you dance the polko, yes I can,
Not with you but my young man.
First upon the heel, then upon the toe
That's the way the polko goes."

Boys had their own ways of money collecting, not to be outdone. In Blackburn they went through the antics of bear and bear tamer, chanting 'hod-e-hon-con-kay' and 'Catchee polee'. Then came jazz bands, blackened faces and clanging of dust bin lids!

Ever heard of Nick o' Thung's Charity? It sounds olde-worlde but in fact was a Victorian innovation—which makes it almost modern by Lancashire standards, thought up by a home-returned Barrowford man called 'America Tom'. He suggested to the Lamb Club members in his home town, all working men, that they and their families should make a trek towards Pendle every first Sunday in May—a field day plus 'barbecue' in a pleasant spot above Twiston. Any excuse for a day out if good eating was involved!

As the years rolled on this 'Charity' developed into a feast of gargantuan proportions. The men members, aproned for their chores, built improvized hearths, cooked ham and eggs, steak and chops, onions and mushrooms, which were handed round in thick mouth watering 'hamburgers' between thick slices of bread. At the same time the pièce-de-resistance was being prepared, a giant nettle pudding, into which went no less than 100 eggs, 10 pounds of onions, 11 pounds of sausage meat, great lumps of dripping—and from a large sized clothes basket, tender, succulent young nettles.

It did not much matter what beverage was to follow on, when each initiate had adequately repeated the necessary formula to become a full member of Nick o' Thung's. It was a tongue twister on the doings of Thimblerig Thistlewaite who after "thinking to thrive through thick and thin by throwing his thimbles about was thwarted and thwacked by thirty thousand thorns. . . ."

If some wandered off into Twiston Clough where beeches dip green branches in a slow stately pavane, bluebells drift under tawny oaks, lambs race round white thorns and 'cuckoo, cuckoo' is shouted from clough to clough, it was but natural.

There was any amount of traditional ceremonial in May concerned with Mayor Making, especially in old boroughs with long memories like Clitheroe. A civic dignitary we called 'Colonel Blood' because of his red robes—he was in fact the Town Sergeant —went from school to school announcing in stentorian voice, with 'Oyez, oyez', and ringing of his bell, that we were to have a day's holiday. Alas! The last of the old-style Mayor-makings took place in 1973, for Mayor, council, borough and all disappeared in administrative changes.

The Cockle and Mussel Feast, the shellfish fresh from Lancaster in the old days of packhorses, is now dependant it being May, on tinned variety, but the pattern is the same, the 'colts' at the meeting drinking a potent punch from a large loving cup.

On Thursday 12th May 1966—the seven hundred and first year after the creation of the Earldom of Lancaster—I was witness of a most colourful ceremonial occasion, the Hanging of the new High Sheriff's shield on the walls of the Shire Hall at the Castle. It is said with truth this is the most splendid heraldic display in Britain. Many times I had walked along the raised court scanning the arms and names of the families who made our county history, but what went before the placing of those shields I did not know.

The Countess Peel was first to insist I ought to see what happened, Lt.-Col. Owtram the 1965–66 High Sheriff agreed—a Portrait of Lancashire without a mention of it would be incomplete. The Under Sheriff sent me the new High Sheriff's formal invitation.

The Secretary to the Mayor of Lancaster told me of the courtesy visit the City and County paid on the Judge at his Lodgings prior to the Summer Assize. At 10 o'clock, she said—.

So, as the priory clock was striking I stood at the Town Cross—puzzled that no one else should be watching. The City was perfectly calm, no cheering crowds, no watching tourists. Understandable maybe, after over 800 years of sheriffs, and over seven centuries of visiting Assize Judges, this was mere routine. But nothing is 'forever'. Now Lancaster's Assizes are no more. What follows is now past history.

The Civic Party arrived with all the splendid insignia of this ancient town, the Mayor, the Town Clerk, the Mace Bearer in crimson and gold lace leading the procession, the brilliant sun flashing on the magnificent silver-gilt mace, the largest in England it is claimed, and I do not doubt it.

On the three occasions each year when Assizes were held in Lancaster one could tell by the uniformed police outside the Judges Lodging, the clean curtains at the windows, the tubs of flowers by the door. This morning the interior was ablaze with lights. On the heels of the City, came the County—the new High Sheriff, his Under Sheriff and chaplain arriving in a sleek limousine with its pennant, in unheraldic terms, three golden lions on a scarlet ground. County after City, and the doors closed behind them.

Courtesies exchanged and the two parties in turn filed out, followed by the Judge's procession, under the motto 'In Concilio Consilium'—three cars in cavalcade away up Castle Hill to the Priory and Parish Church. By a short cut up the stone staircase I reached the churchyard just ahead of them, bells ringing, the Vicar waiting in his most splendid vestments in the shadows of the porch and all prepared for what is a great occasion, City and County taking the Queen's Justice to church.

A row of plain clothes police, no heralds in sumptious tabards with trumpets at the ready, waited the signal for the fanfare. The bells continued pealing. The sound of choristers' voices and organ music issued from the church. The birds in the limes and the great beeches went on singing as though this day was like any other; and a boy and girl lying on a table-topped tomb did not even turn their heads but fixed their gaze on the far away sea and mountains.

The church service is all things to all men at all times. Today how the words Mercy, Righteousness, Truth, were pinpointed.

Whalley Abbey: a Summer 'Open Day'

"Submit yourselves to the ordinances of man" was the lesson, most fittingly. And for the Judge we prayed he should be granted the spirit of "uprightness, discernment, love and mercy".

The first act of a new High Sheriff as Her Majesty's deputy at the Crown Court is to hand to the Judge the document declaring that the "court of oyer and terminer and goal delivery" is thereupon to be held. The High Sheriff sits at the judge's right hand. Since 1176 courts have been held here at Lancaster and always sheriffs have watched the course of justice, and made sure no attempts succeeded in preventing the doing of it. In the bad old days when the judge on northern circuit was at the mercy of desperate men, ambush and reprisals for unpopular sentences, the High Sheriff with escort of all nobility and gentry in the shire, saw he was handed over at the county boundary safe and sound.

We sat for two hours listening to the 'hearing and determining' of the judge, waiting for each new prisoner brought forward in the 'goal delivery'. The small court is close and intimate. No voices are raised, nothing but reasoned cadences, a level voice explaining, as a wise headmaster to an erring pupil, just why crime, forgery, cheating do not pay; that the British pattern of life, finance and commerce depends on individual honesty.

The ceremonial hanging of the new High Sheriff's shield followed the adjournment of the morning court. We all gathered in the vast Shire Hall to watch Colonel F. W. Jones, in a simple, but impressive ceremony with eight centuries of tradition behind it, hand over his new shield—five red roses upon it representing his five tall and stalwart sons—to the Queen's Constable of the Castle, the Earl of Sefton. The Shire Hall is a lofty place but the six hundred shields, over 540 of them Sheriffs'—from 1129 when Bertram de Bulmer was presented on behalf of Henry I, the rest, shields of sovereigns and of Constables who hold their office for life—extend in four rows round the circular court and space is almost exhausted.

Early power-conscious sheriff's 'hung on', and when strong men were welcome, in time of war, stayed in office for years. Henry II decided his deputies should be chief tenants of the emerging shire.

Edward I made sure of his sheriffs; his head men were the Crown's chosen guardians of the north-western approaches, empowered to raise men and supplies for campaigns in Wales or Scotland. The earldom was created for his young brother Edmund

14

Hunting morning with the Holcombe harriers; midwinter grips the Holcombe country

Crouchback, already sheriff in his own right. As an hereditary sheriffdom it passed through Henry the first Duke, to John o' Gaunt his son-in-law, who later, with Palatinate power chose his own deputy sheriffs. Until his son, Henry IV, merged Duchy and Crown, but chose to keep the Duchy as his own quite separate possession, the sheriff was purely a deputy. Now the king allowed him to play a much more important role, as High Sheriff. And so it goes on, this office as king's deputy.

The Duchy of Lancashire—and Cornwall too—being separate from the Crown, their High Sheriffs are chosen by the Queen who, in council, 'pricks' from the three names submitted by the Chancellor of the Duchy.

And how are the three in the short list chosen? *Not* from the peerage, the clergy, officers on active service, barristers or solicitors – or any who claim poverty! He must be a man of honour, integrity, held in esteem among Lancastrians, for his duties include attending the judge at Assizes, and at election petitions. He executes writs and death sentences, is returning officer at parliamentary elections; he prepares jury panels and sees to safe custody and delivery of prisoners.

When a former High Sheriff took up residence for a short time in one of Manchester's largest hotels to be near the Law Courts and a spate of work in connection with his office, the manager regretted that the rooms most suited to his rank were taken by an American couple. But how quickly they offered their suite to Lancashire's High Sheriff, possibly envisaging the familiar film-type H.S. with gun and posse behind him!

In the past the gentry of Lancashire had to ride with the Sheriff to Assizes to ensure his safe arrival; they supplied his lodgings with wine and victuals for he had to entertain the judge. Certain estates in the county were held by 'Sherifftooth'; their owners contributed food and lodging for the sheriff when he, about the king's business, rode to attend the judge. Magistrates contributed towards his 'out going'.

Later the High Sheriff's considerable expenses during his year in office were met in *very* small part from Duchy moneys.

Does any other county indulge so wholeheartedly in Walking Days? These are a Lancashire speciality, processions of witness 'on the Church's birthday', and continue throughout Whit week. I remember myself in white with a shepherdess basket full of yellow anthemis and trailing smilax walking behind Clitheroe St. Mary's Golden Banner. And the Sunday Schools are still walking!

Manchester's Whit Walks are worth going many miles to see, the Anglicans on the Monday, the Roman Catholics on the Friday; and a spirit of rivalry aiming to outdo each other in lavish spectacle imbues the thousands. Mothers save up in weekly Walking Day Clubs to buy finery for small sons and daughters; they are turned out on the day like little princes and princesses and no one objects to waiting along the route for hours on end. At Preston, too, the forces are separated by police control. One morning the Protestant 'Orangemen's' processions lead off, each of the many component parts led by a King William in curled wig, regal riding costume, mounted most handsomely, at the forefront of a bloodless revolution; the Roman Catholics walk through the afternoon.

If you have not watched them you can have no conception of the magnitude of Sunday School walkings. Bolton discontinued the Church of England's round-the-town, stop-all-traffic and cordon-off-the-town-centre processions. Instead the various churches walk through their own parishes and combine the parochial promenade with the annual sermons; they take up every weekend through May and June. Trinity Sunday remains the great day for 'the Romans'.

I like what is done at outliers, Turton and Edgworth; the congregation sallies forth to do the rounds of all the scattered cottages and farms in the parish, combining all the faithful, and the strays, in very simple (and appealing because of their simplicity) open-air services and hymn singings. With blue sky above, birds joining in and farm animals leaning over the fence taking an interest, one feels very conscious that there is a God and from Him blessings continue to flow.

North country non-conformists have always had midsummer feasts and joint religio-social events. Lune Valley methodists hold camp meetings; combined churches gather in some field or farmyard, listen to good preachers, let themselves go in rousing, uplifting congregational singing—what volume, what verve! Later they adjourn to a nearby barn for a spread which must be seen to be believed, the result of combined operations of all the local 'chapel' women.

Great interest in folk music and the publication of the quarterly

Lancashire Wakes for enthusiasts have led to numerous local outdoor 'happenings'. May sees Morris Men performing the intricacies of their dancing in market place, shopping precinct and on village green, and adding colour and life to many a rural fête. Look out this month for the Furness and John o' Gaunt Morris Men, and the famous Garstang and Leyland teams.

Who does anything about the 29th? "Royal Oak day, the 29th of May", we used to chant, and "If you don't give us a holiday we'll all run away". We have Royal Oak Inns by the score; King Charles II peeps from his oak tree in the painted sign on Allithwaite's inn.

Did any other inns do as the 'Dog and Kennel' at Tong near Bolton? There the effigy of the Merry Monarch was garlanded with oak leaves and saluted with fitting ceremonial by the oldest patron. We have many 'Kings Heads', and where the dark-visaged Charles is portrayed they possibly possessed earlier signs, 'Black Lad', or 'Saracen's Head', easily altered when patriotic zeal reached its height at the Restoration.

Perchance anyone believes that Whitsun and Trinity being over the highways and byways of Lancashire are to be cleared for free flow of traffic, think again. Notices appear on buses based on Manchester and South Lancashire:

> "With the approach of the season for holding Church Processions of Witness passengers are warned of possible delays to services particularly on Saturdays and Sundays during June and July. Every endeavour will be made to maintain scheduled services. Passengers should make some allowance. . . ."

Could this happen anywhere else? So many churches holding their 'birthdays', preserving their right of slow marching to martial music down the centre of their main streets, banners waving, drums beating—and impatient traffic queues lengthening.

"And why not?" ask the walkers and their parents on the side line. "It's only once a year. And whose street is it anyway?"

On the Feast of Corpus Christi, the Thursday after Trinity, or on the following Sunday, slow and reverent processions accompanied by singing, and with small girls in their white communion veils and dresses strewing flowers, make their way through town parishes or along quiet lanes. The Host is borne aloft by four men, its canopy swaying as they pass. The priest goes before in his richest vestments, altar boys swing censors, the men leading the procession, the women bringing up the rear. Another patch of bright colour in the Lancashire kaleidoscope!

Open Houses—For May and June

May gadding green and gay across Lancashire and beauty flooding in with June, makes us restless. No wonder everyone wants to be out and about, going places. The urge seizes town and country. Countryfolk flock to town; townsfolk off for the day realize our stately homes are opening their doors; their season is well and truly launched.

Lancashire for noble mansions, historic halls, parks and gardens —now at their best. Cars and coaches are rolling along sweeping drives, under ancestral trees, pulling up in parking places once stable yards or tourney grounds. Teas are laid on in orangery, converted coach house and buttery.

The best are homes of the old families; the coppers, the five- and ten-penny pieces are dropped into the till and we know we are helping to keep alive what otherwise—with crippling taxes and upkeep beyond any but the near-millionaire—might perish. Great houses and their parks and estates must pay their way these days, or go under. They are very precious, those homes founded by Tudor, Stuart and Georgian gentry who, knowing they themselves could never see the fruit of their plans and labours, left the future to inherit. That is where we come in.

Holker Hall is farthest north, beautifully sited in a deer park fringing Leven Sands. The Prestons, then the Dukes of Devonshire, made it what it is. Mr. Richard Cavendish now lives here with his family. Produce of farms, gardens and greenhouses are on sale in local shops; it is a vast well-run undertaking. The Hall is filled with treasures, world famous pictures; and 'Royalty has slept here'. Queen Mary loved it. The Cavendish family were great tree planters; the first larches were grown at Holker, and eleven seedling monkey-puzzle trees, germinated from seeds a Liverpool sailor brought back from Chile, here grew into giants, as did cedars of Lebanon from seeds brought from the Holy Land in 1789. The gardens are superb, especially in May and June when azaleas and rhododendrons are in full display.

Very near Leighton Moss and Keer sands is Leighton Hall, home of Major and Mrs. Reynolds whose ancestors were the Gillows. It is a most romantic neo-Gothic mansion, a jewel in a perfect setting, with Sir Walter Scott's influence evident. Period furniture of the Gillow's creation is—naturally—a reason for visiting the Hall. The gardens are charming. The family welcome visitors at the door, always a pleasant experience.

Gawthorpe Hall opens its doors on Monday, Wednesday and Saturday afternoons between Easter and September; a new look college, but some relics of past times. A gift from Lord Shuttleworth to Lancashire.

Other houses now in National Trust or town and city ownership—saved for posterity with public money behind them, and every penny well spent—include two near Liverpool. Speke Hall is on Mersey bank, and Rufford Old Hall on the Ormskirk-Preston highroad, a splendid timber framed house with magnificent great hall, hammer-beam roof supported by angel corbels and unique 'spere', a folk museum, armour, costume and period furniture, an excellent half-crown's worth! Also, for Shakespeare's devotees, a possible link with the poet's 'lost years': a young William Shakeshafte was a player here in Hesketh's Company.

A number of public spirited Blackburnians and Prestonians saved Samlesbury Hall from demolition by a timber merchant in 1925. The Southworths lived here from the fourteenth to eighteenth century. The romantic can weave tales about priest's hides and the possible appearance of the White Lady's ghost.

A ghost rocks a cradle at Turton Tower, one of three ancient halls very near Bolton and open to the public. The Tower has Tudor additions to a medieval pele, and Victorian improvements to the whole. It is a fascinating place with an enthusiastic curator enamoured of his charge. Equally informative is the caretaker of Hall i' th' Wood now enclosed by Bolton housing developments—but a shrine if ever there was to old families of the town's pre-industrial past, and to Samuel Crompton who in a small room invented such great improvements for fine cotton spinning; surely it is Bolton's greatest pride. So easily one may forget the present, for the centuries roll back in passing from room to room. It is, as I wrote in *Lancashire Landscape*, as though having pressed a time switch we are guests in an eighteenth-century home, waiting—in a quiet room with clock ticking and bird singing in its cage—for our host to put in an appearance.

Smithills Hall, above a wooded Dean, plays two parts, the Victorian wings are an old people's home, the rest, great hall, Tudor rooms and chapel well restored, a valuable picture of Lancashire Past.

Astley Hall's gallery has the unique and enormous shovel board table, so large the house would need to be pulled about to remove it. Chorley is fortunate in its possession and surroundings. Towneley Hall also—wonderful things to see in a mansion ancient, historic and bringing for our pleasure riches of many generations of Towneleys. It is Burnley's contribution to local culture. A wonderful restoration by Salford of the Tudor Radcliffes' Ordsall Hall is worth seeing.

If these are not enough to fill May and June, then make a beeline for Wigan's Haigh Hall where plantation and gardens excel themselves. Or share with Mancunians the varied splendours of Heaton Hall, Platt Hall and Wythenshawe Hall, each a valuable contribution to the rich and pleasant side of the county's life.

And look out for scores of private gardens—open for charities.

June

June days and all the country working up to its full glory and all the midsummer pomps. We dream of days on the fells, the incense of crushed wild thyme, blue pools which are not sky-reflecting tarns but bluebells, shores not flushed by sunset but blushlike with acres of sea thrift, growing grass in meadows running like silvery waves under the wind. We think of idling on our beaches, sunbathing in the creeks of Silverdale, enjoying other people's gardens—and the scent of new cut grass on our own lawns; garden parties, open days, school sports—and cricket.

We expect so much—and what happens? Cold weather holding back the flowers—not an open rose for our Women's Institute 'best red rose' competition one third Monday in the month; spectators huddled from driving rain in pavilions, garden parties whipped into the school hall.

Completely unpredictable! More like March we say. Only the lengthening of the days is certain and that on Midsummer Night there will be no more than an hour or two of darkness.

Advance notices in the papers—"Midnight Hikers. Sunrise Service on Ingleborough at 3.30 a.m." and enthusiastic walkers from Lonsdale, led by energetic clergymen, strain upwards to the summit. And with them Carnforthians whose ancestors practised pagan rites on Hell Bank on Midsummer Eves long ago!

Around Clitheroe they lift up their eyes to Pendle, and from a dozen towns around it. "Once," they say, "we couldn't sleep for the sound of crowds of folk walking by—all off to climb the hill."

Pendle is grand for seeing the sunrise, but everyone's nearest hill is better than not attempting it at all. Rivington Pike, Holcombe Hill, Jeffrey Hill, the skyline of Knotts-in-Bowland and Cross-o-Greet descending into Lancashire with the growing day.

A daily miracle; why do we not enjoy it more often? There is no sudden pop-up of the sun or daylight rioting over a sleeping world, but a slow imperceptible creeping in of the dawn; enchanting! And especially so if the curlew's clarion call puts the night to flight, crying at the gates of the morning. As the first pink flush steals along the cloud edges and daybreak trembles on the brink so do all the birds tune up, small soliloquizings and at last, full chorus.

In early May we saw the wild cherry trees hung in snow the length and breadth of Cartmel and Furness. Now cherries hang along the bough, ready to be picked, at Claife and Cunsey, Sawrey and Wray. Years ago families made an occasion of it, flocking over Windermere for three successive 'Cherry Sundays'. With baskets filled they returned across the ferry and on an overlooking hilltop sat to rest, eating and strewing their stones around. Which is why so many cherry trees line the lane sides on the way to Crook and Winster.

Now is the time to see public spirited action in our villages—cottagers weeding between cobblestones, hedge trimming, tying up gadding ramblers; men and boys scything the common and verges and churchyard grasses, mowing the green—and removing broken bedsteads from the village pond. Painting here, beautifying there, putting up of new notices and tearing down of the old; and careful scrutiny of incoming motorcars with happy families ready to spill out of them and coaches about to unload their mystery tour cargo. Who knows, they may be potential litter bugs flicking a toffee wrapper here, a cigarette packet or lollystick there. Every stranger is suspect.

Look for the reason—a notice, "We are entering the Lancashire Best Kept Village Competition. Please help us to win." Former winners include both Ecclestons, Wrea Green, Inglewhite and

Chipping, Caton and Hornby, Hawkshead and Cartmel, Edgworth and Whalley. Smaller communities among the best-kept are Barley, Newchurch-in-Pendle, Withnell Fold (a cul-de-sac immaculate off the Blackburn-Chorley highway), Halsall, Outgates and Caldervale. Some have been several times champion—and champion among champions!

If your pet village is not in the list maybe it did not enter, or maybe it had a pretty face and no more—which does not count. Making the most of itself, as with homely girls, wins the prize!

At the month end, long before the rest of the United Kingdom, holiday fever seizes the county. One town after another is getting ready for its staggered fortnight; Bolton, Oldham and Rochdale lead. Nowhere is there such a complete evacuation of towns; silent as the tomb, footfalls sound loud. The cotton towns are virtually dead on their feet.

July

July, a very full month with more and more towns adding to the holiday exodus, and countryfolk so throng with haytiming—the natural follow-up of sheep clipping—you would wonder how they had the time or patience to be pleasant to visitors.

This is the time of happiest sounds—the hay mower, flapping sails, swish of waves on shingle, cool music of moorland streams, bees in lime flowers and grasshoppers 'nicking' the glad minutes. And of most delicious perfumes, for our new mown and gathered hay smells sweet, honeysuckle scent travels down every lane, there is the blossom on the elders, the most delicate hint of sweetness from wild roses, honey sweetness from fields of the small white clover, wild thyme crushed underfoot as we climb the fells, and in every damp hollow in the High Furness dales, incense from the bog myrtle. All these are everyday sounds and scents anywhere 'north of the Sands' and down many a lane and moorland path farther south.

There is a full programme of events too. As the Agricultural Show reporters say, 'the country comes to town'. Take your pick from Liverpool's at Wavertree, Lancashire Royal at Ribby Hall. Losses from successive rainy show days have eliminated some, but stalwart survivors carry on. The attractions: sheep-dog trials, horse shoeing demonstrations, W.E.A. displays of exceptional standard, morris dancers, and maybe the local huntsman and hounds on display too. Flower lovers, growers of and arrangers of, have their great time of homage to the queen of flowers at Grange Rose Show, "on the most beautiful natural site in Great Britain", but if the visitor seeing roses everywhere gets the idea an overspill has been staged—well, it is just because the bay-edge towns and villages are always embosomed in roses throughout the summmer.

Prick a pin on the Lancashire map, and something exciting is on; the Mystery Plays staged against the majestic ruined walls of Furness Abbey at the beginning of the month; on the 12th, no need to cross the Irish Sea to Ulster to see Orangemen in action—Liverpool celebrates the victory of the Boyne and transports its tens of thousands to finish off the day at Southport.

For a complete contrast, there is a purely Lancashire occasion in memory of a Lancastrian, on a lonely moorland which might be a hundred miles from mankind, yet is on the fringe of the most densely peopled industrial belt—the annual pilgrimage early in July to Waugh's Well at the heart of the ancient Forest of Rossendale—quaffing of the clear cold water, laced with something stronger perhaps, for the poet was no spoilsport—

"But he that would leifer drink wayter
Shall never be stinted by me."

There will be a reading of his best loved poems—'Moorland Breezes', "I've worn mi bits o shoon away", and a rollicking rendering of "A lift on the way" which is sung wherever trueborn Lancastrians meet on windy hills, moorland ways, with the great outdoors before them.

"There's some folk at mun trudge it, an' there's some folk at may
ride,
But, never mortal man can tell what chance may betide;
Today he may be blossomin' like roses i' May;
Tomorn he may be beggin' for a lift on the way."

Now is the time to see how trim the Best Kept Villages can be; the final judging follows the preliminaries of June. And how we wish it was not necessary to remind visitors to KEEP LANCASHIRE TIDY and LITTER SPOILS LANDSCAPE—the very notices detracting from the most enchanting scenes.

Lancaster is this month plastered with notices announcing

'Admission of Freemen', a ceremony dating back over three centuries—most interesting, and admirable to encourage loyal townsmen over sixteen to take on the responsibilities involved. To qualify, old style, one had to be the son of a freeman or for seven years apprenticed to a freeman; but, new style, any resident for seven consecutive years and any native over sixteen may also apply for admission and appear at the Town Hall on a Saturday morning in mid-July to take the customary oath.

Applicants swear to "bear faith and true allegiance to the Queen—pay due obedience to Mayor, Magistrates and others in authority in this City and Town—to maintain and support the Franchises Priveleges Rights and Customs thereof—to contribute to all duties, Scot, Lot and other charges—keep the Queen's peace in their own person—."

For aiding the Mayor and Corporation, reporting unlawful assemblies, meetings and conspiracies, suppressing offenders, and doing as much as in them lay for the good of Lancaster, freemen in the seventeenth and eighteenth centuries were allowed to pasture beasts on the moor and enter goods toll free to Lancaster Market—but not "colour fraudulently other men's goods".

During July Lancashire folk are seen in all shades of brown, the depth according to whether the holiday fortnight was 'a real scorcher' on the beaches of Spain, Portugal or Yugoslavia, or 'it rained everyday' on home shores. Everyone is becoming foreign travel minded, 'chasing the sun', they say; but I can get as much as I want in my own garden unprotected, as after weeks in the Alps protected; and those spread-eagled to the beneficent rays on Blackpool prom or golden sands acquire the tan as surely. Spectators' faces redden round a hundred Lancashire cricket fields.

Tales of how generations ago Lancashire folk behaved with regard to their annual holiday week read like tall stories: the careful mother putting her return cab fare on the dresser—to ensure enough to pay the cabby when they arrived home, spent-up; and to make sure he spent up every penny of his holiday money, the young man looking round his boarding house to see what would add up to a few shillings worth of damage.

Annual Holidays, Town Holidays, Wakes Weeks—which term to use? For economy in words newspapers prefer the last, though it is quite alien to all but south-east towns like Ashton, Oldham,

Hindley, Eccles where their patronal saints' days, in this month, developed through festivals and holy days to holidays.

August—For More Shows, Sports and Club Days

The national newspapers and magazines never seem to realize that holiday hints in August fall flat on most Lancashire ears. What good to be told how to acquire the perfect suntan, avoid travel sickness, prepare for beach and plâge when they are back at work, tan fading, and idle days by blue seas—just like the travel brochures—either memories or recorded on colour transparencies?

The crowds enjoying our sands and sea breezes, from Southport to Morecambe and Grange are non-Lancastrians, most of them.

We are most likely to be found, en masse, at one or the other of the local shows, at Chipping's or Garstang's or among North Lancashire folk at those pleasant occasions held annually in Cartmel, Hawkshead or deep within the vale of Rusland. Shows, sports, flower shows, and for knock-me-down-colour blazing fiercely as forest fires, Southport's, the most spectacular in the north. Flower lovers are there if they own no bigger garden than a window box and are still so raw that they have not yet put the spade into the clay soil and builder's rubble of a bungalow garden in a new estate; and the old hands and lifelong addicts to gardening are there. It is the best place to learn from experts and go home and try and begin again, dreaming of patios and rose arbors, rock gardens and alpines, pools and fountains, and lawns of velvet pile.

August must have been a jolly month in the old days when towns did enjoy their feasts 'as of yore'. Not only rushbearings were on the calendar but guild or club days—very popular in the Fylde and neighbouring places, similar to the Wakes in that they came near the saint's day and involved two blessed days of holiday derived from holy days. Longridge Club Day died hard, but what were two days fun culminating in a grand trip to Blackpool when every one could go off for a week, and later a fortnight, if they wished? Horse racing from the Dog Inn to the Quarryman's Arms on the fell road—the prize a new saddle—foot races, processions and sports were no longer the looked-for excitements. A fancy dress parade for the children, a rose queen with her retinue of pretty little girls, and a field day, and maybe a dance and the choosing of the local Club Day princess is quite a pleasant way of filling in a summer Saturday. So, the traditions give way to a modern Festival and no one is concerned.

One village still enjoys all the old traditions, only slightly modified. Come to Broughton-in-Furness on the first of August and join in with Charter Day crowds gathered in the square around obelisk and fishstones. Mounting excitement as the Bailiff declares in time-worn phrases,

> "Oyez, oyez! The Lord of the Manor of Broughton and of this fair and market strictly chargeth and commandeth on Her Majesty's behalf that all manner of persons repairing to the Fair and market do keep Her Majesty's peace upon pain of £5 to be forfeit to Her Majesty's pleasure and their bodies to be imprisoned during their Lord's pleasure. . . ."

All very necessary when Furnessian tempers flared at the fair and in settling of old feuds up flashed forbidden 'bill, battleaxe and other such weapon'. Today Furness folk are particularly peaceful and law abiding—the police are hardly needed except to deal with visiting offenders.

The declaration over, the children, wildly excited, scramble for ten shillingsworth of pennies thrown among them, the Lord of the Manor—now the Lancashire County Council—retires with the guests for sherry and biscuits at the inn and the rest to a glass of ale, as from the Earl of Derby's first proclamation in 1593.

The first few days in August coincide with what are known as Maudlin rains, which can bring the wettest, stormiest week of the summer over Cumbria, and the edge of it to High Furness; it sets in about the time of the old Bank Holiday and persists with great perseverance, gales, flooded rivers, high tides and deep gloom, for two or three days, non-stop.

Fortunately, by the Twelfth, a date important on the grouse moors about upper Wyresdale, Bleasdale and Longridge, if nowhere else, the weather has usually 'faired up'. Then it seems that all the pent-up perfumes of the heather hills are suddenly released with the return of the hot August sun. A drowsy intoxication is in the air as anyone knows after idle hours on Harrisend Fell, or Beacon Fell, on the moorlands anywhere between Bolton, Darwen and Chorley, or when wandering over the empurpled tops of Nickey Nook or Scorton Fell.

Royal forest much of this was in the Middle Ages, and royalty enjoyed good sport until 1972 as guests of the late and last Earl of Sefton at his Abbeystead shooting lodge. It was a Lancashire lad, young Drinkall, who got in the way of the guns above Marshaw one August day. Someone shouted a warning "Hey, George, look out!" It was the Duke of Lancaster, King George V, who jumped, alarmed!

At the month end, Rochdale St. Chad's used to hold its annual rush-bearings—when after much festivity, rushes at their ripest were cut and strewn on the church floor. When annual holidays grew out of the old feast they were still called Rushbearings though ne'er a rush was to be seen. The third week in August seemed over late for 'going away' and, envious of early holidaymakers, the town decided to put forward its fortnight into late June. Since when folk have had their doubts, for not-so-good to bad weather, they say, has dogged them just the same.

Late August has its advantages, coinciding with that annual Feast of Lights which throws a diamond necklace half way round Morecambe Bay and jewelled brilliance against blue dusk and velvetty night skies shows up Blackpool's seven mile sea front.

The 'switch on' follows months of behind-the-scene preparation and, more often than not, a week of frantic reparations after stormwinds have done their worst to batter down stands and tear away miles of fairy lights from their moorings. After which the weather behaves itself. In flows the multitude; year after year the people come, though every time they say, "Well, it's really very pretty, but once you've seen it you've seen it!" A visit to the lights is as good an excuse as any for a day and night out. They even make plans a year ahead to come up by the coach load from places like Bath and Wells, and they come down from the Clyde and Midlothian with not a sign of waning interest. Ask any farmer's daughter from one of the remoter beauty spots of Lakeland or the Yorkshire dales what is the highlight of the season. "A night out at Blackpool Illuminations," is the answer, with great conviction.

The Illuminations lengthen the season and therefore please landladies and all who cater, within Blackpool and Morecambe. Coaches rolling up at their doors bring in the money to roadside cafés and bars with the largest accommodation—but the more select hotels put up discouraging NO COACHES notices. Local councils reckoning up what twenty times forty-one pulls on chains means in water consumption—counting up the calling coaches at the village inn or café—twice a night for the month's duration—know why local water supplies dwindle so rapidly. "Spending half a pint and wasting two gallons," as the Duke of Edinburgh remarked.

Residents fade into voluntary retirement. They are not part of the nightly goggle-eyed multitude. They come out of their hiding places again with October, and the return of peace and quiet.

Golden September

September has a golden glow about it—and a nip of frost in the mornings. Everyone makes a desperate last attempt to soak in the sun, as a camel faced by Sahara takes in water, to 'last the winter'; a blessed long weekend holiday to do it in. They trek to Blackpool where the lights glitter more brightly against the darker skies.

They begin to say, "Nights are drawing in".

Stay-at-homes organize family blackberry-picking expeditions; in blissful concentration bent figures stand by every lane edge from Winter Hill to Cartmel Fell. In the Winster valley damsons like black pendants bow low the branches of the trees we saw starry white in May, and the merchants arrive with their vans collecting from the farms where they bought in 'the futures' a year ago. In country places jam-making sessions are the order of things; we prefer it 'home made' in Lancashire, and 'reckon nowt of shop jam'.

This was a great month for fairs, charter fairs of great age, horse fairs and such. Most of them have degenerated sadly into rather watered down 'dos'. Old folk remember Turton Fair which welcomed the crowds, when inns were thronged and every cottager prepared gargantuan quantities of hot-pot, potato pie and pickles· They arranged stalls along the street, or at open doors invited the hungry to buy their good food by the plateful. For the children—a toy fair, free roundabout rides, and a climb up a ladder to take off, holding on to a long cable, on the 'aerial railway'.

Primarily it was a horse fair: the first day for Irish horses suitable for doctor's gig, children's carriages and greengrocers' carts; but the second day—nothing but worn-out old nags! A nonegenarian told me of a lad who held a horse for a buyer while he adjourned into the 'Chetham's'. The man was interrupted by the boy announcing the horse had fallen. "Then tha mun had been leaning against it!" was the new owner's retort.

It became rowdy with lads wrestling and boxing, and over-indulging in cruel fighting in iron shod clogs, 'punching and purring and throttling a chap so he nearly died'. Men were branded for manslaughter following such brutality in the 1800s and Bolton men transported, later, for life. Such 'sport' put an end to Turton Fairs. To show their fair had a religious origin Turton, without its jollifications, continues its Sermon Sunday.

Another 'lapsed' fair was at Ormskirk, with cattle and horses for sale in the main streets, pavement-edge stalls and favourite fairings among the children—why, gingerbread donkeys bought from the gingerbread women in their three cornered shawls, who hawked them in baskets through the town. A pity old streets, old inns and the Gingerbread Shop have been swept away in Ormskirk's desire for progress.

A most interesting survival continues, modified, around Wigan and Westhoughton. At the month end when nights were drawing in, local inns began preparations for the traditional 'Pasty Eyting' or Pastry Feast. In turn each 'pub' hired expert women cooks from the neighbourhood to see to the making and baking of large turnover-shaped pasties of chicken, pork or rabbit. In each they put a small, jelly-baby shaped, pot doll as a good luck charm, the finder being expected to 'pay for a round'. The 'Eyting' was also occasion for entertainment. Here as elsewhere in Lancashire—with everyone a natural comic, mimic or entertainer—the concerts were a great feature and many a man sported with pride a smart neckerchief won in talent-spotting competitions. Silk kerchiefs for the star turn, and for the best comic costumes—bunches of black puddings!

Those who did not frequent the 'pubs' could buy large pasties at 5s. family size, or smaller 2s. 6d. ones, and still smaller individual pasties without the pot doll; these were eaten with much relish round the family table.

If you are in Low Furness on the Sunday nearest St. Michael's Day, make your way to Urswick and the venerable church of St. Michael and St Mary for the annual rushbearing. The nearby tarn supplies the tallest of rushes, at their best for cutting. The women have gathered them by the armful, the queen's crown has been plaited, her robe edged with rushes and every child armed with garlands and sheaves called 'bearings'. This is nothing of the tourist attraction, as at Ambleside and Grasmere on the feast of St. Anne and St. Oswald, but a very simple village occasion. After the procession and service the church floor is strewn with the rushes and out go the children into the sunshine all carrying flowers to be placed on every unadorned grave of the forgotten dead.

St. Michael, caster out of devils, is a popular North Country patron of ancient churches, many it is thought on sites of pagan worship. Croston still holds its Wakes, but on Old St. Michael's Day, in October. As at Eccles and Goosnargh where cakes are an essential part of any festivity, Croston Wakes cakes, 6 inches diameter, with scalloped edges, are made and stacked in piles. The inns used to sell such quantities all the village women were kept baking batch after batch a week before the Wakes. They look and taste not unlike the Goosnargh Cake, 'and keep well, if you let them.'

In the olden times the Wakes on the Eve and Saint's Day, were kept with much solemnity, followed on the morrow by great merrymaking. In later centuries the religious side became less obvious, but from what old Crostonians tell me the feasting and merrymaking were not allowed to lapse. More like bacchanalian orgies, the processions, led by brass bands each heralding one of the Friendly Societies, the Oddfellows and the Good Shepherds—accompanied by a lamb washed and brushed-up for the occasion—their members in full regalia and red faces behind resplendent banners; decorated lorries followed on, and the more forward of the local girls dancing with abandon to the blaring trumpets.

Later the village folk assembled on the field by Yarrow side below the rectory garden, the bands struck up for dancing, and preparations were made for the day's 'great event'. Once a huge balloon was launched into space; inflated by heated air it rose above the heads of the wondering crowds and was wafted to the sky to a burst of triumphant brass band music.

The members of the Friendly Societies were not always present. Some had fallen by the wayside. Croston had many inns and after the annual carousel there were some to whom dancing on the green and cheering the balloonists offered small attraction. It was over-indulgence put an end to the old style Wakes. And now a new generation is not interested in a complete revival.

Many of us are interested in hearing of such old jollifications but, being completely honest and not in the least 'folksy', few Lancashire towns or villages are likely to mourn their end.

October's Jolly Days

October's month and mood suits me well. Now for the final flourish of flowers, more and more roses blooming, working up to that magnificent grand finale, oriental in its scarlet, orange and tawny gold which makes of Lonsdale north of the Sands and in High Furness a glory indescribable.

The towns and cities have their autumn touch too, yellow leaves gently falling, red-gold screens of foliage thinning day by day in the avenues and gardens of great mansions in the suburbs, the brighter gold of the leaves contrasting with the smoke-begrimed branches. Beyond the town streets the moorlands have turned brown and bracken-rust; too eager winds pick off the leaves on ash and oak, strip the coppice trees on the gale-swept windward side of every hill. By mid-month townsfolk are resigned; summer has indeed gone on swallows' wings, and "earth has buried all her flowers".

Or maybe those precious golden days granted by St. Luke, his 'little summer', have brought out old folk to sun themselves and with a nodding of heads they all say, "This'll put winter on nicely". So it does, but how are they to know, in towns, that there are parts of their own county where the gold will persist for weeks to come, and no autumn mist nor rains will quench it?

In the Ribble valley we are still picking blackberries, though 'they say' the devil has put his mark upon them now October has come. For hazelnuts, range the copses around Silverdale or Winster and Coniston to pocket your fill after winds have kindly done the picking for you. Neat piles of halved shells show red squirrels have beaten you to it—but plenty is left for everybody. Gather the shining chestnuts too, to hand over to the first small boys you see back in town; I always do, for now the conker season is at its height and conker championships will be played according to the traditional rules.

October nights are for shooting stars, for screech owls scaring you out of your wits. There is great activity on the hill farms, with the hoggs—the year's ewe lamb crop—sorted to be sent to winter feeding grounds. The fathers of next April's lambs, the patriarchal tups of High Furness fells, go in pairs, horns linked by short chains, until mating time arrives.

In Rusland Woods and Dale Park are realms of red-gold glory. But beware, for this is rutting time and lordly males resent intruders. It is not uncommon for ramblers to be 'treed' for hours before being rescued. So—keep out of deer parks!

Everyone is planning for when 'winter nights close in', for fireside nights, cosy sessions with the 'tele', or in bettering oneself from the large selection to be made from evening classes. Posters are up in every town library and every village butcher's window. My own sphere, the W.E.A. from the Extra Mural departments of Manchester and Liverpool, lists scores of subjects for the winter session, their range an eye opener for those who hold outdated ideas of what W.E.A. means.'Workers'? Of 8,000 and more students enrolled in the Liverpool-Manchester area nearly 3,000 are likely to have technical and supervisory jobs; around 2,300 housewives; many retired or not doing paid work—over 1,000; about 800 teachers, 300 professional people—civil servants, bankers, doctors, lawyers—and about 600 manual workers. The movement changes but the name is the same!

I remember an elderly member at a Manchester University reception who eyed the 2,000 students assembled. "How many of them," she queried, "have ever done an honest day's work in their lives?" To her a worker was one whose brow was perpetually wet with honest sweat and at the day's end was dog-weary with physical exertion. Fifty years ago W.E.A. was made up of hard working men and women who had barely time to wash and change before they were off to classes, eager to make up for lost time and early school-leaving. Not now! What kind of people tear themselves from their television sets to sally forth on cold winter nights to classes? The more intelligent who want more than the 'tele' can give them.

The young find their own fun. Having a reputation for witches we get a special kick from Hallow E'en parties. Women's Institutes indulge in witches gatherings by candlelight and hear spooky folk tales. Young Farmers' Clubs round Pendle design lurid posters for their 'WICHES REVELS AND WICHES BREW. LEAVE BROOMSTICKS OUTSIDE'. The 'ton-up boys' roaring round Pendle on Hallow E'en rallies make such a hurly-burly no self-respecting broomstick riding witch could compete. The landlord of the

Pendle inn at Barley, heavily disguised as Old Demdike, ladles out a witch's brew from a cauldron. And from the dark night flaming eyes goggle at the passer-by and eldritch screams from the young turnip lantern holders rend the air.

So, out goes October; the hunter's moon has waned, but the glory lasts in Cartmel and High Furness, bracken rust glows on the fells and until leaf-stripping gales and frosts arrive beauty lingers on into November.

November

1st November, All Saints and usually golden sun the day long. All Soul's Day on the 2nd no longer haunted by the singing of the Soulers who once made their way through the streets of Lancashire —and Cheshire—begging

"A soul cake, a soul cake, please give us a soul cake."

Never no more, though the poignant, melancholy tune is remembered.

Any townsman who believes that countryfolk now go to sleep for the winter could not be more wrong. Why, the weeks have not enough nights to do all that is on the village programme. Dances, whist and domino drives; classes for drama, soft furnishings, local history, folk dancing; money-raising efforts for the Hunt, the hungry, the church, the band club, the football club and the pensioners—no one need be idle.

Especially in Cartmel and Furness, country matters have a good send-off on the first day. At appointed centres—as Torver's Church Inn, the Blacksmith's at Broughton Mills, and Newfield in the Duddon valley—the bringing in and claiming of stray sheep is an excuse for a day of business combined with pleasure. Shepherds Meets are an essential part of Lakeland life, though the farmers are more likely to bring in the stray sheep in trailers behind cars rather than walk them over mountain passes as of yore. The eating, and talking and hound trailing, the Tatie Pie Supper, the drinking and singing are all part of the day. If a foxhunt can be combined with it so much the better. Like their Norse ancestors, any opportunity for conviviality must be seized upon and prolonged as long as possible. What staying power these fell farmers possess!

To a townsman's untrained eye all sheep look alike, but not to a hill shepherd. In every Lakeland farm a well thumbed "Shepherd's Guide" is part of his stock-in-trade. It contains matched pages of outline drawings of sheep, near and far sides marked in dots and dashes—'pops and strokes' to the initiated. Each pair carries the name and address of the owner so that quick identification —'Red pop on the far shoulder' or 'black stroke on the near rump' and the finder is on the phone to inform the owner.

There is sheep business of a different kind away in Pennine Cliviger where at the Ram Inn the Autumn Lonk Fairs are held. The rather doleful looking creature, who looks as though he spent every day breaking through quickset hedges backwards way, when he comes to the Fair is handsome as the patrician Wensleydale tup. This is the best place to meet the Pennine hill farmers on their own hard ground.

Being hill sheep the Lonk are not encouraged to bring forth their young until late March whilst the fell sheep of Furness, the Herdwicks and Swaledales, by traditional family planning do not lamb until mid-April. That is why tups mooch around so mournfully, in couples with horns linked by chains, until the grand release comes and with November they are free to lord it, each over his flock of ewes.

Hunting is now in full swing. Any day on the high fells can be heard the winding of the horn, the belling of hounds and loud hallooing echoing across the vast silences. Over High Furness the Coniston pack is busy on missions of extermination. When evening shadows lengthen in deep purple on the fells—but birches like flaming torches light up the gills, a patch of moving scarlet appears and very rapidly, with a clatter of rolling stones growing louder as it draws nearer, down the rocky slopes comes huntsman in his scarlet coat, the whipper-in and a following stream of hounds and terriers. They flow by, intent for home, and silence 'surges softly backwards'.

Silence sits in faded bowers! Silent, save for the jay's fishwife racket, magpie's rattling warnings, and the robin's sweet piping from every damson orchard. Poplars shudder and drop their yellow dresses, beeches disrobed stand beautifully on red-gold drifts of their own fallen leaves, larches shake golden tresses and birches still shimmer like flickering flames with every breeze.

This is the time to come north of the Sands, putting the seal on beauty. Colour soaked in by Duddon, Crake and Brathay will carry us on to spring.

One morning, from Hampsfell or Bigland Brow, or maybe from Tawtop or Warton Crag—from Morecambe promenade also—we see the mountains have their first powdering of snow, on the Old Man, Wetherlam and Langdale Pikes.

Soon friends will report arrivals of mute swans in greater numbers—to the quiet bays of upper Windermere and where Brathay slides towards the lake—and wintering whooper swans which honk like hounds.

Half-term holiday—the last break until Christmas—Teachers Rest some call it, but for the children it is 'bonfire time', and little else matters. Guy Fawkes and his plotters did well to time their grand blow-up for this time of year. All the garden rubbish, loppings and prunings is to be burnt and the litter of tree branches brought down in October gales to be tidied up. The framework of old beds and bedding, barrels and boxes, poles and planks—and unlimited debris from demolition sites—are covered up by more and more combustible material as Plot Night draws near. Village greens, rocky hilltops, and down back streets and open spaces in the towns are scenes of great activity. It would take more than Acts of Parliament to stop Lancashire's bonfire building.

In North-east Lancashire, Mischief Night precedes the Fifth; we bring indoors any moveable garden furniture the day before. Children range the villages like a host of mischievous imps borrowing, without knowing, their antics from the Lancashire boggart, rolling away dustbins and hiding lids, lifting gates and wheeling away barrows and, of course, raiding the bonfires of rival gangs.

Guy Fawkes Night and scores of red fires pierce the darkness; Orion and the Great Bear are put out by the fireworks and rocketting stars. There are still grand 'dos', traditional, large scale and small, with potato pies, jugs of coffee, roast potatoes, parkin and sticky treacle toffee consumed by the fire watchers. And the memory lingers on, long after the scent of wood smoke and smell of gunpowder has gone; on the day following the fifth small boys still poke the embers into flame, feed little fires and crowd around for evening games.

Poppy sellers go from door to door. Small knots gather around memorials on Remembrance Sunday. Martinmas comes and goes

—but with none of the old hirings. And, before we know where we are, comes a Saturday afternoon when town streets are crowded more than is usual, with eager children dragging one or more parents to line the pavements, waiting for the arrival of Father Christmas. He may come in sledge, stage coach, aeroplane moon rocket or space missile to show, in spite of his red robes and long beard, that he is 'with it' in the latest interplanetary form of transport. There is frantic cheering, a civic reception, and he takes up his residence in Grotto or on the Fifth Floor for the coming six weeks.

Six weeks! Christmas comes round more quickly every year, we all say.

The Twelfth Month

December in Lancashire; as in every other county, more lights, tinsel and temptation in the shops and each Saturday the buying panic more obvious; arrival of van loads of evergreens from the country, holly and mistletoe from the Midlands, loppings of spruces for Christmas trees from Manchester plantations at Thirlmere.

After Advent hundreds of parlour windows spring into twinkling light; a cheerful sight, these little Christmas trees. In the week before Christmas comes the uprearing of tall trees in Town Hall squares throughout the county, cribs appear outside chapels and churches, in public places—and at Clitheroe's Castle Gate. Drab towns for a while are transfigured with festoons of lights. Over the milling throng in Manchester Market Street and Picadilly, cherubim and seraphim blow out their cheeks to make silent music above the traffic noise. Shopping crowds shuffle along.

"Christmas is not what it used to be," folk say. But *Messiah* is rehearsed in a score of halls, children practise their carols and not a school with church connection but has its Nine Lessons and Carols service or a nativity play in production.

Never again, say city fathers when word comes of more light bulbs being smashed or stolen by hooligans. But the next day a myriad fairy lights delight the eyes and not a gap to be seen!

Everybody is 'trimming up' with the miles of paper chains eager sticky fingers are turning out in infant rooms; silver bells from egg boxes, and frosted boughs and powdered twigs in the junior schools, paper angels and nativity murals in the secondary moderns.

Trimming up is traditional in the factories too; fairylands are made of weaving sheds! And the old game of chasing the tackler with a twig of mistletoe proceeds with great hilarity. The weekly whist drive in the village school specially for Christmas has prizes of 'Fur and Feather'. Neighbours' children tune up at our front door. "Wait," we say, "till we turn down the radio—and begin again!" Then with 'Hark, the herald angels singing' and 'Good King Wenceslas', 'Silent night, holy night', there is a knock at the door and a ring of the bell; a coin rattles in a tin and with "We wish you a merry Christmas—and a Happy New Year" away they run.

Customs change, people change, but not the fundamentals. The 1970s on paper may not sound so jolly as the 1570s—but we enjoy ourselves, using slightly different words and music!

> "So blithe and bonny now the lads and lasses are,
> That ever as anon the bagpipe up doth blow,
> Cast in a gallant round about the hearth they go.
> And at each pause they kiss, was never seen such rule
> In any place but here, at Boonfire or at Yule;
> And every village smokes at Wakes with lusty cheer,
> Then 'Hey' they cry for Lon and 'Hey' for Lancashire."

Maybe such enthusiasms will survive in Merseyside, greater Manchester and in Cartmel and Furness, where the Queen will continue to be their 'Duke of Lancaster'. With the folk of Bowland Forest and Ribblesdale north of Sawley, loyalties will probably be to Yorkshire for generations to come.

INDEX

D

E

F

Y